"A courageous memoir of breaking free from a fa[...]
and how poetry can be a salve against chaos." —*The Guardian*

"BREATHLESS"
—*The New York Times*

"Sinclair's striking memoir is a testament to her craft and
her capacity for self-preservation." —*The Atlantic*

"In addition to the deep love, courage, intelligence, and compassion of
her writing, what caused me to well up repeatedly was the understanding
that I was in the presence of an enormous soul."
—Tracy K. Smith, Pulitzer Prize–winning poet, *The New York Times*

"MELODIOUS"
—NPR

"[A] vivid and poetic memoir." —*The Christian Science Monitor*

"With this book, Sinclair joins the pantheon of great writers of the
Caribbean literary tradition, standing alongside authors like Paule Marshall,
Edwidge Danticat, and Jamaica Kincaid. Simply stunning."
—Imani Perry, author of *South to America*

"RIVETING"
—*Harper's Bazaar*

"Sinclair is a gifted and poetic voice whose lyrical story of personal
reclaiming will inspire generations." —Tembi Locke, author of *From Scratch*

"A TOUR
DE FORCE"
—*The Washington Post*

"A narrative marvel, the testimony of an artist who literally writes her
way out of a life of repression, isolation, and abuse into one of art, freedom,
love, and wonder. To read it is to believe that words can save, words
can heal, and words can imbue us with near-divine power."
—Marlon James, author of *A Brief History of Seven Killings*

"REMARKABLE"
—*The New Yorker*

"One of the most gut-wrenching, soul-stirring, electrifying memoirs I've ever
read. It shatters every perception we have about Rastafari and lays bare our
postcolonial wounds as Jamaicans with lyrical power, unflinching truth,
and grace." —Nicole Dennis-Benn, author of *Here Comes the Sun* and *Patsy*

"MOVING"
—*Time*

"From the material of history and mythology, both personal and political, Safiya
Sinclair has gorgeously and lovingly assembled a story with radiant, trans-
formative power. I couldn't put it down." —Nadia Owusu, author of *Aftershocks*

"Essential . . . This book is lit from the inside by Sinclair's determination
to learn and live freely, and to see her beloveds freed, too."
—Jesmyn Ward, author of *Let Us Descend*

"A TRIUMPH"
—*The San Francisco
Chronicle*

37INK

SIMON &
SCHUSTER

Also by
SAFIYA SINCLAIR

Cannibal
Catacombs

HOW TO SAY BABYLON

A MEMOIR

SAFIYA SINCLAIR

37INK

SIMON & SCHUSTER

New York   London   Toronto
Sydney   New Delhi

An Imprint of Simon & Schuster, LLC
1230 Avenue of the Americas
New York, NY 10020

First 37Ink/Simon & Schuster trade paperback edition July 2024

37Ink/SIMON & SCHUSTER PAPERBACKS and colophon are
registered trademarks of Simon & Schuster, LLC

Simon & Schuster: Celebrating 100 Years of Publishing in 2024

For information about special discounts for bulk purchases,
please contact Simon & Schuster Special Sales at
1-866-506-1949 or business@simonandschuster.com.

The works of Louise Bennett Coverley are copyrighted, and permission to use has
been granted by the Louise Bennett Coverley Estate. fcoverley@gmail.com.

The Simon & Schuster Speakers Bureau can bring authors to
your live event. For more information or to book an event, contact
the Simon & Schuster Speakers Bureau at 1-866-248-3049
or visit our website at www.simonspeakers.com.

Interior design by Lewelin Polanco

Manufactured in the United States of America

1 3 5 7 9 10 8 6 4 2

Library of Congress Cataloging-in-Publication Data
is available on file.

ISBN 978-1-9821-3233-0
ISBN 978-1-9821-3234-7 (pbk)
ISBN 978-1-9821-3235-4 (ebook)

For Ife and Shari and Cataleya
and
She who is yet to come

Sun a-shine but tings noh bright,
Doah pot-a-bwile, bickle noh nuff,
River flood but water scarce yaw,
Rain a-fall but dutty tuff!

—LOUISE "MISS LOU" BENNETT

By the rivers of Babylon, there we sat down,
yea, we wept, when we remembered Zion.
We hanged our harps upon the willows in the midst thereof.
For there they that carried us away captive required of us a song;
and they that wasted us required of us mirth,
saying, Sing us one of the songs of Zion.

How shall we sing the Lord's song in a strange land?

—PSALMS 137

Caribbean reality resembles the wildest imagination.

—GABRIEL GARCÍA MÁRQUEZ

Contents

III
LIONHEART

IV
MERMAID

Author's Note

Memory is a river. Memory is a pebble at the bottom of the river, slippery with the moss of our living hours. Memory is a tributary, a brackish stream returning to the ocean that dreamt it. Memory is the sea. Memory is the house on the sand with a red door I have stepped through, trying to remember the history of the waves.

In telling this story, I have followed my river all the way down to the sea, treading as closely as I could to my memory of the people, places, and events that shaped my life. Outside of my family, most of the names and identifying characteristics of the people who appear in this book have been changed. May each of you find your way back to the water.

Prologue

My Life had stood—a Loaded Gun—

—EMILY DICKINSON

BEHIND THE VEIL OF TREES, NIGHT'S voices shimmered. I stood on the veranda of my family's home in Bickersteth in the small hours after midnight, on the lonely cusp of womanhood, searching for the sea. My birthplace, a half speck of coastline hidden by the tangled forest below, was now twenty miles away in the dark. When I was a girl, my mother had taught me to read the waves of her seaside as closely as a poem. There was nothing broken that the sea couldn't fix, she always said. But from this hillside town fenced in by a battalion of mountains, our sea was only an idea in the distance. I pressed my face into the air's chill and listened.

Out here was the bread and backbone of our country. The thick Jamaican countryside where our first slave rebellion was born. These mountains tumbling far inland had always been our sanctuary, hillsides of limestone softened over time, pockets of caves resembling cockpits overgrown with brush, offering both refuge and stronghold for the enslaved who had escaped. Echoes of runaways still hung in the air of the deepest caves, where Maroon warriors had ambushed English soldiers who could not navigate the terrain. The English would shout commands to each other, only to hear their own voices bellowing back at them through the maze of hollows, distorted as through a dark warble of glass, until they were driven away in madness, unable to face themselves. Now more than two centuries later, I felt the chattering night wearing me mad, a cold shiver running down my bones. A girl, unable to face herself.

The countryside had always belonged to my father. Cloistered amidst towering blue mahoes and primeval ferns, this is where he was born. Where he first communed with Jah, roaring back at the thunder. Where he first called himself Rasta. Where I would watch the men in my family grow mighty while the women shrunk. Where tonight, after years of diminishment under his shadow, I refused to shrink anymore. At nineteen years old, all my fear had finally given way to fire. I rebuked my father for the first time, which drove him from the house in a blaze of fury. What would happen to me once he returned, I did not know. As my siblings and mother slept inside, frightened and exhausted by the evening's calamity, I paced the dark veranda, trying to read the faint slip of horizon for what was to become of me.

As I stared past the black crop of bush into the night, the eyes of something unseen looked back. Something sinister. A slow mist coiled in the valley below. The air shook across the street, by the standpipe where we filled our buckets with water when the pipes in our house ran dry. There, emerging from the long grasses, was a woman in white. The woman appeared like a birdcatcher spider ambling out of its massive web. Her face, numb and smudged away, appeared to me as my own face. I stood unmoving, terrified as I watched this vision of my gray self glide down the hill toward me, cowed and voiceless in that long, white dress. Her head was bowed, her dreadlocks wrapped in a white scarf atop her head, walking silently under the gaze of a Rastaman. All the rage that I burned with earlier that night had been smothered out of her. She cooked and cleaned and demurred to her man, bringing girlchild after girlchild into this world who cooked and cleaned and demurred to her man. To be the humbled wife of a Rastaman. Ordinary and unselfed. Her voice and vices not her own. This was the future my father was building for me. I squeezed the cold rail of the veranda. I understood then that I needed to cut that woman's throat. Needed to chop her down, right out of me.

There, I could see where these fraught years of my adolescence had been leading—with each step I had taken into womanhood, the greater my hunger for independence. The more of this world I had discovered, the more I rejected the cage my father had built for me. There, in her frayed outline, I saw it, finally: If I were to forge my own path, to be free to make my own version of her, I had to leave this place. If I were to ever break free of this life, I had to run. But how would I ever find my way out? How would I know where to begin? Here, in the same hills that had made my father, now sprung the seed of my own rebellion.

I was being called to listen to what the land already knew. To unwind the hours that led to this catastrophic night, I had to exorcise the ghost of its making; I had to first understand my father and the history of our family. To carve my own way forward, I had to first make my way back. To where the island's loom and my family's yarn made one knotted thread. I had to follow until I could find just where this story's weaving began: decades before I was born, before my father was born. Before he had a song for this strange captivity, and a name for those he longed to burn. And before I learned too well how to say it.

Babylon.

I

BUDGERIGAR

A cage went in search of a bird.

—Franz Kafka

1
The Man Who Would Be God

Look to Africa for the crowning of a
Black King, he shall be the Redeemer.
—MARCUS GARVEY

BEFORE THE MUSIC CAME THE RAIN. Familiar and relentless, its torrent lashing hard and showing no signs of slowing, falling for hours on the heads of the hundred thousand Rasta bredren who had overrun Kingston's Palisadoes Airport, waiting since the first horn of dawn's red-letter arrival, praying for the storm to finally break. Some came barefoot, came on crutches, came by the truckload with whole families and tribes, framed with thick manes of dreadlocks flowing about their faces, sprouting wildly, or piled into crowns atop their heads, everywhere a black shock of overgrown beards and a loud ululation of tongues. Each was fueled by a higher purpose from bredren to bredren, and the sea of worshippers sprawled beyond the sight line. While some Rastas packed into the upper gallery of the airport for a better view, the more resourceful bredren among them climbed the air traffic towers and scaffolding, some scaling the few poinciana trees, every single bloom and broadleaf shaken loose in excitement. The Rastas pushed dangerously against those barricades of Babylon, tentatively eyeing the officers armed with bayonets as they flashed the heavy rain free from their dreadlocks. Their hopes buzzing near-electric, they watched the sky for the first glimpse of the Ethiopian airliner that carried the man they believed to be a living god, the emperor Haile Selassie.

On this damp April morning in 1966, the acting prime minister and his party studied the scene before them in disbelief. Settling above the gathered flock like its own heady stratosphere, a thick fog of ganja smoke hung on the air. The ministers expected some Rastas to attend, but they did not anticipate that every single Rasta on the island would pack natty to natty into Palisadoes. No visitor to Jamaica had ever received such a welcome; no dignitary or celebrity, not even Queen Elizabeth II, who had visited only a month before, was greeted with such jubilation. The minister's party had laid out a red carpet for the Ethiopian emperor, and cordoned off reserved seating for VIPs, all of which was now occupied by unbothered members of Rastafari, necks craned skyward, studying the thundering sky. The Rastas outnumbered the police officers more than ten to one, and while the PM's delegation had rehearsed an elegant ceremony for the emperor, I can imagine now their panicked huddle, trying to decide how to improvise a welcoming ceremony against the eyesore of these loud and unkempt madmen chanting unintelligible edicts about Jesus being a Rastaman.

This rambling legion of Rastas came from as far away as Negril's westernmost point, from the shores of Lucea and Savanna-la-Mar, the banks of Milk River and Black River, from Oracabessa, and the remote eastern villages near Port Antonio and Morant Bay, down from the verdant hills of Cockpit Country and the scarred mountainsides of Clarendon; they traveled hundreds of miles from the seaside coasts of Ocho Rios and Montego Bay. Dressed in regalia fit to meet their deity, the faithful were emblazoned in holy garb, flanked head to toe in the roaring red, gold, and green of the Ethiopian flag, the adopted symbol of Rastafari, worn by Rasta bredren in dashikis, rain-soaked tams, and military insignia, and Rasta sistren in ankle-length whites, bright scarves, and tasseled headwraps. The weather did not stop them from devoutly waving palm fronds and dancing, trance-like. Here and there they lifted portraits of His Imperial Majesty, carefully painted giant pictures of His coronation, or stenciled passages of Christ's resurrection from scripture as evidence of Haile Selassie's validity. Many lifted banners and signs sky-high, bearing messages to their Messiah:

WELCOME TO OUR GOD AND KING

HAIL TO THE LORD ANOINTED, GREAT DAVID'S GREATER SON

UNTO THEE WILL I PRAY ALMIGHTY

JAH COME TO BREAK DOWNPRESSION TO SET THE CAPTIVE FREE

Voices could be heard chanting the psalms of Rastafari, as loud kette-drumming rumbled throughout the airport. Now and then a cry of *Jah! Rastafari!* bellowed out from the crowd, causing a boomerang of rallying cries of *Jah! Rastafari! Jah! Rastafari!* to crack and roll across the mass of bodies like a wave. Hallowed Rasta elders from the Mansion of Nyabinghi blew the curved war-horn of the abeng, the sacred instrument of the unconquered Maroons who fought and defeated both Spanish and British colonizers. The horns' groans shook the warm, wet air.

These were the nation's downpressed and downtrodden; outlawed and persecuted since the Rastafari movement's creation in the early 1930s, when a visionary street preacher named Leonard Percival Howell heeded Marcus Garvey's call to "Look to Africa for the crowning of a Black King," who would be the herald of Black liberation. Howell followed Garvey's arrow back to the Motherland and found Haile Selassie, the emperor of Ethiopia, the only African nation never to be colonized, and declared that God had been reincarnated, walking among them in the form of a Black man, born Ras Tafari Makonnen. From the man came both myth and mountain, a seismic cultural shift that made the Rastafari a lasting colonial threat. It was a movement that hardened around a militant belief in Black independence inspired by Haile Selassie's reign, a dream of liberation that would only be realized by breaking the shackles of colonization, and unifying the African diaspora. And though the Rastafari movement was nonviolent, they were the nation's black sheep, feared and despised by a Christian society still under British rule, forced to live on the fringes as pariahs. These were the involuntarily landless and homeless, their encampments sacked, their fields burned by a government in service to the Crown. When Howell built Pinnacle, the largest-ever Rasta commune and a peaceful self-sustaining society, the British government razed it to the ground, staunching the movement's message of unity and Black independence. They were the unemployed and unemployable, the constant victims of state violence and brutality, the ones the government jailed and forcibly shaved, the ones brutally beaten by the police. In 1963, when a group of Rastas refused to relinquish the farmlands they lived on to government seizure, Alexander Bustamante, the white prime minister then, ordered the military to "Bring in all Rastas, dead or alive!" This triggered a devastating military operation where Rasta communes were burned island-wide in a weekend of terror, where more than 150 Rastas were dragged from their homes, imprisoned, and tortured, and an unknown number of Rastas were killed.

For decades they had been maligned as boogeymen, as madmen, as the monstrous Blackheart Man—a bloodthirsty caricature invented to scare children away from the Rastafari. They were kicked out of their homes, abandoned by their families, turned away at every door. So, when Rastas read the biblical accounts of Jewish persecution and strife, they recognized a similar suffering in their own tribulation. From those psalms of Jewish exile came the Rastafari's name for the systemically racist state and imperial forces that had hounded, hunted, and downpressed them: Babylon.

Babylon was the government that had outlawed them, the police that had pummeled and killed them. Babylon was the church that had damned them to hellfire. It was the state's boot at the throat, the politician's pistol in the gut. The Crown's whip at the back. Babylon was the sinister and violent forces born of western ideology, colonialism, and Christianity that led to the centuries-long enslavement and oppression of Black people, and the corruption of Black minds. It was the threat of destruction that crept, even now, toward every Rasta family.

But on this day, Babylon could not stop the Rastafari. On this day, they moved in a fervor of hope. They came to be heard, to be seen, to be legitimized. Today they came to witness God look Babylon in the eye.

In defiant contrast to the prim-starched suits and pearls of the welcoming delegation of Kingston uptowners, and in disobedience of the governor-general and the acting prime minister's calls for decorum, the Rastas continued to dance and chant.

When God come, the rain will stop! they yelled. *When God come, the rain will stop!*

All kept pious watch for his plane in the blackened sky.

According to Rasta folklore, what happened next was sudden. Like a scorched wind out of Eden, seven white doves burst out from the clouds, and behind them emerged the first silvery tip of the airplane. The plane was white and bore a streak of red, gold, and green, with the roaring Lion of Judah insignia emblazoned in the middle. As the first glare of sunlight reflected off the emperor's approaching plane, illuminating the entire Kingston sky, the rain instantly stopped, and the tarmac at Palisadoes erupted in an ear-splitting roar of pandemonium.

Like a battle cry ripped from some epic poem, a charged howl of voices ululated across the airport as men propelled themselves over the stunned heads of soldiers in a damp stampede. Rastas flattened the VIP area and trampled the PM's red carpet with mud as they tried to get a closer view of the landing plane. Hearts thundering, heads floating light with unreality, they danced as if this was the first day of their known lives. All were speaking in tongues, singing fevered spit-fueled chants of *Hail the Man!*, *Lamb of God!*, and *Black man time now!* Their day had come. And when the plane's wheels finally touched down, one hundred thousand Rastas charged the tarmac, running underneath and around the taxiing plane, with disregard for the moving wheels or still-in-motion propellers. They rose with a singular purpose, in zealous pilgrimage to swarm and crush the silver bird from all sides, hungry for a chance to touch the Black hand of God.

Believers surrounded all sides of the plane. "God is with us. Mek me touch the hem of his garment," they pleaded. This was as close as they would ever get to Zion, the Rastafari's name for both the promise of liberation and the soil of Africa, to where they believed it was their destiny to repatriate. Rastas leaned on the wheel of the emperor's plane, smoking ganja from giant chalices, chanting *See how God stop the rain! See how God stop the rain!* Fearing for his safety, Haile Selassie, seventy-four years old then, did not exit the plane, and instead waited on the tarmac for nearly forty-five minutes. Some Rastas began to stir with doubt. Unable to convince Haile Selassie to disembark, and concerned for the emperor's safety, the PM had no choice but to enlist the help of a Rasta leader, Mortimer Planno, who boarded the plane with his hands shaking. The words that passed between Planno and His Majesty are cloistered, a lost relic. Planno returned and beseeched the crowd to calm.

At last the emperor's airplane door opened. When Haile Selassie finally stood in the doorway and studied the screaming sea of believers before him, he wept.

Rasta bredren, sistren, and children cheered and waved beyond his bleary eyes, as His Imperial Majesty descended the plane's stairs and waved back, regally, his hand moving ever so slightly. At the last step, instead of walking on the half-cleaned red carpet leading to his waiting motorcade, Haile Selassie stepped instead onto the muddy ground of Kingston town. This caused the Rastas to erupt into even more deafening cheers and chants of *Jah! Rastafari! Hail the Man!* To them, this was stark evidence of his humility, that his first footstep on Jamaican soil was on the very same ground they walked upon, and not on Babylon's red carpet.

The scripture, in the end, would write itself. Among the crowd waiting out the day's rain on the island was a young singer named Rita Marley, who prayed all day for a sign of the emperor's divinity. When Haile Selassie's motorcade went by her in the jampacked Kingston street, he looked her directly in the eyes and gave a nod, waving his hand, where she saw the mark of a black stigmata in the center of his palm. "This is the Man!" she screamed. "This is Him!" By the time her husband, Bob, returned a few months later from Delaware, where he had been visiting family, she had grown her dreadlocks and set them both on a path of staunch devotion to Rastafari, believing they should spread His Imperial Majesty's message through music.

So went the benedictions of the living God, hailing his presence through Kingston from his motorcade, where all along the roads the crush of onlookers spilled out into traffic, manifesting myriad gospels and good old-fashioned Jamaican folktales. Each account was more outlandish than the next, with signs and wonders to be gleaned from every action. Most infamous was the tale of what Rastas believed were miniature coffins disguised as cigar boxes that Haile Selassie gave the PM's delegation—evidence of the edict that *Babylon must fall*—versus the seven gold medallions he gifted the Rastafari leaders: plain-as-day proof of his approval of Rastafari. Stranger still was the fervent belief that it was the emperor's cigar-coffin that caused the acting PM's subsequent death a year later from a brain hemorrhage.

When the emperor, who was an Orthodox Christian, finally sat down with Rastafari leaders, he told them very plainly he was not God. But his message, instead of deterring them, was widely seen by Rastas as irrefutable proof that he was in fact a living god, because only God would be capable of showing such humility. Only God Himself would deny His divinity. Somewhere on the emperor's last rail stop in the town of Montpelier, in the countryside where my father was born, I imagine the radio of his train car playing reggae's future ragged and discordant tune. On this journey, perhaps the emperor recognized himself in the long claw of history, saw himself caught between the weight of being the heir to the Solomonic dynasty and the true freedom of being Chosen as the Messiah. What did it mean, after all, to be the living answer to the fraught question of Black survival?

Speeding along with Haile Selassie through the Jamaican countryside, my lifeline curves back on itself. I imagine the emperor quiet, observing from the royal coach of our now-defunct passenger railway, passing the crumbling green towns of the island's countryside, lush and Edenic, discovering with surprise his own image painted on the modest shacks, on the sides of schools, his golden lion roaring unexpectedly from another humble shanty, then another. As I grew up, his stern and silent face would become as familiar to me as a grandfather's. His portrait would be gilded and exalted in the many rented homes of my childhood, every detail of his life more closely known to me than prayer. How serene he seemed, this man whose existence would come to unstitch my family. Hurtling along with the man who would be God, on a railroad that no longer exists, in a country that nestled its dark ache in me—the moment is ephemeral, illusory. I, too, am searching for a sign.

Before my father came to believe he was God, a man named Haile Selassie walked here, among the same blue ferns he did, following that one blue note between rock-steady and the clink of the country river. Haile Selassie's visit, eventually forgotten by most Jamaicans, would shepherd a generation of Rasta bredren to birth whole gospels in the emperor's name, and my father would become the most devout among them. And though he was only a toddler when the emperor visited, Haile Selassie's influence would take staunch roots in him, irrevocably changing the course of his life, and my family's life with it. Long after the emperor boarded his holy airliner and waved against the cheering hordes, he remained with us. His message stalked the wet leaves and salty palms of my youth, growing until he was a colossus, wading out to the sea where my mother was born, where I was born. Long after his own people rejected him in a coup, he was still here, at the airport next to the tiny fishing village of White House where my family first made a life. His flame burned alive in my father, who was god of our whole dominion, who slept with one watchful eye on my purity and one hand on his black machete, ready to chop down Babylon, if it ever crept close.

2

Domain of the Marvelous

WE LIVED BY THE SEASIDE UNTIL I was five years old, in our tiny fishing village called White House, which belonged to the fishermen of my mother's family, her father and grandfather. Hidden just beyond the margins of the postcard idea of Jamaica was our little seaside community, a modest hamlet shrouded behind a wall of wind-gnarled trees and haphazard cinder blocks, a half mile of hot sand browned from our daily living and sifting between bare toes, glittering three hundred yards in every direction to the sea. Our village was impossible to see from the air, unless you knew exactly how to catch this pinprick of shantied blue, and just as hard to find on land. Down a little dilapidated lane, shrouded with hibiscus shrubs and poinciana trees drumming the car roof, was our tucked-away cul-de-sac, named for my great-grandfather's house, which he painted white himself when he first came to this beach almost a century ago. Here there was no slick advert of a "No Problem" paradise, no welcome daiquiris, no smiling Black butler. This was my Jamaica. Here time moved slowly, cautiously, and a weatherworn fisherman, grandfather or uncle, may or may not lift a straw hat from his eyes to greet you.

Here, my mother and I drew our first breaths in salt-air and measured our seasons by the sea breeze. From the village entrance, at certain slant angles, the sea's view was obscured by small wooden houses, no more than thirty in total, modestly crafted by the men who lived here, men who died here. My family lived in close quarters and knew the subtle dialect of each other's dreams. Under a zinc roof held together with sandy planks and sea-rusted nails, we lived in the shrinking three-bedroom house my grandfather had built with his own hands. I shared one room with my parents and my brother Lij, who was two years younger than me, all four of us sleeping on the same bed, while my newborn sister Ife, who was four years younger, slept in a hand-me-down playpen next to us. My aunts Sandra and Audrey shared a room with my cousin, while my grandfather and his nineteen-year-old girlfriend slept with their three young daughters in their own room. Somewhere in this house, or the next, is where my mother keened her first cry, and my grandmother keened her last.

Along this cluttered shoreline is where my uncles anchored their boats, handmade and brightly painted, bearing names like *Sea Glory*, *Morning Star*, and *Irie Vibes*. Most mornings I watched for hours as they patched up their fish traps made with chicken wire, scaled buckets of fish to sell, or arranged them on large ice blocks for roasting later over a coal fire. Our little half mile of sea often fed the entire village—fishermen hauling heavy, glittering nets filled with sea turtles, dwarf sharks, red snappers, bonito, and the sweet flesh of a conger eel. People from all over Mobay— our nickname for Montego Bay—would come to buy fish, shouting and haggling at this makeshift market for our riches fresh from the sea. Then came the meager scavenge of the hungry and curious: children, ducks, and mongrels waiting for a bone, a bite of flesh, a fish head to suck on. When the smell of cooking wafted through the wooden walls and floorboards of every house, the villagers would gather around the Dutch pot, mouths watering.

Whenever my mother's sisters fell down on their luck, or one of them got pregnant, they returned from the sweltering inland cities to the beach, packing into the always-warm house with the red polished floor that stained my bare feet crimson, our breath rising and falling with the waves outside. We had no electricity, no running water. With the windblown houses and ramshackle beach, indoor plumbing was a luxury, so none of the houses in the village had bathrooms. Instead, all the villagers shared a pit-latrine, about three hundred yards away from the farthest house. Children were not allowed to use the latrine, since we were in danger of falling in, so we were each tasked to keep a plastic chimmy in the house instead, emptying it into the sea every morning. My parents showered outside in the sand in one communal shower hastily built with thrown-away plywood, while my siblings and I bathed in basins set down close by, next to a standpipe in the yard.

The sea was the first home I knew. Out here I spent my early child-hood in a wild state of happiness, stretched out under the almond trees fed by brine, relishing every fish eye like precious candy, my toes dipped in the sea's milky lapping. I dug for hermit crabs in the shallow sand, splashed in the wet bank where stingrays buried themselves to cool off. I slept under the ripened shade where the sea grapes bruised purple and delicious, ready for sucking. I gorged on almonds and fresh coconut, drinking sweet coconut water through a hole my mother gored with her machete, scraping and eating the wet jelly afterward until I was full. Each day my joy was a new dress my mother had stitched for me by hand. She and her sisters each had a distinct laugh that rang out ahead of them like happy sirens wherever they went, crashing decibels that alerted the whole village to their gathering. Whenever the sisters sat together on the beach talking, I clung to their ankles and listened, mimicking their feral cack-ling, which not even the herons overhead could escape.

I never loved any place more than this. At night my mother read to me by the light of a kerosene lamp, upon which I, born stubborn and accident-prone, would often burn my hands. Each scar on my body be-came a fixed reminder of what was lost, what would never grow back—the hairless scar on my left eyebrow that I got from falling off the tiny bed I shared with my parents, the burn on my temple from the lit mosquito coil I dragged down on my head, the bites from mosquitoes that grew to giant itching wounds, pocking my legs, or my tender mouth, shat-tered from a fall on paved concrete, where my tooth had ruptured my gums. For months after that, my mother had chewed all my food and fed me from her mouth like a bird. "You were born too sensitive for this world," she told me, as I sucked my thumb and pawed at her long dread-locks, listening to the rushing pull of the waves.

My father was not from the seaside, so he never felt at home at White House. He was a man who lived among fishermen but did not eat fish, adhering in all ways to an ascetic Rasta existence: no drinking, no smok-ing, no meat or dairy, all tenets of a highly restrictive way of living the

Rastafari called Ital. Already at twenty-six his thick beard and riverine dreadlocks gave him the wizened look of an augur whose tea leaves only foretold catastrophe. Some days he would bring his guitar to the sand and belt out his reggae songs, forecasting the impending peril of Black people with a stormy austerity that must have seemed misplaced at the seaside. There was no time for idling with Babylon on the prowl, he would warn, often trapping villagers into long talks about fortifying their minds and bodies against the evils of the western world. "For a weak mind is ripe for the worms of Babylon," he would caution, slowly sharpening his look into a gaze that could overcloud the sun. A gaze that my siblings and I would later come to know all too well.

Even at this young age I knew that my parents were unusual. They were the only ones at White House who had dreadlocks, and the only people I had ever heard call out the name of Haile Selassie in reverence, though it would be some time before I questioned why. Most days my father journeyed far away to the hotels lining our coast, where he played his reggae music for tourists, his guitar and dreadlocks heavy dreams slung over his back. When he was gone, my pregnant mother spent her few free hours while my baby brother slept scouring the beach for empty conch shells, or chopping mounds of almonds to make a sugary confection called almond drops to sell to tourists, supplementing the family's income. Before he left for work, my father would always stoop down, hold me eye to eye, and warn me to stay away from the sea. I promised him that I would. As the light grew longer with the passing months, I grew more curious, roaming ever closer to the boundary of the shoreline, away from my mother's watchful eye, testing how far along our beach I could go.

Firstborn of four, I had claimed this beach as much as it claimed me. As a toddler I would wade into the shallows to wash my chimmy with my mother, while the steady clamor of Concorde jets shrieked across the sky, their white contrails crisscrossing our blue. Each one an iron bird, a bird of Babylon. Nearly two decades after Haile Selassie's silver jet had departed, I had grown accustomed to the constant roaring of planes leaving from the airport next door, a place forbidden to us. Next to the airport, looming along the borders of our village, were hotels with high walls made of pink marble and coral stone, flanked on top by broke-glass bottles, their sharp edges catching the light in cruel warning: To live in paradise is to be reminded how little you can afford it.

Those high fences first went up in 1944, four decades before I was born, when the government spent years paving our wetlands to build an airport next to the village, while more and more hotels crept up on either side of us. Each new hotel they built was larger than the last, until the resorts resembled our still-standing colonial houses and plantations, many of which served as attractions and wedding destinations for tourists. This was the fantasy tourists wanted to inhabit, sunbathing at hotels along the coast named "Royal Plantation" or "Grand Palladium," then getting married on the grounds where the enslaved had been tortured and killed. This was paradise—where neither our history nor our land belonged to us. Every year Black Jamaicans owned less and less of the coast that bejeweled our island to the outside world, all our beauty bought up by rich hoteliers, or sold off to foreigners by the descendants of white enslavers who earned their fortunes on our backs, and who still own enough of Jamaica today to continue to turn a profit.

But my great-grandfather would not sell our little beachside. He held on to his home, even as the hotels grew grander on both sides of the village, even as we lived deeper and deeper in their shadow, until eventually the coral reefs he fished in blanched and disappeared, his livelihood gone. Now most of Montego Bay's coastline is owned by Spanish and British hoteliers—our new colonization—and most Jamaicans must pay an entrance fee to enter and enjoy a beach. Not us. Today, no stretch of beach in Montego Bay belongs to its Black citizens except for White House. My great-grandfather had left the land title and deed so coiled in coral bone, so swamped under sea kelp and brine, that no hotelier could reach it. This little hidden village by the sea, this beachside, was still ours, only.

Living at the seaside meant wonder and danger arrived frequently on the same wind, tugging at me from the horizon. Like an eager kite, I was constantly drawn to danger. The first time I disobeyed my father and walked into the sea alone, I was four years old. The afternoon heat was perishing. My father had already left for work, and my pregnant mother was sweating somewhere out of sight, bathing my baby brother in the same red plastic basin she'd use to hand-wash our clothes, or bending over to feed her own baby sister, her father's newest newborn, who she'd delivered from his scared teenage girlfriend on our bedroom floor only a month before. While cooling down under the palms outside in the sand, I spotted something glinting in the water, caught under the sun's glare. Calling me. I slipped away from the shade and walked to the shore.

I stood barefoot at the water's edge and watched the waves heaving, its million eyes glittering, staring down the blurred horizon where I was forbidden to go, and waited. I waited for my mother's familiar grasp, to be pulled back to the safety of the sand, waited to hear a grown-up screaming for me to get away from the water. But no voice came for me, except a strange echo on the wind, sweeping sweet nothings in my ear.

Hello and *I love you* said a reedy voice from the sea, speaking the kind language of a small child, and so I stepped in, first one foot in the sinking sand and then another, warm sea froth snaking around my tiny ankles, then rising quickly to my knees. It didn't matter to me that I didn't yet know how to swim. I turned one last time to look at our house—my grandfather's house—a hundred feet away, crouched small on the sand, sun glinting off its zinc roof, the ripe almond trees on either side, and saw no one reaching for me, so I threw myself quietly into the rollicking waves.

The seawater rose to my chest, the waves splashing against my torso, my dress clinging frantic to my skin. Salt water filled my nostrils and mouth as I kicked my arms and legs uselessly, my body sinking in slow motion, my hands reaching up, reaching out, and feeling only sea, touching nothing and nowhere but the darkening blue below.

What I remember next was red. Red shirt, red in the water. Blood. Suddenly my mother's arms were around me, lifting and gasping, and the world unsealed itself and sang every song in my ear. My mother held me tight, too tight, and screamed my name. Against me her body was warm and wanted, her pregnant stomach firm. I could hear her heart pounding in my ear, the world quiet, the world loud again. She sobbed and looked into my face, darted between my eyes, touched my head, counted my fingers, kissed them, and sobbed and sobbed.

"Are you okay?" she cried, breathless. "Are you okay? Are you okay?"

She had briefly gone to the latrine, missed me when she came back, then saw me out in the distance bobbing in the water. She had flown to me from hundreds of yards away. As she dashed, something in the sand had ripped through her bare foot, a broken bottle or old tin can, and now she bled all over the sand, all over me. She didn't seem to notice or feel it, as she touched me gently here and there, pleading, "Are you okay?"

"Yes, I'm okay," I told her, with what my mother has described as an unnatural calm, before I slipped my wrinkled thumb into my mouth and sucked, looking away from the horizon. I placed my head against her heaving chest, relieved to gulp the rush of air, and breathed when she breathed.

She never told my father about my near-drowning, I discovered nearly three decades later. They had both wished for a Rasta family for so long that she could not bear to name the danger we'd only narrowly escaped—danger that my father soon began to foresee in every corner. My mother didn't want to upset him, or perhaps she didn't want to stoke his worst fears. So began our first secret, mother and daughter, our own little creation lore, cloistered as a clamshell around us. This was the first time my mother had saved me from my own calamitous devices, but it would not be the last.

Months later, down our half-mile strip of coastline, under the scattered shadow of a palm tree, you could find her still clasping me on that shore, weaving the tale of my glorious rescue from drowning, rewinding each family tale like a pop song, like myth. This is how she taught me to read the sea. Almost every afternoon, after my father had picked up his guitar, kissed me goodbye, and trod out again to face Babylon at the hotels, I would follow my mother down the sandy path that led to our secret beach, studying those old waves foaming and hissing, as she showed me how to look into the water and find its rhythm. Our history was the sea, my mother told me, so I could never be lost here. And, if I listened closely enough to the water, it would always call me home.

I played with her dreadlocks and listened, watching the day's surf rush in with my head nested against her chest. I asked her to tell me the story of how our lives began, again. She would take on a peculiar glaze and look out beyond me whenever I asked this, retracing the threads of my birth story so frequently that it had become her own origin myth. I was always moved by the way she began. "If I never had you, I would have been a beach bum," she said, walking me out into our languid history, neck thrown back, her laughter naked and familiar. She would say it began under the gaze of a white Catholic nun. Or it began with a rainy afternoon, a catch of fish, the warm grasp of a hand. It was here at White House, in my unlikely arrival, that my parents' journey into Rastafari began.

3

Fisherman's Daughter

I F I STAND ON MY TIPTOES and peer hard enough into my family's past, I can see the tea-black leaves at the bottom of my mother's rusting tin cup. My parents were both born in the wail of rebellion in 1962, when Jamaica first gained independence from Britain, and found each other eighteen years later in 1980, two parentless teenagers searching for some higher purpose. They'd always felt outcast, their burdens singular, driven by a profound belief that they were different. Chosen. Years later, while retracing the history of my family's journey into Rastafari, I would eventually come to understand that my mother felt called because she wanted to nurture, and my father felt called because he wanted to burn. Somewhere in between her hope and his fire, there was a united belief. A miracle.

My mother was born with six fingers on each hand, and constantly probed for anything good. Her mother, Isabel, had died unexpectedly from a botched black-market abortion when my mother was only four, leaving her all but orphaned at White House. Her father would disappear without warning for long stretches at a time, abandoning my mother and her many siblings, most of them younger than twelve, to the mercy of the sea. While my mother's half-siblings from Isabel's side were sent to live with relatives scattered in other houses along the beach or in faraway parishes after Isabel died, my mother and her younger sister Audrey—her only full-blooded sibling—were dropped off at the doorstep of her father's current wife and left to contend with their eleven half-siblings from his side. There were days my mother went without being fed, subsisting on nothing but a mixture of sugar and water. There were weeks she wore the same donated clothes for days in a row because that shred of cloth was all she had. There were months she could not go to school because her one hand-me-down pair of shoes fell apart, leaving her barefoot. Most days she walked the beach, trying to remember her mother's face. She had been so young when Isabel died that for a few years afterward she didn't know where her mother had gone and had been waiting for her to come back. No one bothered to tell her the truth until she was seven, when a man offered her a ride home on a bicycle. As soon as they rode off, she felt his hands sliding up her skirt. She swiped his hands away, and he flung her off his bicycle onto the gravel, sneering, "Gyal, yuh mumma dead!" and pedaled away. She cried all night, realizing her mother was never coming back. Every few months her father would return with a new whimpering child in tow, drop them off at the village's doorstep, and disappear again, leaving children like little land mines in his wake.

Though she was not the eldest of her father's many children, my mother's striking resemblance to her gone mother Isabel—her father's mixed-race mistress—had fostered the cruelty of his current wife, who made a point of picking on my mother, often pulling her away from playing with her siblings to make her do hours of housework every day. By the time she was eight years old, my mother had fallen into the permanent role of housekeeper, cook, and laundry maid in her stepmother's house. As she got older and her father's countless wives came and went, it fell to her to raise her many half brothers and sisters, which she did without complaint, cooking and cleaning and bathing all who she could not bear to see helpless and uncared for. She has been warming the world with those hands ever since.

I can see her now at eighteen years old, her hands patient and familiar, folded against her lap as she waited in a makeshift clinic in Montego Bay, watching the sky through concrete blocks arranged into the shape of a few latticed windows. The illusion was just-sufficient, letting scant light and air into the room, where several women—sickly, poor, old, and the frightened teary young—waited to be seen. The free clinic was a converted classroom in the back property of an all-girls' high school run by American nuns, cloaked in long brown habits that swished as they walked from here to there. The other women gazed at my mother, who was used to garnering unwanted attention wherever she went in Mobay. Much of what made her an oddity she had inherited from her mother Isabel; she was tall and light-skinned, with long auburn hair that fell to her shoulders in loose silken curls that framed her gentle face and brushed against a mole on her right eyebrow and the prominent dimple in her chin. Waiting on the long wooden bench, my mother scoured the women next to her with the same curiosity with which they studied her. Here they all were, relying on the kindness of white nuns, after herbs, tea, and plain old-wifery failed to cure whatever ailed them.

My mother had never been seen by a nurse or doctor for her issues "under there," but on this unsuspecting morning in 1980, at eighteen years old, she clasped one hand within the other and waited. For most of her adolescence, her period's gnarl-fisted ache had wrenched her inside out, leaving her bedridden for days, and had once even caused her to pass out in the street. She had missed her crucial final Caribbean Examinations Council exams, and her own graduation because of it. Some days the pain throbbed so hard she threw up, then blacked out. Today she had come with her last hope.

Finally, her name was called. My mother did as she was told and entered a cramped side room, a converted bathroom now serving as an examination room. There was barely any space between her and the friendly nun who ran down a cursory checklist of medical history in a gentle American accent, then asked her to disrobe. My mother had never been touched by a white person before. As she lay down on the shaky exam table and spread her legs apart, she studied the lucent outline of the nun's kind face, then closed her eyes tight.

The nun inserted two gloved fingers and pushed. The whole world flooded through this dark puncture. When the nun finished, she unpeeled her gloves, then reached out to hold my mother's hand. At first she said nothing. Then—

"I'm sorry," she said. Too quietly.

My mother waited. Endless hours seemed to pass before the nun spoke again.

"You have a condition that prevents women from having children. I'm really sorry. It's unlikely that you will ever—"

"No," my mother said. "But—" Then choked on the salt of her own words.

"I'm sorry, Esther," the nun seemed to say, her voice already inaudible, her face gone blurry as a massive wave of water crashed through the clinic roof and flooded this moment, submerging the examination room, sending desks and papers floating, the blue sky upturned, its vast wave filling my mother's ears and lungs, heaving her out the clinic door, washing her down the busy overpass we call Top Road, down past the airport, flooding out to White House, tossing her past her waving sisters, past the watery lurch of her future life, until she was washed onto the foamy seashore and rolled out into the waiting sea, where she kicked her legs, ducked her head into the blue, and swam.

After her encounter with the nuns, my mother's infertility sat heavy in her chest, where her hurt circled. Even though she was so young, she had been a natural nurturer for most of her life, and always wanted to be a mother one day. After raising nearly half of the village's children, she couldn't imagine not having her own. She turned her mind to the mystics. She spent the next year reading about yogis, trying to project herself to another plane. Her sister Pansy gave her a book about Indian shamans and rolled her a ganja spliff for the first time, saying, "Smoke this, it will mek yuh feel bettah." Down into the heady green of the sea my mother went, losing herself to the torpor of the days, chasing a high that might unmake her hurt. When she wasn't reading poetry or swimming, she was smoking, walking with the yogis who subsisted on sunlight alone, plastering a brown mixture of egg yolk and honey on her head, a concoction to help soak up the sun she was always chasing. She turned nineteen years old, and graduated high school with top marks, but with any future of further schooling swallowed up by her father: "unnecessary money," he called it. Like many young women born into poverty, the scarcity of her choices made her easy prey. Her life's prospects must have seemed more or less predetermined: She could be a maid or secretary in the guesthouse next door, or she could play a maid or secretary at Ocean View, the brothel next door. "Everybody wanted to be like *Dynasty* and *Days of Our Lives*," she told me. "All the women were pressing their hair and wearing shorts. But not me. I prayed every day that I wouldn't end up like some of the girls in the village, at the whorehouse next door." She decided to chase her own kind of rebellion: She stopped wearing makeup and started to cover her hair. She smoked her days away on the beach instead, trying to learn the slant mysteries of the chakras that might unblock her infertility.

She was the family's outcast. She'd been born an oddity, a little strange and bookish, her straighter hair and lighter complexion marking her visibly different from all of her twelve sisters. In high school she had dreamed of being a chemist and had scored excellently enough on her exams that she was invited to study in Scotland, but there was not enough money to get there, or anywhere. She thought of that mournfully as she pushed her toes into the sand, watching her life wash away. Every day she watched the cruise ships come in and the American sailors disembark, and shuddered. She could see into the windows at Ocean View. She saw all the women who lived there, all the men who came and went. One by one she watched the young women of her village slowly burn away.

On her darkest days, it was always books that gave my mother's world a clear sort of hope. She couldn't leave, but she could still escape. She would rummage through the rubbish bins of the adjacent hotels on the beach, looking for old books left behind by tourists, their pages stained with discarded coffee grinds and fruit peels. Into their pages she went, always searching for something greater. "Why yuh head forevah inna book?" her sister Audrey would ask her, trying to coax her to leave the village and go downtown with her, or to watch television with the family instead. Audrey was my mother's closest sister, and the only sibling, of more than twenty, with whom she shared the same two parents. "Look how long we done with school!" Audrey would tease, always trying to lift my mother's mood. But my mother kept to herself and retreated from the world entirely. Her mouth clamped around something else that dampened her days and that she could not share with Audrey, something she would spend decades trying to escape. A few weeks after her visit to the nuns, her own grandfather, now bedridden, had groped at her and pulled her, facedown, into his sickbed. My mother ran from his house and as far as possible from him as she could. It would be years before she told anyone about what he did. She drew into herself and kept away from the world, searching for something that might transform the tenor of her adolescence. Something to give her a true sense of purpose. Or someone.

Across town, waiting for the bus with his guitar slung over his back, my father liked to say he was born a wildflower. Long before he ever reached for the fire, he was untethered and alone in this world, searching for something to belong to. At eighteen, his life had already seemed overwhelmed with a series of false starts and new hopes; with every disappointment in his reggae career, he put all his faith in the next break, the new day just over the horizon. His old band, Future Wind, had been wildly popular in Jamaica in the late seventies, when he was a sixteen-year-old heartthrob, chased around the island by throngs of screaming teenage girls. They packed arenas, played television shows. Growing up, he was teased for being too broad-nosed, and for the keloid scar on his forehead, but he was the star and lead singer of the band. Though he was naturally skinny and stood no taller than five nine, when he was onstage, he was a giant. He would wave his hand over the crowd and watch them swoon. Future Wind was managed by James Hewitt Sr., the keyboard player's father. Mr. Hewitt was a businessman who boasted a big house and a car in Montego Bay. The band stayed with the Hewitts when they rehearsed, and were accommodated by them when they traveled. After a year of Future Wind shows, Mr. Hewitt had a new house and car in Miami, and his wife's wrists were stacked to the elbow with gold bangles, but my father hadn't seen a penny. One afternoon he finally demanded his royalty money from Mr. Hewitt, who claimed there was no royalty to pay. All my father's share of royalties had been taken as payment for a year's worth of rent and food. And just like that, the band imploded. My father jumped up and swung, accusing James Hewitt Sr. of being an "exploiter rat," then threatened to bomb their house if he never got his money. As sudden as a flare, the band and its fame vanished, along with its future. And so, he looked ahead again to a new day, and its music.

Like a rite of passage for every Jamaican youth, my father went searching for his fortune in America and met his misfortune instead. He ran into trouble with the law and was deported after a year. Before he left the

United States, he'd also found his future calling. As a boy, he'd watched one Rasta bredren walking around his country town of Montpelier with quiet admiration; instead of being scared off by the legend of the evil Blackheart Man, the fictitious child-killing Rasta, he had been drawn in. The Rastafari seemed peaceful to him, living as one with nature, and not the frightening cannibals his Christian family had warned him of. While that Rasta bredren had sparked his boyish interest, it was his passion for reggae music that first planted the seed of Rastafari in him. My father had always been a gifted singer and had even sung in church when he was a boy. In his late teens, once he began listening to the records of Rasta musicians like Burning Spear and Bob Marley, who sang about Black liberation and the fight for equal rights, his "third eye opened." In the potent message of their songs, my father began to understand that his own anger had a name. Through reggae music, he began to identify his own helpless rage at the history of Black enslavement at the hands of colonial powers, and his disgust at the mistreatment of Black Jamaicans in a newly postcolonial society. In the island-wide abuse lobbied against the Rastafari, my father soon began to see himself.

On his ill-fated trip to the United States in the winter of 1979, while spending hours in New York City's free libraries, he discovered the speeches of Haile Selassie and Marcus Garvey, then read about Leonard Howell and the history of Rastafari. It was there, with his nose pressed into stacks of books, that his mind slowly awakened to the racist downpression of the Black man happening all around him in America, that inescapable shock of firehoses and police battalions and the battered corpses of Black boys like him. He understood then what Rastas had been saying all along—systemic injustice across the world flowed from one massive, interconnected, and malevolent source, the rotting heart of all iniquity: what the Rastafari call Babylon.

Just as a tree knew how to bear fruit, my father says, he knew then what he needed to do. On a cold day in February, on his eighteenth birthday, fourteen years after Haile Selassie had stepped onto the screaming tarmac in Kingston, my father stood before a mirror in New York City and began twisting his Afro into dreadlocks. When he returned from New York, his mother took one look at his hair and refused to let him into the house. She told him he could only live with her under the

condition that he cut his budding dreadlocks. It was shameful to have a
Rasta son, she said. All her neighbors at Kerr Crescent would worry that
he would brainwash their sons and turn them into Rastas, like Bob Marley had done all over the island a decade before. Talking bout Africa this,
Africa that. My father had nowhere else to go, so he reluctantly complied,
cutting his hair back down to an Afro. While living with his mother he
continued to write his reggae songs and play his music, and spent the next
four months ignoring the silent glare of her new husband, Gifford Craw-
ford, whom my father called Giffy, and who my siblings and I would call
"Uncle Clive" a decade later.

My grandmother Pauline had been a star student and her family's
shining hope, until she got pregnant with my father at thirteen, the origin of a hardship that seemed to hound her and my father, even now. My
father had never known his father, not even his name, which created an
emptiness that would forever haunt him, a void that my grandmother was
unwilling, or unable, to fill. After my father was born, my grandmother's
family treated both of them with the kind of cruelty that sent mother
and son running as far from each other as they could. When he was still
a boy, my grandmother left him to the mistreatment of her family for
months at a time, staying many towns away while she worked and studied
for her teacher's degree. She became a penitent Christian, and my father
grew up to be a rebellious antiestablishmentarian. All his youth he'd been
searching for an anchor, the austere paternal grounding that he eventually
found in Haile Selassie.

When he returned from America that year, my father began spending
time around the drum circle with Rasta elders in Montego Bay, sitting in
on the philosophical and spiritual discussions that Rastas called reasoning, and there he felt the seed of Rastafari grow roots within him. "Rasta
is not a religion," my father always says, echoing the edict he drilled into
me and my siblings growing up. "Rasta is a calling. A way of life." There
is no united doctrine, no holy book to learn the principles of Rastafari,
there was only the wisdom passed down from the mouths of elder Rasta
bredren, the teachings of reggae songs from conscious Rasta musicians,
and the radical Pan-Africanism of revolutionaries like Marcus Garvey
and Malcolm X. My father found himself most called to the unwavering

discipline of the Mansion of Nyabinghi, the strictest and most radical sect of Rastafari, and constructed the man he would become around it. Eventually he would plunge himself headlong into its unbending tenets of asceticism, which taught him what to eat, how to live, and how to fortify his mind against Babylon's "ism and schism"—colonialism, racism, capitalism, the temptations of greed in white American and European culture, the mental chains of Christianity, and all the evil systems of western ideology that sought to destroy the Black man. "Fire bun Babylon!" the Rasta bredren chanted every night. And my father turned it on his tongue like prayer. It was never the hope of building Zion that called out most to him, but the fire, the fight against Babylon, and now he was ready to decimate any heathen who stood in his way.

At eighteen, my father stood on the threshold of fully embracing Rastafari, but it was his mother who gave him the final push. Four months after his return from Foreign, under an overcast sky in June, my father packed up his guitar, made rehearsal plans with his newly formed second band, and headed home. When he turned up the road to Kerr Crescent, he found a moving truck parked outside his mother's house. Strange, no one had told him they were moving that day, but luckily he didn't have many possessions so he would be ready to hop in the car and go. He looked at the gray sky and knew the movers would need help if they were going to be done before the rain came. He put his guitar away and started helping to move boxes, lifting furniture and heaving barrels. Everyone moved in an impenetrable silence back and forth, ignoring the tense static, which could have been the oncoming rain, or something more. Before they were finished, it started to pour, so they moved as quickly as they could, stacking settee and fridge and stove until everything fit into the back of the truck.

When they were all packed, my father followed his mother and her husband, Giffy, to the car, with the moving truck prepared to follow. Giffy's two young cousins, Sheena and Cara, who'd been staying with them, were waiting in the back seat. In the corner of his eye, he saw Giffy say something to his mother. My father opened the car door to get in, and his mother got out and stood between him and the car.

"There's no space for you in the car," she said.

"Okay," my father deferred. Maybe she meant he should ride in the moving truck instead.

"Howie, the situation is going to be different. Where we're going to live, there's no space for you anymore." She looked out far past him, and not in his face.

"What do you mean?" my father asked.

"There is no room for you there. And I don't want anybody sleeping on my settee."

"But I'm your son."

She said nothing.

"Where do I go, who do I stay with? I have no other family out here," he pleaded. He was trying to look her in the eye, even as the rain was coming down.

She shifted on her feet, glancing back at the car where Giffy had his hands on the steering wheel, looking dead ahead. She looked past my father again. My father had bucked heads with Giffy a few times over his interest in Rastafari, and more than once he'd overheard Giffy telling his mother that he "didn't want no Rasta in his house." But he never believed his own mother would turn him away because of it.

Finally, she said, "Howie, I don't know where you're going to go, or what you're going to do, but here is ten dollars."

He looked at the ten-dollar note. Two days' worth of dinner, at best. All he had was a small duffel bag filled with his clothes, which had been left on the pavement by his feet.

"But I'm your son."

"We have to go," she said, walking back to the passenger side of the car.

"But you're leaving me in the rain. I'm your son." He thought if he said it enough times, the words might reach her.

She got in the car and closed the door. Giffy, his hands still on the steering wheel, never once looked in my father's direction.

"Jah *Rastafari*," my father cried out in shock as their car started moving, reaching for His Majesty's strength for the first time. The loneliness he felt then doubled him over, and his quivering voice surprised him.

"Jah Rastafari!" He reached past his hurt to call out again. Heart flooded with anguish, his face grew torqued and wet as he called out to his mother from the unguarded place, called out to the indifferent sky, warbling each word like a prayer as their car drove away, with the moving truck following close behind.

After a few months of going from house to house, after spending his nights hiding from friends' parents who didn't want a Rasta under their roof, my father was tired of living like a thief. His mother had already turned her back on him once for being a Rasta, but he'd always believed that was Giffy's influence. If she saw his face just one more time, he thought, she would take him in. But he didn't even know her new address. So he decided to go up to the country to seek out his grandmother, who took one look at his budding dreadlocks and told him he couldn't stay with her, either. She pointed toward the road and told him that his mother had moved into a housing scheme in Bethel Town just down the street. He had nowhere else to go, so my father resolved to small up himself one more time and go see his mother. Evening had fallen and the last bus back to Mobay had long gone, so it was either his mother or the bush.

When he stood at her gate, he couldn't bring himself to call out for her. He stood there waiting, and just as he had turned to go, she walked out into the yard and jerked back.

"Eh eh! Ah wah you ah do yah?" She was so shocked that she tripped back into patois.

"Can I come inside the yard?" my father asked, mustering all his respectful diction.

She hesitantly agreed, and they stood awkwardly on the veranda.

"What you doing here?" she asked him again. "How did you find me?"

He took a deep breath and humbled himself.

"I have no place to live," he said, feeling the words growing hot in his throat. He explained that he'd been hiding out at a friend's house for the past three months, and he was scared of getting thrown out on the street.

She stood motionless. Her face fixed in stone.

"So, what am I supposed to do?" she asked him finally.

He stumbled over his words, although he had rehearsed them in his head.

"Please let me stay here, just for a night, until I can clean up a room in Aunt Sweetie's house."

"I don't know about that, Howie. There is no space in here, and I already told you I don't want anybody mashing up my settee."

My father looked at her and let the silence plead for him. She sighed.

"I will go and ask Giffy," she said. "Since it's just for a night." Then she disappeared into the house.

My father waited there for some time, his heart kicking in his chest.

Finally, she came back and looked down at her feet.

"No. You can't stay here. He doesn't want you here. And the settee—"

Just then, all the air seemed to leave the yard. My grandmother barely raised my father. Whenever she had left him as a child, to the cruelty of her family, for months at a time, he sat for hours at the windows of their houses, frightened and alone, waiting for her to return. But she rarely came back to collect him. She had always left him to face the world by himself and here it was happening again. Only anger moved through him now as he stared into the void of her face, and his body shook. She was no mother to him. She was no different than the sinister forces of this world that moved against a Rastaman—those who wanted to break him, to crumble him to nothing. She was Babylon. And there was no true family for him now but Rastafari. My father mustered all the voice he had and shouted.

"FIRE BUN!" he screamed in her face.

Like lightning had struck and scorched the earth at their feet, a chasm cleaved open at last between them.

"FIRE BUN!" His voice echoing down the street, booming into the house, rattling Giffy's teeth, as his mother flinched and backed away.

His eyes were wide and rabid.

"FIRE BUN!!!" he spat again, growing taller. "FIRE BUN!" he repeated, like an incantation, each syllable pronouncing his abjuring, breaking every bind. She was still cowering as he turned to leave her for the last time. Walking away, he hoped to Jah she'd been incinerated right where she stood.

With no home, my father moved into the dilapidated house up the hill from his grandmother that once belonged to his great-aunt Sweetie, before she emigrated to Canada. For months he cloistered himself from everyone he knew, lived on mangoes, breadfruits, and bananas from the yard, and slept on the littered and moss-covered floor. It wasn't the first floor he had slept on, nor would it be the last. His selfhood was a garden, flourishing some days, withering on others. To him, this was all living proof of Babylon's wicked ways, forever persecuting the Rastaman. All he wanted was to be free of the mercy of others. He tended to his dreadlocks and his flourishing precept, what a Rastaman called his beard. He rooted his belief in Jah, always aiming to reach higher heights of consciousness and righteousness, to enrich his livity, which was Rasta dialect for the tenets and principles of living Rastafari. Rastafari didn't use terms like "faith" or "religion," as those were Babylon's terms for worship. Instead, Rasta had livity, his trust in Jah, and his way of life. There, with the hills as his witness, my father found he needed nothing but the earth and its god-sent green to nurture his livity. Alone he could create his own temple of Rastafari, forging a private understanding of Jah that lived only within him, strengthened by his connection to nature, and separation from society, which was Babylon incarnate. This was the one thing he could control, his discipline—the way he lived his life as Rastafari. He knew a righteous livity would eventually set everything else right.

One day he walked up the main road, a stone's throw from the old house in which he'd been living. He hadn't touched his guitar since he last saw his mother and had instead let the silence eat mournfully away at the strings. A car zipped past him going down the road, but before it turned the corner and dropped out of sight, it squealed to a stop. Someone jumped out of the car and screamed his name.

"Howard Sinclair!" the man cried. When a car stops abruptly on a Jamaican road and somebody unseen screams your name, you do not answer. My father said nothing and started running for a place to hide, racking his mind for what johncrow might be coming to his door at last.

As the car reversed up the hill, he saw that the voice belonged to his good bredren Roy Park, with whom he used to play music.

"Man, all ah Montego Bay asking for you. Nobody knows where you are," Roy said in surprise, getting out of the car. "Nobody nuh know weh yuh deh. Yuh just miss up so!"

My father, stunned, mustered up a greeting, but nothing more.

"Why yuh just lock everybody so? Man, everybody ah wonder weh yuh deh. Yuh not playing music again? What happen? You give up on life?"

Here, my father's breath caught in his lungs, and all the troubles he had been pinning down those past years—the loss of his band, his ruined dream in America, the mute unknown of his father, the blank stare of his mother as she turned him out into the street—came crawling back to life, warped and unwanted. In the honest face of Roy Park, my father wept as if for the first time and told him all. "I have no one, and nowhere to go," he said. "I just don't want to beg people anymore. I feel like I will just leave it all."

"No, Rasta," Roy said. "Yuh can't do that. Yuh too much of a good musician to do that. I'm gonna to tell everybody where you are. Howie, you have to come back. You have to."

With that, my father turned his mind again to the world. There was going to be a party in Mobay the next week with all his former band-mates, a sort of homecoming for him. He spent the days leading up to it picking breadfruit, digging up yam, and chopping some sugarcane and three hands of banana as an offering to his old friends from Future Wind. Then that evening with nothing but his guitar, Rasta came down from the hills with Jah's music in his head again.

He arrived at the party in Mount Carey to one big excitement. When he walked in, everyone rose in joyous chatter, squawking like the blackbirds that perched on the trees at Sam Sharpe Square, waiting for the emergence of something out of the ordinary to set them alight. In each room he entered, friends grabbed him and dapped him.

My father indulged them, laughing with them as if nothing at all had happened. All night he dodged the girls trying to hug him and stopped them from touching his hair; there was no way of telling if their livity was righteous. He didn't want any unclean women on their monthly cycle touching his dreadlocks. He didn't smoke ganja and he didn't drink, and eventually he grew tired of the crowd and went to find a quiet spot.

My mother's sister Audrey had convinced her to go to the party that night to lift her spirits, but my mother barely knew anyone there, so she looked for a tucked-away corner of the house. She went out onto the balcony and looked out at the lights of Montego Bay below. She heard the commotion about Howard Sinclair arriving at the party, but she kept to herself, even though she'd loved Future Wind and had noticed the lead singer—like everybody else. She knew something about him was special, something unsaid in his face.

When he stepped out on the balcony for some air, my father was relieved to see it was empty. He hadn't noticed there was someone else there until a voice disrupted his thoughts.

"Hello, young man" were her first words. He turned to face the playful voice and saw a beautiful young woman standing there. She was simply dressed in a long skirt, no makeup, smiling. She looked like a modest woman, one not drawn in by Babylon's guiles, he thought.

"Irie, sistren. I'm Howard. Good to meet you."

"I'm Audrey's sister, Esther. We've met before." Maybe it was the sea breeze out on the balcony, or the heady fact of their aloneness that made my mother feel uncharacteristically bold. She looked my father up and down, studying his budding young locks tucked up under his Che Guevara beret and his green army suit. *He looks like a revolutionary*, she thought. *He looks like someone I can talk to.*

"Forgive the I," my father said, putting on his famous charm and moving closer with a smile. "I and I was meant to meet you this time. This time is the only time." There was no singular or selfish "I" in Rastafari livity, it was always a plural "I"—for Jah's spirit was always with a Rastaman.

"So, this is the famous Howard Sinclair?" my mother said. She never drank, but she felt drunk then. She might never get this night again. "I hear you're a Rasta now," she whispered, and reached out her hand to touch his hair. He shifted away and grabbed her hand, held it firmly, and, as he tells it, never let go.

The night outgrew them on that balcony as they talked until the sun came up over the Caribbean Sea. People passed in and out of their sphere, but my parents didn't notice. They reasoned about Rastafari and about family, about Haile Selassie, about reggae music. They talked about repatriating to Africa, about being born with a sense of loss, living with the amputated history of the Black diaspora; the grief of not knowing where their ancestors came from, or the name of the home they could return to. Mostly they looked out onto Montego Bay growing lighter as the hours waned and talked about the future. They were both searching. Every time someone called after them teasingly, "Young lovers," their hearts said yes. Eventually my father confided in my mother. He told her he was here at a party with a hundred friends but he was alone, he was homeless. She felt for him. By the end of the night he even let her touch his hair. But she could not yet express what heavy stone had held her underwater.

When they finally left hand in hand to grab a taxi in town, she told him, "You could stay with me. I don't have much, but I have a room on the beach at my father's house." For weeks afterward they exchanged letters and tried to see each other as often as they could. Eventually my mother gathered the courage to ask her father if he could live with her at White House. Her father never gave her an answer. Instead, he took my father out to sea early the next morning while my mother paced the shoreline. When the skiff finally returned to shore, my father held up a handsome catch of fish and smiled, and that was it, he was allowed to stay.

One night, weeks later, while my parents lay in bed at White House, my mother decided she would finally tell him the truth before things went any further between them. She was prepared to never see him again, to spend her final days at the beach alone, as her own mother had done.

"Howie," she whispered, and turned to him. "Last year I went up to the clinic at Mount Alvernia and a nun told me I can't have children." She hid a soft cry in her throat as she told him the story.

My father listened as she spoke, then shook his head.

"Rasta don't believe in Babylon system," he said. "The Christians, the nuns, Americans, they're all the same. Their doctors want Black people to be infertile. This is just Babylon's tricks. Don't believe it."

My mother studied his face as he spoke, admiring his eyes, which burned with enough conviction to light the room.

She touched her hands to her stomach and closed her eyes. "Okay," she said, and took a deep breath. When she opened them, she didn't believe what Babylon's nun had told her anymore. When she opened them, she saw only him.

There they went. Three months after they had met, two nineteen-year-olds trekked up to the hills on a trodition, which is what they called the journey of becoming Rastafari. They moved into a small commune with other Rastas, acknowledging Haile Selassie as the Black Messiah and growing their dreadlocks. They accepted Jah as their guide in all things and chanted his name, decrying the temptation of Babylon. For a year they slept on the soil in a bamboo house, eating an Ital diet from the plants and fruits of the earth, and committed to a more righteous way of living. My mother smoked herb every day, cooked and cleaned and farmed the land, while my father went back down to town to spread Jah's message with his reggae music. At night, when my mother sat around the fire drumming and chanting the Nyabinghi chant, she felt anchored to something at last. She had left her concerned family in White House, thrilled by the chance to get away from her tiny village but not knowing what to expect. Up in the hills, away from her past, away from the hurt that awaited her at the beach, she made a home. Here, she could forget her grandfather's final terror. She could forget that Catholic nun's lies about her womb. Here, Babylon could not touch her. She woke with a spliff in her hand and slept entwined with the hallowed garden she tended. There was peace and love between bredren and sistren, as they reasoned every night about Marcus Garvey and tracing the roots of their African ancestry. This was the higher purpose she had combed the seaside seeking. She could have stayed forever.

This feeling of home that appealed to my parents, the unified livity of Rastafari bredren and sistren, was the vision of Leonard Howell, the radical street preacher who in 1940, inspired by Marcus Garvey's vision for Black liberation and Marx's egalitarianism, built a commune called Pinnacle in the hills of Kingston where Black men and women could live in harmony, uplifting themselves under the banner of hope that a Black Messiah had been born. Garvey had told his followers to look to Africa for a Black Redeemer, and it was in Ethiopia that Howell found proof of him: the Conquering Lion of Judah, the Emperor Haile Selassie I. It was there, in Howell's commune, that the first tenets of Rastafari were established; a nonviolent movement rooted in Black empowerment and equality, aiming to free the poor and downtrodden of Babylon's colonial system, a way to rise out of prevalent poverty through unity, through reaping the natural fruits of the land. Howell, known as the First Rasta, lived peacefully at Pinnacle with an estimated three thousand other Rastas, preaching Black independence and togetherness. But the Jamaican government, still under British rule, thought his brand of transgression dangerous; an empowered Black majority would mean revolution. In 1954, Babylon raided Pinnacle's ganja fields and seized their five hundred acres of land and money, claiming Howell's Rasta commune was a cult, and set fire to the anti-colonial movement by reframing the Rastafari as agents of dread, as madmen, as child-killers, as the Blackheart Man. Rasta bredren, sistren, and children were displaced, and Howell's dream of a unified and self-governing Rastafari movement scattered on the wind. Sections of the movement eventually broke off into three main groups: the Mansion of Nyabinghi, the Bobo Shanti, and the Twelve Tribes of Israel. Over time, a few Rasta settlements and Nyabinghi centers modeled as miniature Pinnacles cropped up over the island, but the true unification envisioned by Howell had been irrevocably staunched by Babylon. This splintering would eventually become the painful undoing of my family a generation later, because it encouraged most Rastafari to individualize their livity at home, with impunity. There, in the privacy of their own households, each Rasta bredren could be a living godhead, the king of his own secluded temple.

Just as Howell's vision had been short-lived, the harmony of my parents' idyll eventually broke after a year, when my father fought a Rasta elder who he thought had made advances on my mother. He was never comfortable in company, even then; his temper was so volatile it made him antisocial, a pattern that would only worsen in the years to come. Soon after that, he told my mother, "Pack your things and come with the I. Because when I man leave, I'm not coming back." And she did. When they returned to the seaside at White House—to what my father now called the "shitty" instead of the city—they both had shoulder-length natty Congo Bongo dreadlocks, with my mother's once-soft and glistening hair now resembling a stiffened bird's nest, coiled into the fixed shape of a fisherman's hat she'd worn the entire year.

When my aunt Audrey saw my mother the day she came back from the hills, she screamed. "What did you do to my sister?!" she shrieked at my father. My mother held tight to my father's hand as my auntie circled her. Her handsewn clothes were ragged, sun-bleached and shapeless, covering her wrists and ankles. Her hair was stiff and unwashed, molded into a flat dome of dreadlocks on her head. "Your good hair!" Auntie

Audrey cried, distraught that she had lost her sister without realizing it. She reached out to touch my mother's head, and my mother pulled away from her.

"Be careful how you talk to the I," my mother sneered at her, snapping the nylon line between them. "I and I is Rasta."

The following months at White House oscillated between tense silence and furious disagreements between my father and my mother's family, who believed she had been drowned under his influence. But Babylon couldn't touch them now. They knew they were fortified and righteous, two youths remade pure by His Majesty's fire. My parents had gone up into the hills as two lost and lonely people, but they returned to the world grafted as one.

The way ahead of them was clear. My father believed "the fullness of God was when a man and a woman came together to make children." In a herb-stalked dream my parents decided that their most righteous duty as Rastas was to make a Rasta family. Under the tenets of Rastafari, a woman's divine purpose was to bear children, so my mother had torched what the nun had told her and tried to conceive anyway. One of the herbswomen up in the hills had told her to drink kombucha tea with a thick culture for fertility. Each day she chanted out for Jah, but only the orphaned sound of doubt crept back into her body. She began to dread each menses that came. A year passed this way; her hope was the faint kerosene lamp she blew out every night, only to light again the next evening. Then one January, she noted her monthly had been several weeks late. She tried not to be too hopeful this time; she'd gone bloodless six weeks before and had celebrated, only for disappointment to come again. At three weeks late she held her breath and decided to head downtown to a lab at the top of the busy hub of Market Street for testing. She would collect the results fourteen days later.

After what felt like a lifetime, the fourteenth day had come. My mother, heart galloping, walked back up the hill to Market Street to collect her results. She considered the envelope in her hands, the weight of it. She slowly opened the seal and looked, then looked again.

She was floating.

Pregnancy: POSITIVE, it read. All the way up in the trees with the blackbirds, her heart was leaping. She checked again. Pregnancy: POSITIVE. POSITIVE, she read the result slip over and over, her mouth gaping at the plus sign. She heard no sounds, felt no sorrows. Saw no buildings. She was the only woman in the world, clutching this slip of paper and laughing.

She laughed until her cheeks hurt and almost danced into Montego Bay traffic. All the way down those long, dreamy avenues she danced, floating out to White House with her head thrown back, laughing past the herons.

"So you see," she says to me now, cradling me tight against the waves and relishing this turn in the lore of our lives. "It was you who showed me the way."

I was the living testimony of Jah, and his conduit on earth, my father. She needed no belief except in what grew within her, needed no guide except her offspring. At twenty-one, my mother looked at my father and saw only the man who had made of her a miracle, and she decided to devote herself to him and this life, without ever wondering what it might cost her. Or her daughters. Ahead of him, my father saw only the clear and doubtless flame of purpose. *Jah is with me*, he said, taking the first step of our family's long walk through the fire. *Jah is with us*.

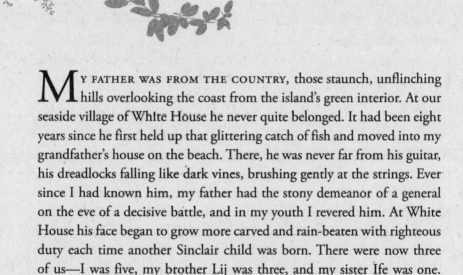

4

Unclean Women

MY FATHER WAS FROM THE COUNTRY, those staunch, unflinching hills overlooking the coast from the island's green interior. At our seaside village of White House he never quite belonged. It had been eight years since he first held up that glittering catch of fish and moved into my grandfather's house on the beach. There, he was never far from his guitar, his dreadlocks falling like dark vines, brushing gently at the strings. Ever since I had known him, my father had the stony demeanor of a general on the eve of a decisive battle, and in my youth I revered him. At White House his face began to grow more carved and rain-beaten with righteous duty each time another Sinclair child was born. There were now three of us—I was five, my brother Lij was three, and my sister Ife was one. Though my father had a naturally frail frame and was no taller than my mother, he could quiet the whole house just by walking through the door, with an air as perishing as His Majesty's. Under Selassie's scorpion-gaze, I was small. His portrait hung high from our living room wall, searing into me whenever my father spoke.

We lived in a noisy tangle, packed under zinc with my mother's family, who my father called baldheads and heathens, the unprincipled men and women of Babylon. Living in the same house meant there was no gate to guard me and my siblings from them, and there were no fences to keep the other villagers away. This troubled him. Steadfastly devoted to Rastafari, my father had a strict binary of rules by which he measured everything. What was righteous and what was wicked. Who was blessed and who was heathen. Though my siblings and I were all under six, the purity of our spirits obsessed him because there was no way for him to know that my livity was righteous—that I followed the true path of Rastafari—once I scampered away from the heat of his gaze.

Throughout my life, my father was the main breadwinner in our family, and was always gone to the hotels for work. Six nights a week, he traveled for hours by bus to the resorts, then often stayed overnight, so he was gone when we left for school in the early mornings, and gone again when we came home in the afternoons. There was no other option. Being a musician was just about the only way a Rastaman could be gainfully employed in Jamaica.

By 1989, when we lived at White House, reggae's promise of cultural revolution and freedom for Black people had waned, becoming little more than a sideshow over resort dinners. Bob Marley had been dead almost a decade, Haile Selassie dead for almost two decades, and the Rastafari movement had gone back to the fringes of society, with most reggae musicians relegated to performing cabaret shows at the new palatial resorts devouring our northern coastline. Just like Leonard Howell's commune, reggae's original mission of anti-colonial rebellion and spreading the message of Rastafari had been defanged. My father was convinced that reggae's erasure by dancehall in the 1990s was a deliberate ploy by Jamaica's white right-wing prime minister, Edward Seaga, and the CIA, an agency he believed to be the villainous heart of Babylon itself.

Though my father sang at these hotels to make a living, first and foremost for him, reggae was a religious experience. He believed that if he kept playing his reggae with righteous conviction, this crooked world would wake up and change. If he kept playing, he could save Black people's minds, and we would reach Zion, the promised land in Africa. Some days it was enough for him to commune with Jah, to spread His Majesty's message, and so he continued to play his holy music for tourists at popular resorts in Negril and Trelawny, feeding the vast appetite of the white and foreign imagination, all while Jamaica shunned him and his message. What the tourists couldn't discern, as they drank and ate dinner while my father sang and flashed his dreadlocks onstage, was his true motivation for singing. Night after night he sang to burn down Babylon, which was them.

At the seaside we had a small radio but no television, so we got our news of Babylon like roots wine and bitters from my father's mouth. He was our god of history, god of media, and high priest all in one. Every week my brother, my sister, and I kneeled in front of him like disciples as he taught us Black history; all the crucial knowledge that Babylon kept from us, he said. He told us of African kings and conquerors, of unsung Black inventors and pioneers, proof of our glory, our greatness. He wanted us to know we were mighty. Like most members of Rastafari, my father's most enduring wish was repatriating to Africa, and he sang us psalms of the motherland so we would know ourselves. "Africa for Africans!" was his frequent rallying cry, quoting Marcus Garvey, and we would bellow the words back to him in response, feeling our power.

Whenever the spirit of Jah flowed through him, my father pointed his hands into a sacred Rasta symbol called the Sign of the Power of the Trinity, and my brother would follow along, both of them looking regal and militant with their index fingers pointed down into a diamond, like the emperor did above our heads. Once, I tried linking my fingers into the sacred sign as well, but my father reached down and firmly peeled my hands apart. He shook his head at me, his gaze stern as His Majesty's above me, and said, "This is not for you. This is only for bredren." I crumpled away, wondering why I was unworthy, and let my hands hang limp as a soaked flower.

When he wasn't exalting the majesty of Haile Selassie, my father would deliver hour-long lectures about the evil white men who ruled and ruined the world, the men he imagined every time he said "Babylon." He wanted us to guard ourselves from them, to watch out for the bloodsuckers and baldheads. At night in our bedroom he chanted *Fire bun!* at those duppies out to get us, thorned to anger by those he called cattle, those "simple people" with "simple minds," telling me and my siblings that Jamaicans were enslaved by Christianity, by America, and by that "damn bugu-bugu noise," which is what he called dancehall.

"These people are in chains and don't even see it," he told us. My mother, listening with her sewn-up silence, smoked her spliff and nodded along. "Nyamin pork and chicken, ingesting all kinds of dead flesh, drinking rum and poisoning their minds with dat bugu-bugu noise. I man cyaan even call it music. It's not music. This is why Black people will never be free," he said with painful conviction, as if it burned him alive at night. If my siblings and I were unable to escape before one of his lectures began, we were forced to sit in the cramped bedroom and listen to it in full, nodding often and bleating out agreement. And yet, loving him was so easy. It was something I'd learned from my mother all too well—there was only one answer to whatever he said. *Yes, Daddy.* Whatever lecture or conjecture, *Yes, Daddy.* A keen face of listening, then *Yes,* to whatever he said. Accepting his bitters like spring water.

When he was feeling particularly loving, he called me Budgie, after his favorite bird, the budgerigar. "Because of how sweetly you used to coo as a baby." But my interior was volatile, he said. My giddiness was a weakness, which made me susceptible to the wiles of Babylon. I needed discipline. Like most members of Rastafari, my father believed that a person's body was Jah's temple, and should remain pure and uncorrupted, just as the mind should remain vigilant against encroaching evil. Inching ever closer was Babylon and its temptation.

It was baldheads who posed the gravest danger to my purity, my father said. A year before, my family had survived Hurricane Gilbert, which came raging from the sea in 1988, destroying our boats and fish traps, demolishing our house, unpeeling the whole roof, and splintering our furniture to dust. But we had survived. It was not the sea or the hungry mangroves that brought down darkness on I and I, but the heathens right here in the village. Chief among Dad's accursed heathens were my two aunties. Their livity wasn't right, my father said, denouncing them as Jezebels who wore too much "jingbeng"—dangling gold earrings and bangles, false fingernails and bright red nail polish. They had chemically processed hair and wore makeup and tight jeans shorts. They were pork-eaters and rum-drinkers. They liked dancehall and gossiped about the men they dated. To my father they may as well have been the grand architects of Babylon. *Unclean women,* he called them, and skirted them with a screwface and his nose in the heavens.

When he first arrived at White House, my father had tried converting my aunties to Rastafari. He spent hours lecturing them on the evils of Babylon—telling them to stop straightening their hair, to stop wearing makeup, to cover their bodies. Then he tried to convince them to stop eating meat. "Rasta don't eat flesh," he told them, refusing to touch the pots they cooked meat in, leaving the house in disgust. He covered his hair with a woven tam, even indoors, to preserve his dreadlocks from their iniquity. My auntie Audrey pushed back against his rants, sparring nearly every day with my father. When she could no longer endure his lecturing, she rolled her eyes and told him to shut up, pointing toward the road, telling him to "Galang back where yuh come from!"

Auntie Audrey, who had known my father long before my mother did, was distressed by my mother's radical changes after meeting my father, and was a frequent and outspoken critic of his control. Despite what my father told me about her, I loved my auntie. She was beautiful and kind and would loom bright as the North Star in my sky. Of the entire village, even the men, she was the only person who ever matched his conviction, standing firm to challenge him, which angered him even more. A rebellious woman like her was "an instrument of Babylon," as I would eventually come to learn for myself—and though I was too young to understand their quarrels then, as I grew older, her refusal to be diminished would subtly come to shape my own sense of place in this world.

"Yuh brainwash my pretty brownine sister and hide her 'way," Auntie Audrey yelled one day in an argument with my father. "I saw *you* kissing up another woman in the back seat of the taxi while my sister sitting there in the front seat listening to the two of you, silent like stooge." Her voice quavered at the memory. She could not reconcile this voiceless disciple my mother had become.

"Say what you want," my father countered, "Esther is the cleanest woman in White House, in every sense of the word. Spiritually free and clean. That's why you all jealous of her. Jealous of I and I!"

All of this would come to mean a great deal to me later, but for now it hovered somewhere just out of reach, unintelligible to my young mind. On and on they went, thrashing tears and fire and salted earth. My mother took me and my siblings to the sea and stayed out of it.

I remember my mother in this time as perpetually silent, her lips pursed as if she might never speak another word. She began smoking ganja the way my father played his music—what began as her way to commune with His Majesty soon became a way to escape the daily strife of living in Babylon, and before long, it became a fixed aspect of her character. She followed the smoke into a state of calm and avoided all conflict. At White House she had been pregnant with three children in four years, and was wary of thinking even a single bad thought, lest it affect the child growing inside her. She wanted none of the nasty argument, so she stayed serenely away, and I was grateful for her quiet shelter, the steady tide of her tranquility.

When the walls between my father and auntie scorched, my father grabbed his guitar and sang a less peaceful song. Back straight as an ancient tree, he jolted pen to paper, and chanted out *Fire bun!* from the depths of his lungs before he strummed his guitar, decrying his hatred for Babylon, baldheads, and bloodsuckers at top volume, pouring his lava into song lyrics. In times like these, his reggae music was also his firebomb, a way to obliterate whatever evil corrupted his and Jah-Jah's green earth.

He started singing a pleading croon, his eyes closed:

> *Come by here, oh Jah*
> *Cause we need your intervention*
> *Babylon is getting from bad to worse,*
> *Jah we need your protection*
> *Batter, Shatter, Scatter the heathen away!*

I stood outside our bedroom window and listened. As he sang I felt hot coals, burning underfoot. The emperor's black gaze, even out of sight on the living room wall, made my stomach lurch.

When my father was finished singing, I heard his voice rumbling through the bedroom window as he talked to my mother. Gruff and muffled, I picked out the particular tenor he used whenever he talked about unclean women. "Lay down with mongrel, you ketch flea," he said. "I man daughters cyaan grow wit heathens and idolize their ways."

My mom shook her head gravely as he spoke, assuring him that would never happen. He had already forbidden me from playing with my cousin and baby aunts because they were too rough and kept bruising me. But he still rustled awake in his hotel room at night, worried about my adult aunts being around me while he was gone.

"All the sistren dem lost now," my father said, voice hushed. "Lost. Because they fall under the spell of Babylon." He pulled on his precept and shook his head. "I man tired of living with Jezebel," he said.

As he spoke, the words blazed against my mind, fear rattling me as my father cursed on, terrified that I, too, would fall under an evil spell of Babylon and get lost.

"This world has no place for an unclean woman," my father said, and turned to leave my mother in the bedroom.

I scattered out of sight down the beach and found the hull of an empty sea urchin with which to trouble my hands. I was five years old, heart skittering as I sat alone with this thought, hazy and unformed. The unclean woman. It sounded bad, and dirty. It made my father angry. The idea that I could be someone like that frightened me. My fear nudged out of its shell, waiting for some darkness to be borne of me. While that shining world of ruin and temptation jangled in the sky like gold filaments, a legion of wanton eyes, beckoning.

Though I was too young to understand that my father believed the sanctity of my soul was at stake, I was petrified of becoming unclean. It was almost a decade before I learned my ruin had been fixed all along. Rasta bredren believed women were more susceptible to moral corruption because they menstruated. I was destined to be unclean. But at five years old, I wanted only to be good for him. I wanted to be worthy. Though I was born a daughter, I still believed I was a salvageable machine; the correct cogs and automation would someday make me right. At night, I imagined Babylon ramming its three-horned beast into my unsoiled interior and then Jah riding in to purify me. Then down came the woodpecker's hammer and the day reset itself, as I raced out into the sand again, watching how carefully each night twisted its long tongue into a folktale.

It was Babylon that drove us away from the sea, in the end. The longer we lived with baldheads who didn't share my father's beliefs, the worse his distrust of outsiders became. Growing ever more preoccupied with the encroachment of Babylon, he decided we'd outgrown White House. My mother, still shaken by my near-drowning even a year later, agreed. My father had found us a new place to move, a place free from Babylon's system, where we didn't have to "deal with no ism and schism." About two weeks later, the moving truck arrived in the closed throat of evening. My parents told no one, neither my aunties, nor my grandfather, nor my cousins, that they were moving that night. In less than two hours we were ready to go.

I don't think I understood the truth of it then—that we wouldn't ever be coming back.

It was pitch-black when we moved away. The houses were barely visible, and the crickets, I remember, were the only things that sounded against our departure. My parents rolled our life up in the small shell of the pickup truck and told the truckman to start driving as if we had never lived at White House at all. I looked back at the seaside as we left, but it was ink dark. All that was visible was the ghost outline of the waves I knew were there, waves I felt watching as the distance grew between me and the sea. I said goodbye to my village of the lonely and unclaimed. The only place I still call home.

Years later, while cloistered in the countryside and aching for my birthplace by the sea, I would come to understand. There was more than one way to be lost, more than one way to be saved. While my mother had saved me from the waves and gave me breath, my father tried to save me only by suffocation—with ever-increasing strictures, with incense-smoke. With fire. Both had wanted better for me, but only one of them would protect me in the end.

I curled into my father's lap in the passenger seat and studied his face, the way his eyes only looked ahead. His paranoia that I would be invaded by Babylon would dominate my childhood for years to come, but none of us, not even my mother, knew how far he was willing to go to prevent it.

"Don't worry, Budgie," he said to me, smiling. "The next place will be better."

5

Bettah Must Come

WE MOVED TO BOGUE HEIGHTS, A hillside community that overlooked Montego Bay and its looming hotels, and, beyond that, the sea's constant blue. There we lived in the golden hour, measuring the months by the birds living in the trunk of our plum tree. When the parrots left, the doves moved in. Soon the doves were gone and we awoke to a fat hedge of owls. Finally, when the owls were evicted, all that remained was a single knock-knocking woodpecker, our crack-of-dawn alarm. When I first saw our new house in the daylight, I was stunned. It was an empty two-story house with upstairs and downstairs, flanked on each side by wide moss-covered steps that rushed down to a sprawling backyard, then up again to a wide front yard full of noontime buzz and bright-winged things fluttering.

"Wow! It's a mansion," I said to my parents, as my brother Lij and I skipped in and out of the rooms downstairs. Looking up there was a long veranda and wide windows verged by curtains you could just see into, showing all the spacious rooms upstairs whose doors were still locked. We rented two rooms on the ground floor, a modest bedroom and living room separated by a folding partition. Inside the bedroom was an indoor bathroom that flushed. When I first saw the toilet, I squealed and pushed the metal handle, standing there to watch the water swirl away. I laughed. Then I did it again. I used a public toilet at school, but this was the first inside toilet that was just for me.

When I moved to flush again, my father stopped my hand.

"Stop wasting water, and mind you break it," he scolded.

Outside I twirled around in this new space and gawked, making my hands wide wide. "Is this all for us?" I asked my parents.

"No," my father said, his face knitting stern. "We are only renting these rooms downstairs." He gestured around me. "Remember, upstairs is off-limits. That's where Ms. Gordon lives. None of us are supposed to go up there."

Ms. Gordon was our landlady, a retired Jamaican émigré who lived in the United States for six months at a time. How rich she must be, I thought. How fancy, living up there in Foreign. I conjured pearl earrings and red nail polish and a whole glittering lifetime for her.

The forbidden places didn't matter one bit to me and my little brother, because Bogue was a paradise of firsts. Though we occupied only the smallest portion of the house, for the first time, the yard was all ours. Our living room opened out onto a lawn that galloped downhill into a sloping jungle, a sprawling backyard bursting with fruit trees that undulated for almost an acre. Exploding in a verdant spray were navel oranges and three types of mango trees, branches and leaves a-chatter with birds and insects, our whole world crammed to the teeth with possibilities. Each day my widening eyes filled with things to climb and eat, sometimes in that order. There was a massive breadfruit tree, a bristling Otaheite apple tree, and stooping avocado trees in bloom. Detached from the main house and up the moss-covered steps was our kitchen, its windows facing the beloved lignum vitae, our national flower, which bled maroon beneath its thin bark. Our gate was rusted copper, painted over white, flanked by a driveway outdreaming itself into a flush lawn of tall grass.

This was our private kingdom. We would let no one else in. On weekends we sat outside on the terrace overlooking the lawn with our parents, while they unfurled each note of Haile Selassie's magnificence again and again in the sun, key after key, composing a rhythm. We listened until we knew Haile Selassie's name meant Power of the Trinity. Knew Ethiopia was the only African nation never to be colonized, despite the efforts of Mussolini and the Vatican. We knew the pope blessed Mussolini's army and their poison gas, blessed their bombs and bullets before Italy invaded in 1935. We knew white people were evil. Knew Christianity to be wicked. We knew Margaret Thatcher and Ronald Reagan were white devils. That Gorbachev bore the mark of the beast. And Queen Elizabeth, in Rasta wordplay on her villainy, was Queen "Eliza-bat."

All of this was the heart of Babylon, my father told us. He pulled on his precept as we kneeled in front of him, his long dreadlocks draping his shoulders, a titan's black roots, unshakable. Behind him was the large map of Africa we spent our rambling days studying, memorizing all the countries on the continent and their capitals, my brother and I rassling at his feet to show who was the brightest. Haile Selassie's birthplace was always first.

This was part of our livity, my father reminded us, the source from which Rastafari flowed. "For a people without the knowledge of their past history, origin and culture is like a tree without roots," he said, quoting Marcus Garvey. A moist hiss pressed in through the double doors that led out into the yard. "You overstand?" Rastafari rejected any English word with a negative connotation, and took every linguistic opportunity to upend Babylon's language, so "understand" became "overstand."

"Yes, Daddy," we said, repeating the Marcus Garvey quote like a family motto. Under our rented roof, in this hand-me-down life, these lessons were our daily bread.

"Jah," my father called out to us, stroking his precept.

"Rastafari," my siblings and I answered.

"Jah."

"Rastafari!" we shouted.

There we were. I was six years old, my brother four. Mouths open in the rain. Eager to be filled.

My father looked over our heads and out into the yard, and clasped his hands into the sacred Rasta sign.

"I and I not goin by the names Babylon gave me no more," he told us. "The I is now called Djani." He said it with a flourish, strong and certain, pleased with the power of his new name in his mouth. Gone was Howard Garfield O'Brien Sinclair, the ghost name of a ghost boy. A renouncement of his mother and his unknown father, whose face and name were still a mystery to him, at twenty-eight. Djani was a solid Swahili name, meaning simply, *King*.

"Power starts at conception," he told us, gazing out as he spoke. Much like the reggae lyrics he used as spells to chant down Babylon, the names we called each other meant everything.

My parents had inherited their names from enslavers, like most citizens of former colonized nations, and descendants of the enslaved. They wanted to ensure my siblings and I were free of those chains, so they used an African naming book for all of us. Each of our names was like an amulet, worn against the known and unknown evils of the day. If anyone ever teased or questioned our names, which they often did, we would walk into the world like lionhearts, for we knew ourselves.

"Safiya Jamila," my father said, calling out my full name as if he were announcing royalty. I imagined him placing my name like a crown atop my head. *Clear-minded and pure. Beautiful.* It lay heavy and lovely about my ears.

"Lij Tafari," he called out next, turning to his only son, and my brother grew taller. Lij was named after Haile Selassie himself, from the emperor's boyhood honorific, a fact my brother wielded like a spear thrown skyward whenever my father called his name. *Blessed Child. One who is highly respected or feared.* My father also called him Fire or Fireball, so that he would remember his earthly power.

"Ife Kibibi," my father continued, singing out sweetly in the direction of my baby sister, who had been born two years before, in 1988, in the middle of Hurricane Gilbert. *Little Lady of Love.* Perhaps the truest meaning of all, for she had none of the storm and only the sweet calm that came after, as she toddled around meekly, always observing, still unaware of herself.

I studied the sated quiet of my mother's face as she listened. The sun had bleached her hair sienna. I loved the mole on her right eyebrow and the dimple in her chin, the warmth of her hands and the six fingers she was born with on each of them. She had also taken a new name, a name only my father used: Makini Nassoma, meaning *Strength of Character. Queen.* But she had always been Esther Norman to me. She never took the name Sinclair because my parents never married. "Rasta don't believe in marriage," my father told me firmly. "That's just Babylon brainwashing."

The next day the sky shook with the news of the birds and my mother blew ganja smoke in the air, eyes squinting. The humidity bloomed thick in our lamb's-wool hair. My father looked over us, his flock and his king-dom, and he was pleased. At last, we lived away from the heathens. In our own yard, with a gate that he could use to keep Babylon out. Here, where he was godhead and architect of our new world, he would create the purest Rasta family.

Those early days at Bogue were the most blissful of my life; we woke in harmony under sunshine and birdsong, the world's chaos held safely away by my parents' arms. The day's half-light glinted off the smooth scar on my father's forehead and he smiled. "A family living in *umoja* can overcome anything," he said, using the Swahili word for unity. My mother hummed out in agreement. Here everything, even happiness, was possible.

Our closest neighbors, we would soon discover, were all versions of our landlady, Ms. Gordon—retired, well-off, and mostly well-meaning women we called "Aunt." There were the elderly sisters Aunt Vye and Aunt Ess who lived next door, there was our family friend Aunt Si and her daughter who lived up the hill, and there was our one neighbor who was too rich to be on familial terms; we called her simply Ms. Martin. Farther up the winding hill were people whose homes seemed more like the ones we'd left at White House—no electricity, crumbling interior, always on the edge of nature's mercy. It seemed to me that my family's life always orbited somewhere between these two realities at Bogue, caught between the massive two- and three-story houses with giant satellite dishes at the bottom of the hill, and the modest cobbled-together cottages with over-grown yards at the very hilltop. Our existence between these two worlds was borrowed, transient. My parents were the only Rasta people living in Bogue, and our neighbors on both sides of the hill took note.

It was here, on our verdant hillside, that my mother first taught me the poetry of greenery. She showed me how to suckle language from each bloom. It was a blessing, she told me, to live as one with the earth. This is how Jah intended it. On weekend mornings, when the dew was still on the grass, she took us on nature walks up the hill, pointing out the neon bush lizards and giant swallowtails we encountered there, quizzing us on the names of the trees and plants we saw on the way. Soon we knew a petunia from an oleander from a bougainvillea, all of them nourishing the garden of ourselves.

While my father molded our view of the wicked world and its hidden history, my mother shaped our love of learning and our sense of wonder. While he warned us of Babylon, she showed us Zion. My siblings and I were the top of our class at our schools, skipping several grades along the way. Soon my mother became known in Montego Bay as the light-skinned Rasta lady with the three bright children. Children drew to her like a flame and trailed behind her like ducklings when she came to pick us up from school. Along in a line they went, waddling behind Mom and Ife, chanting, "Ife modda! Ife modda!" She was a wild wonder to us. When we were older, my siblings and I would jest that while my father was forever behind the joke, my mother was always in front of it, ringing out her distinct laughter wherever she went, breaking the rules long before we noticed. Every Saturday she took us to the public library, sometimes checking out books that she never brought back, tailoring instead her own private library collection for us. After she checked out the heavy leatherbound volume of a general knowledge *Encyclopaedia Britannica*, we kept it for years on a shelf in our living room.

A book, I soon learned, was time travel. Each page held irrefutable power. When the sun burned so bright it made me drunk, I opened the giant encyclopedia and fell right in. On weekends I pretended to be a teacher, strict and insistent, drilling my siblings with facts from the encyclopedia. Feeling electricity spark alive in my fingertips, we learned of cuneiform and Mesopotamia. Imagined Hannibal on the Alps. We floated along the Danube and lived under the shadow of Timbuktu. We knew the birthdate of Marcus Garvey—one day before Mom's. And Bob Marley's—one day before Dad's. More proof of our power. We studied the lives of Black pioneers like George Washington Carver, Mary McLeod Bethune, and Madam C. J. Walker. Every Sunday we pored over the week's spelling bee list, guzzling each new word like soursop juice, and studying the map of Africa, so we'd be ready when my father quizzed us next.

We were the only Rasta children at school, and our parents were the only Rasta people at the PTA meetings. My parents had only graduated high school, but they had higher hopes for our future. Academic excellence, they always told us, was a way to escape a run-down life. "We likkle but we tallawah," my father said. We may seem small, but we can move mountains. My siblings and I took this maxim to heart. We were all spelling bee champions, we won elocution contests and dance competitions. For my father, our intelligence was a gold token. We were his living proof of Jah's blessings, proof that Rastafari could outwit Babylon any day of the week. Soon friends and acquaintances wanted to know my mother's secret. Strangers were less subtle, telling my mother straight to her face that they thought Rastas couldn't read, so how come we were so bright?

This gave my mother the inspiration to start something she had been dreaming of, an idea she stashed away like a seed of hemp. An educational program for other children, based on how she taught us, with a curriculum of word games, poems, songs, and trivia, taught through time spent outside in nature. She called it S.P.I.C., after her favorite cleaning product:

Stimulation
Program for the
IQ-raising of
Children

Parents all over Mobay rushed to sign up their children. Mom taught S.P.I.C. from our empty garage after school. Her classroom was barebones because she couldn't yet afford supplies. In the beginning, she taught for free because she believed this to be her civic duty. "All children deserve a great education," she told me. My father couldn't stop talking about it. "See how Babylon system can't make no yute smart as ours?" He wouldn't say he was bragging, because Rasta don't brag. "Esther not even a trained teacher and she have baldhead from all ovah the place begging for the secret! I-man apprecilove that."

My siblings and I helped Mom perfect her new lessons, which made us experts by the time those afternoons rolled around. When all the children gathered, we were ready to show them all that we knew and we weren't subtle. We each took turns being the "Computer Man," a robot who was supposed to know the answer to any question you asked, cycling through our knowledge at lightning speed. Every time we played, I out-maneuvered everyone with my final question, gloating: "How do you spell Czechoslovakia?"

Finally, out of kindness for the other children, my mother told me I wasn't allowed to play Computer Man anymore.

"Why?" I whined.

"Because you're the oldest and you know the most."

It pleased me so to hear it.

On weeknights my father played at a resort named Hedonism II, then he took the public bus three hours to Mobay to see us on his day off, burning incense to cleanse himself before stepping through the gate. He was most peaceful in my life when he was first with us at Bogue, happiest to know that we had a gate that kept Babylon out, and we were all overjoyed to be with him, my siblings and I eagerly awaiting the squeak of the gate announcing his return to us every weekend. But the longer we lived there and the longer he worked at the hotels, the more he changed. Or the more apparent his change became to me. Soldiering wearily through the gate each weekend, he began to return to us with a screwface and a heavy mood. Leaning his guitar case against the wall, he shooed me and my brother away and barked a familiar tune to my mother. He didn't get the respect he deserved. He wanted to play his own songs, not just Bob Marley's. The volume of his voice bellowing louder as he spoke. He was tired of the nastiness at the hotel, the nastiness of the dancehall music on the radio. He couldn't seem to escape the heathens. He couldn't protect us from Babylon. His anger and frustration shook the walls, and we cowered under his helplessness without escape, the whole sky and roof bearing down on us.

Even as he thundered in our cramped two-room apartment, he stood tall as a mountain in my six-year-old eyes. In my mind, he was one of the last true reggae musicians in Jamaica. If not for him, my relationship to reggae would be tenuous at best. By 1990, when we moved to Bogue, the island had moved on. None of the children in my class knew any of the songs that rang out from my family's living room every morning with militant urgency. Songs about the struggle of the African diaspora, songs of repatriation and chanting down Babylon, songs about Zion. My father would say reggae music was the medicine, but all the baldheads wanted was poison. The Rastafari, though still shunned and outcast by their own people, became the living mascots and main cultural export of Jamaican tourism, with barely any profit to the Rasta community. It must have wounded my father to see his entire ethos and spiritual source diluted and commercialized for the foreign masses while painfully maligned at home. Sometimes he raged on for hours as we three huddled in the corner of our tiny bedroom at Bogue, shell-shocked, trying not flinch as he roared out His Majesty's name every time the thunder boomed.

He had no mercy for "false dreads," he would tell us. Many of the youth who had turned to Rastafari at the height of reggae's popularity in the sixties and seventies, when he had—much to their parents' dismay— had now shorn their locks and beards and returned to work in the banks or shops, now that Rasta was no longer in fashion. "But Rasta don't follow fashion," my father would say; he was Rastafari to the bone, and Babylon would have to burn him alive before he conceded even one shred of his livity. He was never going to cut his dreadlocks or shave his precept as most employers required, so he continued playing the music he loved for our family's survival, hoping against hope it wouldn't become the music he hated.

Hanging in his hallowed place on our living room wall at Bogue, forever upright and unsmiling, was the portrait of Haile Selassie, gilded and sceptered at his coronation. His eyes, black as meteorites, never stopped judging me. From our mint-green wall he now chambered a holy trinity— nested between a poster of Bob Marley and a picture of my father, both stage-bound, throwing their dreadlocks like live wires into the air—these were the three fire-eyed men who ruled my waking days. Often it was hard to tell if it was Haile Selassie who struck a fear in me, or his vessel on earth, my father. He had become mutable as the sky before a storm. My siblings and I never knew when the heavens might fall down on us again and he would rail for hours about Babylon, holding us hostage. We learned to scatter early whenever the local news came on, lest we get caught in another hour-long lecture. When his weather changed we three kept away, and my sister Shari, too, born three years later, would learn to read his moods as proficiently as a native language. But by then we all knew what he wanted. A congregation to listen. Most days I lived devotedly like this.

Watching the international news made my father's temper even worse, because it brought nothing but the wicked news of Babylon, making him feel helpless. There was no one my father hated more than Ronald Reagan. Until George Bush. Then George Bush.

"That vampire Reagan hates Black people," he scowled each night in front of the television. "He is a murderer. He killed Gaddafi's baby daughter. She woulda been the same age as Safiya now. Him worse than a mongrel dog." My mother would nod along or mirror his disgust by shaking her head, muttering *mmm-nnn* and *mmm-hmm*.

After the news, he would remind us that white people were devils who did everything in their power to prevent Black people from prosperity. They were bloodsuckers, baldheads, and mongrels. Above all, my father's worst trigger words were "Margaret Thatcher." Hearing "Margaret Thatcher" meant he would rant for another half hour about England and that vampire Queen Eliza-bat, about how they stole from Africa and from us to fatten themselves. Stole our lands, stole our dignity, stole our riches. I imagined her sitting at a feast in her jewels from head to toe—blood diamonds, Dad called them—eating all the food at the table, laughing at me. It was frightening at first to hear these stories, but by the time I was six I'd heard each one so frequently they became defanged, same as all the other duppies who haunted our world, looming outside the gate, waiting.

One day, Dad drove home from Negril with James Hewitt, his childhood friend and keyboard player from his first band, Future Wind, and with whom he'd been playing music at Hedonism II. A decade before, James Hewitt's father had tricked my father out of his royalties, but now that seemed to be behind them. Dad called James Hewitt "Juju," which always seemed to me like a taunt. When they arrived they were cradling two pups, our first real pets; two mongrels to guard us, Dad said. Lij and I squealed and held and petted them. A boy and a girl. The boy was a black and white Ridgeback mongrel mix, and the girl was a brown Alsatian mongrel mix. We were in love.

"You know what you gonna name them?" my father asked us the next day.

"Yes, Daddy," Lij and I said instantly. We'd been plotting all night and had decided on the perfect names.

"So what are their names?" he asked.

"Reagan and Thatcher," Lij and I said in unison, beaming up at him.

Outside our Eden skulked a constant carnival of temptation, all of Montego Bay beckoning this way and that, whispering *follow me, touch me, eat me*. Our neighborhood was no exception. One night, my father heaved through the gate enraged. He set down his guitar and stomped off to talk to Mom up in the kitchen. Lij and I hung outside the steps, pretending to play while we eavesdropped. Something had happened next door that left him shaking with disgust. I could hear my father blustering in anger as he chanted down the dangers of heathens. Spreading their nastiness like wildfire, no matter where we went. Even here, he was saying to Mom, he couldn't keep Babylon away from us, no matter how hard he tried.

"Even the little girl next door bruk out, Rasta," he said to Mom. There was a desperate tone of repulsion in his voice as he spoke. Keisha was the daughter of the yardman next door, and she was eleven, five years older than me. I didn't know she was already being loose with her body. I knew there was nothing worse than a girl who bruk out, for an unchaste girl was lost to Babylon, and unfit to be with a Rastaman.

"I man saw her dancing the lambada," Dad said, then kissed his teeth. Mom shook her head grimly. I'd heard of the lambada from one of my school friends, and I'd seen some of the girls gyrating their hips and practicing the dance one lunchtime. I stayed close and watched them but didn't dare join. I'd already imagined Dad's voice in my head, scolding me about being an unclean girl and a virago, so I kept my distance.

"Keisha is only a few years older than Safiya, Rasta," Dad continued on to my mom, his voice growing lower. "And the construction workers took her down the yard and defile her," he said.

"Mmmm-nnnnnn!!!!" Mom clucked her throat while she cooked dinner.

I was shocked to hear something bad had happened to Keisha. I just wasn't sure what. I was only six years old, but each day I grew taller I felt closer to understanding some buried-away thing about my body, a glance of something dangerous just out of sight. "Your body is Jah's temple," my father would remind me. "Don't let anyone defile it." I had to look up the meaning of "defile," as I often did after some of Dad's lectures. What had they done to defile Keisha?

"Even the little daughters dem gone astray now, Jah," Dad said, his voice hoarse. "All because she dance lambada, skinning out her body for men." He stroked his precept and huffed. "You better not let her step one toe over this fence again," he warned Mom, who went wide-eyed and shook her head.

"Oh no no no. Nevah, evah!" Mom said, wagging her finger in the direction of the yard next door.

These were the trials and tribulations of Babylon, Dad told her. "But like Shadrach, Meshach, and Abednego, I and I will walk through the fire," he said.

Would I, too, walk through the fire? I wondered. What did Jah-Jah have in store for me?

On many of our nature walks we met children who lived at the top of the hill, bashful at first and staring at my mother's dreadlocks, which were long enough to touch her buttocks. Mom would stoop down and talk to them, until somehow they were clinging to her hip by the time we turned down the hill to leave. On one of these walks we met Ummy and Billy, two brothers walking along the hill barefoot. As always, they took an interest in Mom, and I knew something about them really affected her.

"I don't like to see children without shoes," she told me later, when she read to me in bed. "That used to be me once," she said gently.

She invited Ummy and Billy to our S.P.I.C. classes. They came the first day without shoes. But they were polite and listened intently to her lessons, craning their necks dutifully to look at her, smiling whenever she spoke to them. They were shy, but not with Mom, who always made everyone feel like they were a part of her conversation. For the next week they returned, each time a little disheveled, always barefoot. They stared at me but never talked, so I paid them little mind. Lij didn't like them.

A few weeks later, a family friend sent us a barrel from Foreign, which was a long-standing tradition of care among Jamaicans; when friends or family abroad packed a big shipment of things that were too expensive or unavailable in Jamaica—food, new toys, clothes, and shoes—and shipped it to loved ones back home. When our barrel arrived it felt like what I imagined Christmas must be like, if Rasta celebrated Babylon's holiday. Lij had received a pair of brand-new Reebok canvas sneakers that didn't fit, so Mom gave them to Ummy, despite my brother fuming for days. Mom told Ummy to make sure he wore them, especially on the road.

"Yes, Auntie Esther," he promised.

The next time we saw Ummy, he was barefoot again.

"Where are your shoes?" Mom asked. Ummy shrugged and said nothing else.

That evening, zipping past us on a bicycle going down the road we saw Ummy's father wearing the new Reebok sneakers.

"Ummy," Mom asked him the next day, "were those your shoes I saw your father wearing?"

At first he didn't want to answer. Then Mom asked him again, with that kind way she has.

"Yes, Miss. He took them," he told her, visibly upset. I could see my mother thinking for a while about what to say next.

"Please tell your father Auntie Esther said to give you back your shoes," she said, though I really wished she would go up there and take them off him herself.

When Ummy came back to our house a week later for S.P.I.C., he was wearing the sneakers sure enough, but they had been ruined all along the sides and soles with black cigarette burns. When he sheepishly out-stretched his arms, we saw they also bore the pockmarked circles of a snuffed-out cigarette. We were all shocked and saddened, but no one more so than Mom. I felt her shaking next to me as she held me and Lij, both of us gawking at Ummy's arms. Ummy and Billy seemed resigned and aloof at their own scars, already immune to suffering. I felt a small wound opening somewhere within me as I watched them, my eyes opening to how much of Babylon really lived just outside the gate.

"Who did this to you, Ummy?" Mom asked, when all the other chil-dren had gone, already knowing the answer.

Ummy didn't answer. He kept looking at his feet. It was Billy, the more talkative of the two, who spoke up.

"It was our fadda, Miss," Billy told her. "He was drunk." Ummy shot him a frightened look.

Mom let us go and kneeled down and hugged them both.

"I'm sorry," she kept saying over and over, rocking them back and forth.

That night I couldn't shake what I had seen. Who knows how long my mother carried that weight around. After Ummy and Billy went home, I watched her pacing outside, pensive, smoking. Afterward, she sat Lij and Ife and me down in our bed and held us, staring out into what I can only imagine was some past version of herself. She held us against her for many minutes, all of us breathing her breaths.

"I want you to remember that even though we don't have a lot of things, we're not poor. We can never be poor because we're rich in spirit," she told us, her voice soft and soothing.

We nodded against her and lay there, smelling the faint trace of ganja in her clothes, until we fell asleep against her, one tangle of limbs.

After that day, neither Ummy nor Billy came back to S.P.I.C. No matter where we looked, or who we asked, we couldn't find them.

A few weeks later, on the outskirts of the yard, while rambling around with Reagan and Thatcher, Lij and I found blood on the dried mango leaves at the edge of our property, right along the fence we shared with our rich neighbor at the bottom of the hill. My brother and I learned, from honed eavesdropping, that our neighbor had woken up to a thief in his yard, and shot him. Or had it been in our yard? We never knew for sure. But someone had been killed there and all we found was browned blood splatter, his face left to our dark imaginations.

Soon a pattern emerged. Every few months, on the days when Dad was gone to work, there was a break-in on our property or one nearby. First, all our clothes were stolen clean off our clothesline. "They even took the underwear," Mom told us. Then our food and an old toaster were stolen out of our kitchen. We never caught the thieves. "Someone else must need them more," Mom told us nonchalantly when we asked her what happened. We got new locks on the front doors, and Mom started keeping mace in the house, but she never seemed scared, so neither were we. Even though we didn't know who had been stalking our land, we still felt safe in our little hillside paradise.

Then one Tuesday morning only a few weeks later, it wasn't the doves or the woodpecker that woke us. It was my brother's death howl, sending all of us scrambling toward his voice. When I reached him, I screamed too. Lying on the steps at Lij's feet, stiff as a gourd, was Reagan. His belly was swollen and distended, and his tongue hung gray and limp out his open mouth. I couldn't believe it. I stooped down to stroke his belly, thinking he would somehow jump up and run off again. Instead, he was cold as rockstone.

Ife and I joined Lij's crying, the three of us grasping for Mom.

"Somebody poison him," my father said, kissing his teeth. He pointed to Reagan's turgid body. "He has no marks, no cuts, no bites. Look at him big belly."

This sent us wailing, our faces red from crying, as we called out for Thatcher. All day we called out and never found her.

Even as my father dug a hole in the soil at the edge of our yard, we called out for her. *Come, Thatcher!* The sun was perishing and he didn't want to be digging a hole to bury a dead mongrel as his three children cried beside him, didn't want to blister his hands shoveling, the hands he needed to play his music.

Thatcher! Here, Thatcher! my siblings and I still called out. But only the wind rustled back to us. The veneer of our little world began to crack for me then. Because for the first time, I was afraid of what else might come in from the dark. My mother held us tight as we called out for Thatcher again, but only our hiccupping mewls could be heard as we walked back to the house.

There is an unspoken understanding of loss here in Jamaica, where everything comes with a rude bargain—that being citizens of a "developing nation," we are born already expecting to live a secondhand life, and to enjoy it. But there is hope, too, in our scarcity, tolerable because it keeps us constantly reaching for something better. Beyond our hillside, out past the city and its encroaching hotels, was my own marker of hope—the sea and its blurred horizon, the sea wind whispering blithely in my ear. Just as

Mom had taught me to do a few years before at White House, I listened.
As long as the sea was in my sights, I believed that things would always
shake out right. Sometimes I climbed up the exposed pipe by the kitchen
window, inching past the landlady's locked rooms, just so I could catch a
glimpse of it—the waves shimmering from the rooftop in the morning,
when the island's hope still seemed to be rising. If I stood long enough
on the rooftop overlooking the sprawling city at the exact spot the breeze
lifted the waves of the Caribbean Sea, I felt as if I could own the world.
Something better was in the crisp blue mist then, the whole day salved
new. *Bettah must come*, my parents always said. Two decades before, when
Michael Manley ran for prime minister in 1972, his campaign slogan
bore a crucial hopefulness that outlives him even now: *Bettah must come*.
That promise, and Manley's vision, included poor and Black Jamaicans
for the first time, acknowledging those who struggled, those who were
downtrodden, those who were dreaming up a better life. Among those
downpressed and invisible were my parents, who grew up on Manley's
hope and held fast to that belief that somewhere on the horizon, change
was possible. In the blue gong of our sea, bettah must come.

My father's voice rode the wind now, calling me down from the roof
with news. Sitting there in the living room, waiting, he looked to be the
happiest I'd ever seen him. His locks made a curtain of vines down his
shoulders. A rampant energy buzzed off him.

"Jah has blessed I and I," he told us, when my siblings and I settled
at his feet.

Mom had been cooking all morning and was in and out, balancing a
lit spliff on her lip, scurrying from the kitchen to the living room.

"The I them growing day by day," my father said. He inspected us
carefully, as if we were fragile things. "And I and I will need a place just
for us. Our own space, farther away from the heathens."

My eyes darted from his face to the holy trinity on the wall.

"I man is going to Japan," my father said. He snapped back into focus
and my heart leapt.

Lij and I turned to each other wide-eyed, our mouths gaping.

He was going to record his first album, he told us. He met some
Japanese record label executives at the hotel, who were flying him and his
band to Tokyo. They were now called Djani and the Public Works. My

father was the lead singer, recording his own reggae songs and authoring his own vision, after all this time. This was it. His hope on the horizon, his fresh start.

My father's eyes were bright as the rooftop sky.

"Whoa!" Lij said, and jumped up next to Dad on the daybed. Ife climbed into his lap and started singing.

Behind my father, in the corner of the room, I now saw it. The big brown suitcase tucked away and open there. Mom walked back into the living room with a pile of clothes from the line. She folded the clothes and started packing them in the suitcase. As she worked, she looked over at the three of us—me, Lij, and Ife—and in her face, I registered something I was also feeling. Uncertainty, for the first time, under the gaze of the holy trinity.

"Make sure you listen to your mother, and be obedient," my father told us now, his hands clasped in the Sign of the Power of the Trinity. "Jah will guide and protect the I them while I man gone."

"How long will you be gone?" Lij asked.

"Six months," Dad said.

"Are you coming back?" Ife asked.

"Yes, of course, Princess." He brushed his large hand over her head.

"Can we come with you?" I asked, looking my father straight in his eyes like a lionheart, even though I already knew the answer.

"No," Dad said. "The I them have to stay in school and keep doing your best while I man gone."

We all nodded and told him yes.

"When I and I come back, everything will be irie for us," he said. "Everything is going to change."

I didn't ask him to promise because I believed everything he told me then, clinging hard to our little mantra of hope, that *Bettah must come*. But I couldn't shake the look I had gleaned from my mother's face, how worried she seemed about what was next. Now that crack in our little kingdom of Bogue grew wider, and for the first time, my sky grew dim with a whisper of doubt. It was true, too true, what my father had said, though I couldn't yet read the signs falling ashen from the sky. Everything in our family was about to change.

6

Revelations

THE PASTOR WAS SWEATING AND SO WAS I. Seated next to me in the long wooden pew, my grandmother stared ahead at the pulpit, calmly listening to this frantic sermon of hellfire and damnation as if it were just an ordinary recounting of her Friday grocery list. She had dressed me in a fussy cloud of tulle and taffeta that made me boil and itch on the church bench, while Lij and Ife fidgeted and fussed about being bored. It was November, and Dad had been gone far across the sea for less than two weeks, and change had already come. We were visiting our grandmother Pauline for the first time. My father had always kept her away from us. "She's not mature enough to be their grandmother," he told my mother. Grandma Pauline had my father at fourteen, which to him was a permanent stain on her character; she was the original unclean woman, forever fixed in time, his dark star. If he had it his way, we would never see our grandmother at all, for fear that she would pollute us with her stained womanhood, and her "weak Christian mind." But my mother insisted that he reconcile with her right after I was born. "She's the only grandmother they have," she told him, and my father decided that Grandma could visit us for a few hours at a time, with one of our parents present. Now that he was a world and a half away in Japan, Grandma begged to have us come stay with her, and Mom agreed to send us for a weekend.

On this sticky Saturday morning, packed in Grandma's Seventh-day Adventist church, one of five churches on this half-mile stretch of road in her tiny tucked-away country village of Bethel Town, sitting under the dark stare of the pastor, I was terrified. Besides school, where every morning's assembly was set aside for Christian worship, this was my first time in a church, surrounded by those brainwashed Christians I had heard so much about. The pastor read from the book of Revelation: boiling seas and horned leviathans, mangled monsters, death, brimstone. The end of the world. Each word struck me like an arrow. Surely a burning pit would open up beneath my feet to devour me whole. Every so often I looked over at Grandma to see if her expression, magnified behind her thick librarian glasses, changed with the apocalyptic horrors the pastor was describing, but it never did. She smiled, softly radiating from her plump cheeks, nodding along with the pastor, mesmerized. Every time she moved her head, her slick Jheri curls shook to and fro. Grandma, who my mother fondly called Sweet P, possessed a bovine serenity. The pastor spoke feverishly, recounting all the ways the world was doomed, that sinners were doomed, that I most of all was doomed. His tenor and demeanor were familiar, like my father when he raged about Babylon. I hung on to his every word for some recognition of my corrupted soul, but all the while in my ear my father's voice rang skeptical and fiery, reminding me to always *Fire bun Babylon*. When the congregation closed their eyes in prayer, I studied them, looking around at those dressed in their church best, a frenzy of hats and tailored satin, point-of-pride brass and sequined brooches. Women with fans, nodding and *mhmm*ing along with the pastor, men who every so often raised their outstretched palms, bearing witness. So this was Babylon.

After the sermon, they all stood as if on cue and sang along to hymns my siblings and I didn't know. I observed as if from outside a murky window as the congregation sang and swayed, tambourines shaking, faces contorting, watching myself mouthing along with them tunelessly, reading the words from the hymnal, trying to see if I might catch the spirit. If there was one, I willed it to possess me. If damnation was real, I didn't want to be damned. But nothing happened. I spent most of my girlhood this way, longing to feel something miraculous. Doubt, which slept heavy and unexamined at the thought of Jah and my father's conviction, now stirred again within me as the churchgoers prayed.

When the service was over, the other children formed a circle of observation around me and my siblings, the outsiders from Mobay. They were shy and we were shy, and for a short time none of us said anything. Then, cautiously, a young girl from the group approached us.

"Is true your parents are Rasta?" she asked.

"Yes," I told her. She gasped a little bit, turning to look back at her friends with gesturing eyes. We could hear all the children whispering among themselves.

"I told you!" one child exclaimed, pinching another in righteous indignation. All of them now inching a little bit closer to us.

"So how come you wearing shoes, then?" one girl in the back asked Lij.

"Yuh modda and fadda wear shoes?" one boy blurted out, before we could answer the girl's question.

"Of course!" Lij said, his voice loud and ringing. "Yuh stupid, eeh!"

Some children giggled, some moved even closer.

"So how come you don't have dreadlocks?" the first girl asked me.

"I don't know," I said. Once, when I was feeling brave, I had asked my father why he chose Rastafari, why he chose this life for himself, for us. Now I turned his reply over in my mouth like a coin: "I and I don't *choose* Rasta," he told me. "I and I was born Rasta."

That evening when we got back to Grandma's house, we went down on our knees, clasped our hands together, and tearfully begged her to never take us to church again. We knew that neither of our parents knew, and this was now an unspoken secret we would all keep if we wanted to see our grandma again. Everything at Grandma's house seemed this way—its own slant universe, different from our home in almost every sense. The way it smelled like mothballs and perfumed soap inside. The chemical drip of her hair. The strangeness of seeing Grandma wear pants, since my mother never wore pants. But best of all was the food. At home we had to eat an Ital diet: no meat, no fish, no eggs, no dairy, no salt, no sugar, no black pepper, no MSG, no processed substances. Our bodies were Jah's temple. But here, every day our grandmother fixed us a feast of sugar and meats—our plates piled high with foods we were forbidden. She fed us mounds of saltfish, bully beef sandwiches with white bread, bottles of cream soda, clear lemonade with white sugar, giant cups of Milo or Horlicks every morning *and* every night, oversweetened with as much condensed milk as we wanted, and all the curry and brown-stew chicken dinners we could consume. At Grandma's house we stretched and pulled and played around in our new skins.

She said yes to everything, and we loved her for it. We spent the sated hours after dinner laughing and playing Chinese checkers until we heard the sound of Uncle Clive's truck pulling into the driveway, then we all buttoned up our spirits, sat up a little straighter, and waited for the atmosphere to change.

"Hello, children," Uncle Clive said as he walked through the door. His name was Gifford, but we were instructed to call him Uncle Clive. He always referred to us by the collective name of "children," or "you pickneys," a colonial remnant trawled into common vernacular, which he used as if to avoid sounding out our individual names, which he thought were too strange and unchristian. They were a reminder of my father, who he had not said more than five words to since that rainy afternoon over a decade ago when he abandoned him in the exhaust of the moving truck.

"Hello, Uncle Clive," we all replied. My grandmother had already sprung from the table and was reheating and fixing a plate of dinner for him. He didn't greet her.

"So how Howie doing?" Uncle Clive asked, walking over to the kitchen, waking us all from the silence his presence drew like a curtain around us. He had very dark skin that was starkly contrasted against his bright white hair and the glow of his amber eyes, making him look strikingly unearthly.

"He now goes by Djani, remember?" Grandma said gently, watching us.

Uncle Clive smirked and looked at us. My siblings and I all stayed at the dinner table as he ate.

"So Howie getting rich then in Japan, eeh?" he continued, using my father's Babylon name. A dark rum smell misted off him, potent from where I sat.

"I don't know, Clive. All I know is that he's in Japan and he has a record deal. Let's hope everything goes well. God willing," Grandma said.

"Uh-huh," he said, cracking his chicken bones and sucking the insides. "So when yuh children gwine locks up?" Uncle Clive asked us, dropping the subject of riches. "Howie and Esther a Rasta, so when yuh gwine turn Rasta?"

"No. Nnn-nnn. Nnn-nnn." Grandma shook her head at this and frowned. "I don't think so. They will choose what they want to do when they are grown." She sounded convinced.

"Daddy says we *are* Rasta, Uncle Clive," Lij said, sounding as sure as Grandma. He had no doubts. Under the table I could see his hands formed into the Sign of the Power of the Trinity.

"So they brainwash already, eh, Pauline?"

"Clive! Please," Grandma whispered, but he paid her no mind.

"No, man. It's good for dem to learn Christianity. If yuh goin learn bout Haile Selassie from Howie, yuh should learn bout Christianity too. Learn bout good and evil, learn bout heaven and hell. Them should hear di truth from all sides," he said to Grandma. He turned to us and asked, "So unnu believe Haile Selassie a God?"

Lij held his head high. He looked to Uncle Clive and said, "His Imperial Majesty is the King of Kings, and the most High." He said it in the same singsong cadence my siblings and I all used when we'd learned the emperor's title by heart during our lessons with our father at Bogue.

In our house we were allowed to be lions, and nothing else. Anything else made you a weakheart, at the mercy of Babylon, easy prey to an evil world lying in wait. I guarded myself. Ife glanced from my face to Lij's face.

"Yes, Uncle Clive," I said, defensive. "He was a great man. He defeated Mussolini and saved Ethiopia from colonization." We had to be lionhearts, in defense of what, I wasn't too sure. I was only seven then, and didn't know what I believed.

At this, Uncle Clive howled. Lij's face was pulled tight, almost baring his teeth.

"So ah dat what Howie tell you pickney?" He was sneering now, that dizzying smell coming off him.

"Nah nah nah," he said, shaking his head and picking his teeth with his tongue. "Haile Selassie was a wicked man. Him used to have pet lions inna him castle, and him feed the lion dem 'undred pound a meat while the Ethiopian people dem starve to death," he told us, his yellow eyes widening.

My grandma shifted uncomfortably in her seat, but she stayed silent, laying the tablecloth flat with her hands over and over, never looking up at us.

"Oh, Howie never tell you pickney dem dat, eeh?" Uncle Clive kept going. I was sitting up straight, willing myself a shield around Lij and Ife. But I also listened with a kind of shock.

"Him people starve *to death* while him feed him lion dem. Ah'right?" he continued. "And dat's why the people dem overthrow him. So wha kind of God is dat, eh? Him own people don't think him ah God, but Rasta think him ah God? Rasta stupid. Wha kinda man would worship somebody so wicked?" He kissed his teeth, and pitched another rum-breathed laugh, his amber eyes catching mine briefly, slicing me open.

Did he see it? My certainty wavering, my heart a torch flickering as he spoke.

"Haile Selassie is in hell," Uncle Clive said. "I promise you dat."

"No! He's not!" Lij said, his eyes pleading with Grandma to make it stop. Lij put his hands on his ears. Uncle Clive just laughed and got up from the table.

"Clive! I think that's enough," Grandma managed to say.

I could feel a heat radiating from my brother. Lij was kicking the table and shaking his head, while Ife climbed into my lap.

"No . . ." I answered weakly, but no real sound came out. I could not refute him. I had never heard this account of Haile Selassie before, though this was not the last time I would hear it from Uncle Clive. I tried to speak up again, but he had already disappeared upstairs into their bedroom, out of sight. At the table his plate was empty except for a pile of mangled chicken bones, all the red marrow sucked out.

Back in our bedroom at Bogue, doubt clotted sour within me. Every move I made under the watch of the holy trinity was measured. From the living room, Haile Selassie's eyes burned holes into my back. We told our mother about our gallivanting, all the country myths we heard and the duppy stories that kept us up at night. We told her all the things we ate because we knew she would not fuss, but we did not tell her about going to church, or what Uncle Clive said about His Imperial Majesty. We loved Grandma, so we took Uncle Clive like a bitter shot of cerasee tea, deciding it was best to say nothing at all.

But his questions had stuck a thorn in my flesh. I lay restless in bed that first night back, while the dark and its shrill chorus rang out in my ear. Beyond the makeshift partition outstretched in the doorway, my mother curled up asleep with Ife in the living room. Next to me Lij made superhero sketches in bed. I searched the ceiling.

"You believe what Uncle Clive told us?" I asked him. "About Haile Selassie and the lions, I mean?"

"No sah!" he said, shooting me a look. My brother rolled over to my side of the bed and faced me as he spoke. "Daddy seh watch out for false pretenders, don't? Wolf in sheep clothing."

He was not yet six but he already talked in holy riddles like a Rastaman. His Afro made a darker shadow than the dark.

"You think Uncle Clive is false pretender?"

"Yah. And him mean, Saf. Number one," Lij said. Outside the doorway the television droned on, its blue light flickering along the wall.

"True true," I agreed. Uncle Clive was very mean, which made him more likely to be wrong. "But I hope he didn't let his people starve fi true."

"But H.I.M. is the Man, Saf. Daddy said. An emperor can do whatever he wants."

I was surprised to hear my brother say it. I couldn't do what I wanted. I spent most of my waking hours terrified of what might happen if I did. After our visit to Grandma, I was burdened with the guilt of doing what my father told me was wrong. Eating meat, going to church. Hearing Uncle Clive question Jah. Then slowly questioning him myself. My doubt stuck like a rockstone in my shoe. How carefully I had studied the boundaries of this world, navigating each space with my palms out, begging for permission, while in my brother's mind he had already pupalicked over the fence and knocked it down.

I wished I had some way to check what Uncle Clive said. The next time we went to the library I searched the heavy encyclopedia section, found the *Britannica* volume marked "H" and leafed through its dusty pages, looking for Haile Selassie. There was a picture of him in his khaki military suit, his black eyes piercing me. There were facts about Ethiopia, his lineage, and the dates of his rule. There were notes about Orthodox Christianity, which the book said was Haile Selassie's religion, but it said nothing about lions or people starving. It didn't say anything about Rastafari, either. And it didn't say he was God. But my father always told us that Babylon had changed all our history books to hide the truth from Black people. An emperor could do what he wanted. Perhaps that was true. But what about an empress? Could she do what she wanted too?

Maybe I was the false pretender. Every time I walked into the living room or stretched out on the daybed, Haile Selassie's gaze pierced me again with guilt from every side, his face dark and perishing as if he knew my doubts intimately, following me back and forth wherever I went.

In our house our church was green. Holy were the hands soiled with dirt and the blessed herb. Every morning of my youth began the same way—a faint tugging from below, the air a heavy mouth closed over mine, the dizzying smell of ganja slowly pulling me awake. My mother was always up before dawn, communing with the crickets, busying herself with housework and yardwork. Whenever she worked, she smoked marijuana. Dad said smoking herb was how one connected with the Most High, reaching the heights of reasoning, though he himself never smoked. In his youth he had been given a spliff laced with a lizard's tail, which made him paranoid, my mother said, his demeanor permanently shifted. He never smoked again after that.

My mother carried a golden packet of rolling paper wherever she went, stamped with a drawing of the Lion of Judah waving the Ethiopian flag. I watched, mesmerized, awed by the intricacy of her rolling, and how quickly she could do it. By the time I was seven, I could mimic every step in my sleep. The scent of it stuck to her long auburn dreadlocks and all day it clung to me like I clung to Mom. My siblings and I spent a lot of time with her in the kitchen, crowding around her like eager pups. We pawed and pulled at her, spilling juice and paint and fingerprints of grease, but she did not mind. I had never seen her angry. If she was with us, she was ours. But this must have been lonely for her. It had been two years since we moved from White House, and she hadn't been back to see her sisters since the night we drove away. One morning, while she prepared her spliff, I asked her if we could go back to visit Auntie Audrey and my cousin Jason, and my mother went quiet. Her face dimmed as she shook her head. "They're gone, baby. Moved away to Miami." Her voice wavered with something like regret then, and even as she comforted me, her eyes became wet. She must have felt an irrevocable loss as she looked out to the sea from our two rented rooms in the landlady's house; her world growing unbearably smaller just as my aunt's had grown much more expansive. My mother looked away from the horizon and slipped the spliff in her mouth, reaching for the lighter to make a flame.

She took deep solace in the language of the land; she liked pushing her hands into the soil. She took up farming after our father left, clearing the land before planting her crops. Soon enough, as if she planted magic beans, all her crops exploded up and outward in swaths of green. We had new towering stalks of sugarcane she cut into sweet pieces and packed with our lunch. There was a roving pumpkin patch with leaves broad enough to cover my head in a rainstorm, and vines and vines of gungo peas that we shelled and cooked with rice for Sunday dinner. "Eventually everything we eat will come from this land," my mother told me. "Then we can all taste the fruits of our labor."

On early school mornings she and I would fold into each other in the living room, right under the watchful eye of the holy trinity as she combed my hair, often with me wailing and begging for her to stop as she pulled at my thick knots. Sometimes I'd think about the children at my grandma's church asking me why I didn't have locks, recalling the certainty in my grandmother's voice when she said we would be able to choose. As my mother raked the comb through my black thundercloud of hair I felt possessed by the devil. "I'm sorry, love," Mom kept repeating to me. "You just have too much hair!"

But even then, bent under the pain, I wouldn't have chosen dread-locks. For when she was finished, I pulled at my glistening plaits, fitted with blue clips and a blue ribbon to match my school uniform, swinging my hair back and forth, back and forth, pink with delight. I felt it was all worth it then, in the end. My mother made it look easy, corralling three children by herself every morning while my father was away, carrying us preened, pressed, and ready down the hill to school.

By late November, my father's letters from Japan started arriving in the mail. He had been gone almost four weeks. He sent each of us an individual letter, in our own envelopes, addressed specifically to us. We opened them to raucous fanfare on the living room floor. I'd never gotten a letter in the mail before, and Dad had chosen the most beautiful stationery I had ever seen, pink and perfumed, lined with gold-leaf flowers. My father sent money back to my mother every two weeks, envelopes filled with stacks of US dollars delivered by his friends who had international bank accounts. Soon after the first envelope arrived, Mom bought a new fridge and a stove with a big fancy griddle in the middle that allowed her to make three grilled cheeses at the same time.

Mom's letters from Dad were always the thickest, brimming with postcards of Japan, pictures of my father and his band, and long undulating letters in his all-caps handwriting. As she read each page, I watched her face opening, petal after petal. Then she showed us his pictures. Dad in a kimono. Dad wearing a new green tam and cool leather jacket. Dad and the Public Works with their instruments. Dad throwing his dreadlocks upward like a lightning bolt. I clasped on to these pictures like prayer, ignoring my doubt sprouting roots like the soybean my mother kept in water to teach us how things grew.

Babylon would come for us eventually, even in our kingdom of god-sent green. Every Sunday, after hand-washing our laundry, Mom boiled warm water to wash my hair, singing while she poured warm cupfuls over my head. One Sunday, wilting under His Majesty's stare, still thinking about his feasting lions and starving people, I crouched my damp head between my mother and the punishing comb for our weekly tug-of-war. Mom took one drag of the comb and gasped. Two large clumps of hair yanked loose from my scalp by the root, like weak weeds from dirt. I screamed. Black fistfuls were stuck in the teeth of the comb, stray tufts fallen to the ground, sad as a dead animal, dying there without me. My forehead pulsed, tender and bleeding.

"Jeezam peace!" Mom wailed in disbelief. "Oh Jah. Oh Jah. Oh Jah," she said, holding me as I cried, blocking my hand from trying to touch my scalp where I now had a bald spot at the front of my head. She called Lij over and parted her fingers through his Afro to discover that his hair was also falling out in clumps. "Merciful Father!" she exclaimed. She checked Ife's head closely, parting her hair, and told us she was fine, and turned back. "Ah what Djani go say to me now? Oh Jah Almighty!" My father distrusted Babylon's doctors and would never step foot inside a doctor's office, telling us there was nothing waiting there for a Rasta but death. My mother believed this too, until she had children. The four of us raced down the hill in a panic, flagging down a taxi to take us to the doctor. A Christmas breeze blew in through the rattling windows of the Lada, an old Soviet scrap-metal car, donated as postcommunist hand-me-downs that became ubiquitous on the island as our public taxis. "Oh Jah! Oh Jah," Mom repeated to herself. The breeze cooled my burning head as we rode in the jittering can.

The people in the waiting room stared, eyes lingering on the flustered Rastawoman clutching her three children, the messy tassels of her tie-head falling in her face. We had been infected with barber disease, the doctor told us. Mom closed her eyes as she listened, her mouth down-turned in grief. This was a disease that commonly spread from baldhead to baldhead, a kind of contagious ringworm spread first by the barber's tools, then from child to child touching heads at school. Babylon's disease. Evidence that something ungodly was trying to invade us. None of us had ever been tainted by the scissors of Babylon. We were perpetually Samson, before Delilah. My mother was inconsolable for days. The doctor prescribed a thick antifungal cream and chemical shampoo that made me feel sick every time I used it. Luckily, I had enough hair to hide the bald spot when we went out, but in my brother's patchy Afro it was hard to hide. Lij had to shave his head down completely. My mother would only trust a Rasta bredren to do it. Though my brother was out of my sight when his hair was cut, I knew he was crying. Because my heart was crying for him too.

One week after, there was scant improvement. My mother's face wrenched in pain when she parted my hair to look at my bald spot, now smooth to the touch. I knew this had to be a punishment. I had let the baldheads in. The crack had widened each day since Uncle Clive's snickering words fevered me with doubt. Every bad thought and action, the day in church, the sinful food I ate, overripe and falling from the tree. Rotten, rotten, rotten. I had sewn the toxic seed with my questioning, and now I was reaping the crop of iniquity. We were all being punished, and I was the one to blame.

Babylon's medicine was useless, Mom decided. She threw it all out.

"I'm not combing your hair anymore," she told me. "I'm not putting you through that again. I'm done." It wasn't a question. Her spirit fell like a pricked balloon, blue and lonely, as she gathered up every comb in our house and flung them into a trash bag, along with the medicine. Hair for the Rastafari signified strength. My father called his hair a crown, his locks a mane, his beard a precept. What grew from our heads was supposed to be most holy. My mother took our blighted scalps as a moral failure, ashamed that we had fallen ruin to Babylon so soon after my father had gone. So, despite what my grandmother had imagined, it wasn't a question or a choice when the time came.

My mother spoke the green language of herbs fluently and she decided that the only way was for her to cure us herself. We spent the rest of our Christmas break at home, never venturing farther than the gate, while my mother tended to our heads, pushing her hands daily through my hair. This was the first time my siblings and I were deliberately kept inside the gate as a precautionary measure—to be saved from the ruin of Babylon, though we didn't realize it at the time. After only a few days my bald spot healed and my hair started growing back. "Praise Jah," Mom said. Proof of nature's rightful word on the matter of our hair. My mother was then as certain as if she had divined the future from the mint leaves at the bottom of my cup. She would build such crowns atop our heads that no devil would ever prosper. Under the holy trinity's watch she began the process of twisting all our hair into dreadlocks. First me, then Ife, and Lij eventually when his hair grew long enough again. Day after day, it became our new ritual. Snug between her legs, she lathered us in her homemade yolk of aloe vera gel and warm olive oil. Then she spent hours twisting and curling my thick hair between her fingers until little dreadlocks started to take form.

In only a couple weeks my hair stiffened and matted into dreadlocks, sprouts of thick antenna bursting from my head, this way and that. There was no turning back now. I had stepped into the fire and come through like Shadrach, Meshach, and Abednego. We had all stepped through. No one would ever ask again why my parents had dreadlocks and we didn't. I could not have imagined then, my small hands busy with this new hair, what questions would be asked of me next. How much more I would have to give up. We now had Jah's protection, Mom said. This was our crown. But somehow it didn't feel like a crown, not even then.

It would be more than a decade before I combed my hair again. Combing and brushing were now officially among the forbidden things, that growing list of NO. In the beginning we were all young enough to be unplagued by vanity. For now, this was one less thing in our morning routine. No one was more overjoyed than my father to hear we were one step further on the trodition to Rastafari. I ran with my siblings through the yard, ragged and unbothered, flitting here and there, nursing our garden green and flush to honor his return in two months.

The sun scattered light through the branches and grew bright inside our veins. "Look into the camera," Mom said to the three of us, holding a disposable camera.

We crowded around the mound of yellow marigolds we'd been rooting. We looked up into the sun's glare as she prepared to snap a picture of us. There we were. The three of us with three little heads of budding dreadlocks tangled up together.

"This is for your father," Mom said. So we smiled wider.

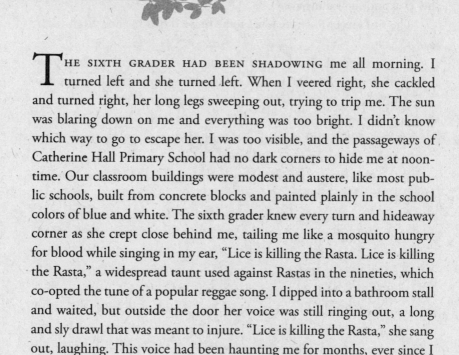

7

As the Twig Is Bent

THE SIXTH GRADER HAD BEEN SHADOWING me all morning. I turned left and she turned left. When I veered right, she cackled and turned right, her long legs sweeping out, trying to trip me. The sun was blaring down on me and everything was too bright. I didn't know which way to go to escape her. I was too visible, and the passageways of Catherine Hall Primary School had no dark corners to hide me at noontime. Our classroom buildings were modest and austere, like most public schools, built from concrete blocks and painted plainly in the school colors of blue and white. The sixth grader knew every turn and hideaway corner as she crept close behind me, tailing me like a mosquito hungry for blood while singing in my ear, "Lice is killing the Rasta. Lice is killing the Rasta," a widespread taunt used against Rastas in the nineties, which co-opted the tune of a popular reggae song. I dipped into a bathroom stall and waited, but outside the door her voice was still ringing out, a long and sly drawl that was meant to injure. "Lice is killing the Rasta," she sang out, laughing. This voice had been haunting me for months, ever since I got back from Christmas break with dreadlocks. It began with this sixth grader pointing at Lij and me and screeching out to everybody, "Lice is killing the Rasta!" then laughing. Then every student in earshot had turned and also laughed.

Now she nipped her shoes at my heels as I raced out of the bathroom and zipped toward the canteen. She leaned in, trying to sniff my locks, as I ducked just out of her reach.

"Please leave me alone," I said, looking around for a teacher, for Lij, for a friend.

"Ey, Rasta gyal," she barked, her mouth foaming. "Yuh tink yuh better than me?"

I didn't answer.

She curved her head to and fro, winding like a petulant cobra, until she was right up in my face. She pinched her nose and pretended to smell something. "Why yuh nuh go wash your hair?"

"I wash my hair," I said.

"Don't look like it to me. Dutty Rasta gyal," she said. Then she cut her eyes and shoved me away.

The sun was in my face. I had to be brave. I had to show her I wasn't a weakheart.

I turned and stepped forward into her, winding my head round and round back in her face and said, "Cut-eye cut-eye cyaan cut me inna two, and penny penny cyaan buy my shoe." I stamped and flicked my hand as if shooing her away.

She stood back and watched me, smiling.

"So you chat patwa after all, then? You red roach." She spat, then wheeled away from me, singing out as she went, "Lice is killing the Rasta . . ."

After she had gone, I lingered in the shadow between two school buildings and pressed my matted hair against the cool concrete wall. My cheeks stung in humiliation. This was another fracture in the Zion my parents had promised. I hadn't felt this unsure of myself since my first day at Catherine Hall the year before. I had been six, about to turn seven at the start of the school year, and less than a week after we had enrolled, the principal told my mother that Lij and I were too advanced and would each have to skip a grade. My heart was a bursting mango as Mom and the principal slow-walked me down to my new third-grade class. Mom squeezed my hand reassuringly and whispered, "You're gonna ace it!" before kissing me goodbye, chuckling as all my new classmates gawked and craned themselves to catch a glimpse of her. After she had left, I crouched gawkily in the corner of the room and fielded all the usual questions about my name, about my parents being Rasta, about why I didn't have dreadlocks too.

But those new-school jitters didn't last long, as Lij and I sailed through our classes with top marks every week, walking tall and trading reports at lunchtime about besting these baldheads. Our teachers marveled at our aptitude as much as they bristled at our candor. We might have had Rasta parents, but our brightness was unquestionable. We liked to flout Babylon's rules, especially at morning devotion. While the principal led everyone else in prayer, my brother and I kept our eyes open and watched; I'd poke my head out of my third-grade line to find Lij in his first-grade line, rolling our eyes and laughing quietly with each other. We had felt untouchable, my brother and I, playing off one another quizzically when our classmates didn't know the capital of Madagascar, or the chemical compounds of rainwater. Of course, they couldn't even spell Czechoslovakia.

When we returned to school with dreadlocks after the Christmas break, there was far less for us to laugh about. We dodged daily heckles from baldheads instead. We'd stepped past our warm veil of safety at Bogue and emerged on the other side, where the eyes of the school shone a cruel spotlight. Now, everyone wore their worst thoughts openly. Even the teachers. Rasta children had not been permitted to attend public schools until the 1980s, so my siblings and I were not only among the first Rasta children to attend school in Montego Bay, but we soon became accustomed to being the only ones. The students at Catherine Hall gawked as if we were a trio of aliens disembarking a spaceship, crowding around and staring at my siblings and me, pointing and trying to sniff or pull at our locks. They followed us and interrogated us. If they could have dissected us alive, I think they would have. And though I was used to children tailing behind my mother like paparazzi whenever she appeared at school, what had once seemed celebratory now felt only like cruelty. Day after day, my selfhood wilted. Outside our gate was a merciless scrutiny, and I longed to hide myself away. For the first time I can remember, I felt ashamed to be myself.

Once the lunch bell rang, I lifted myself from the shady refuge between the buildings and went to find my brother in the canteen. I told him about the girl who'd been following me around all morning. Her needling taunt. My brother shook his head and kissed his teeth like grown-ups did.

"Saf, don't pay her no mind. All ah dem a duppy," he said. "And *we* are the duppy conquerors. One day we gwine blast these crazy baldheads."

I should have chided him for bad language, but that day it made me felt better. He was always trying to sound like a big man, talking like our father. Before Dad left, he told Lij that he was "the man of the house now," much to my brother's delight. This pained me deeply because I was the oldest, so clearly I should be the man of the house. Or Mom.

"You're right, innuh," I said to Lij, surveying the enemy territory all around us. If I was to be the man of the house I had to be strong. I had to make my brother believe in me. So, I talked the hard patois of a man. "We gwine bun down Babylon," I told him. But even as I said it out loud, I didn't believe myself.

While my father was gone, I imagined his voice in my head, speaking through me. He'd only been gone for four months, but it felt like he missed a thousand noontimes, a thousand moons. Already I'd grown taller, and uncertain. I tried to imagine what he would say if I told him what was happening, admitted my weakness. He always told me to be polite but right. If the teacher was wrong, I should correct her. If my classmates were not righteous, I should avoid them. "I man and your mother didn't birth no weakheart," he told me. "Always stand up for what you know is right. You overstand?" Once, my teacher taught me a mispronounced word and he sent me back to class the next day to correct her. He made sure I corrected every teacher every time after that. Miss Clarke chuckled in annoyance and said, "Oh! Well if *your* father says so . . ." and shook her head. *Be polite, but right*, Dad said. *Don't be a weakheart.* Back then there was hardly any decision I made, hardly a thought I formed, without first imagining what Dad would say about it, what Dad would do about it. I tried to remember his tenets of Rastafari like my hundreds of spelling bee words. Even from afar, his mind moved mine like a backgammon piece. I decided to go to the teachers' lounge and tell Miss Clarke about the sixth grader who'd been following me. After listening, she tapped me gently on the shoulder and told me to pay such things no mind.

"God only tests those who are strong enough to be tested," she told me. "And with your grades, Sinclair, you can walk tall in this school. You hold your head up high. You hear me?"

"Yes, Miss. Thank you, Miss." I felt reassured by my one constant.

My gold coin. As I left, I heard Miss Clarke and the other teachers talking from outside. I stayed hidden under the teachers' lounge window and listened, hoping they would say more about my high marks.

"If we chase down every likkle fight we would never have a moment," Miss Clarke was saying. The other teachers joined in agreement. Their voices sailed high with concern.

"Boy, it's such a pity though," Miss Clarke continued, kissing her teeth. "When I tell you the pickney bright? The mother must be doing something right. See how she follow back ah them like shadow? If they say jump, she say how high."

"But it's a shame, innuh," a new teacher's voice chimed in. "I really thought the parents were going to give them the choice."

"It should be a crime to force this thing on the children, as far as I'm concerned," someone else said.

"And what a waste of her pretty skin too," Miss Clarke sighed.

"Such a waste . . ." they all chimed in now. I scampered away, registering the snide tenor of their voices as they used words like *shame*, and *pity*, and *waste* as they talked about me, and I was rattled. Still, it wasn't until I was older that I truly understood the conversation I'd overheard, and the dark sting of the unspoken coiled within it.

Eventually we got used to the harassment at school as part of our weekly routine, salved by Mom's presence when we got home, her warm hands massaging our chakras, only to be hounded again at school the next day. By April I was shaping up to be first in my third-grade class, something I couldn't wait to give to Dad as a homecoming gift. The months without him had stretched like chewing gum between my fingers, sticky and flimsy, its sweetness ephemeral. We counted down the time to his return, pestering Mom about the details of his arrival, while watching the calendar slowly wheel forward. I hadn't realized, until he was gone, how much I needed him to feel strong. Years before, when I was four years old, he stood against the dark fury of Hurricane Gilbert, holding down our zinc roof at White House with his bare hands, just him against the wind, while we slept safely. He was our steadfast guide and guardian; with him I knew no one could ever do us harm. Now every day in his absence was a little storm, and we needed him to dispel our doubts. When he was with us we walked taller, and there was no better way to love him than to be as mighty as he imagined us to be.

We were under our favorite mango tree by the front gate when the car rolled up on that early day in May. Suddenly he appeared like the sun, beeping the horn at the gate with James Hewitt, and flashing his perfect teeth at the sight of us. We jumped on him and cried; the fireworks of feelings had nowhere else to go. We'd been waiting for this moment since he left in November, and now he returned to us with a parade of bags and boxes and a brand-new electric Fender guitar slung across his back. He was buoyant, happier. He even smelled different. All afternoon he kept touching his fingers to our dreadlocks, now completely matted from the roots. He touched us as if we were holy, and he was pleased.

His skin was winter-lightened and his locks were longer. Inside the house he unzipped his suitcases and showered us in mounds of stuffed toys, exquisite notebooks, new clothes and shoes, and a brand-new Nintendo Game Boy with Japanese cartridges. For Mom he brought fancy lotions, a robe, packets of something called miso, and a huge bag stuffed with pungent marijuana. "Had to stop and get this for my Empress Makini," he said. He unboxed a brand-new sound system that could cycle through twelve CDs at once. We yelped at every new gift. The neighbors all the way down the hill must have heard our cheering and screaming for Dad. He was our Santa, if Rasta believed in Babylon's fables.

That evening, after we had calmed down enough to walk with him around the yard, we told him stories of our year. How we had come first in class. How Ife broke her arm. How the children followed us around at school and tried to pull and sniff our dreadlocks. How they sang nasty songs at us. How even the teachers stared. How lonely it was, how isolating, to be hounded and shunned this way.

My father listened closely as we knitted and wove our six-month saga, our voices crisscrossing one over the other. Then he held out a hand to stop us at the mango trees, turned to us and said, "Jah."

"Rastafari," we all called out in unison.

"Remember," Dad said, singing Bob's familiar prayer over us, "Jah would never give the power to a baldhead." He reached out and touched our heads again.

"It will be a hard road for you children," he said, "But it will fortify you. Selah." He closed his hands in the triangular Sign of the Power of the Trinity. Lij followed suit and made the sign as well.

"There is no turning back from the path to righteousness," he said.

We listened and did not speak, as we knew he wanted. He went on for some time about the path to righteousness, and for many minutes he talked way over our young heads, but his conviction was legible to me.

"Babylon cannot touch or hurt the I them now," he assured us. The wind shook through the leaves as if in response. "Praise Jah," Dad said, responding to the wind.

"We can never be a family unit if everybody don't have the same vision," he said. "You pree the I?"

"Yes, Daddy," we all answered. But somewhere deep down I felt shy and uncertain now, picking at the grass. Just then my father pulled on a young sapling mango tree, no taller than me. Its leaves were translucently delicate, its branches thin and still flexible.

"Look at this mango tree," Dad said, "young and green. Anybody can influence this sapling to grow in any direction they want, for the rest of its life."

He bent the tree's branch to make a downward arc. "Just like you," he said, pulling it nearer to the ground. "So I and I have to choose the right direction for my yutes to grow.

"As the twig is bent, so the tree inclines," he said with finality. Then he let the branch go. It whipped back and forth unsteadily in the wind. A few of its leaves were torn away by my father's force. As I looked up at him, his words felt big, bigger than me and the sky overhead. I was daunted by the weight of it, my future held frail and precarious in my hands. I was unsure if I could carry it. My father turned now, with Lij and Ife clasping each of his arms, and went in silence back to the house. I lingered there to watch the mango tree swaying unevenly, flailing and fragile, before turning hesitantly to follow.

My siblings and I crowded around the living room making a fracas and playing with our new toys. My father glided a disc into the new CD player, and instantly his voice came on and filled the room. We cheered. These were the new songs he recorded in Japan, so we turned the volume up and listened to him singing, dancing around to his music. "The I them like that one?" he asked us after each song. And we told him, "Yes, Daddy! That was my favorite one," each time. His voice was clear and crisp and beautiful. My mother closed her eyes and listened close.

After playing his new songs many times over, we sat around the coffee table and listened to him relive his trip. "The Japanese are an irie people," he said. He told us stories of their clean subways, of speeding on the bullet train to Kyoto, of seeing Mount Fuji. He showed us how he drank his tea from a bowl. We were dazzled, in the presence of a god. Someone who had gone all the way to Japan and was now sitting in our living room. My father stared out and saw a glittering road outstretched to glory. And all at once we saw it too. The air was infectious with hope, and we wanted to breathe it all in.

Ife was wrapped up in Mom's lap, watching her roll the mound of marijuana into a spliff, and pulled on her sleeve. "Mommy, can I smoke one too?" she asked, pressing her nose into Mom's bosom, pointing at her spliff. "Like you do? Please, Mommy?"

"Me too. I wanna smoke too!" Lij said, not to be outdone.

"Well, I want to try it too!" I echoed, raising my hand in the air.

Ife touched Mom's face and tugged her dreadlocks, pleading.

"Mommy, can we?" I begged, my chin in my palms.

"Please, please, please," we all said.

My mother looked up at my father and chuckled. We all turned now and looked to Dad for our answer. After a breath, he nodded.

"Alright!" Mom said, excited. She was laughing her high laugh of delight. It rang out and rang out. She rolled us three tiny spliffs, each spindle-thin and about a pinkie's length. Dad picked them up carefully and placed them on a silver tray, before handing them to us one by one. I was seven. My siblings five and three. Each of us took our baby spliffs awkwardly into our small hands and tried to hold them between our fingers the way Mom did. She showed Ife how to hold it between her index and middle fingers, and Lij and I watched and followed her motions. This was another step on our trodition and was supposed to bring us in closer communion with Jah. Dad and Mom kneeled down in front of us with a ritual quiet, each with a lighter in hand, and lit our spliffs. One, two, three.

We puffed and pulled, pulled and puffed. We felt grown-up blowing herb smoke out of our mouths. My mother and father were wrapped in an embrace, looking on and smiling, as luminous as they'd ever been. Our initiation into their private sect was now official. There was no turning back.

My sister Ife and I often relive this moment out loud to each other to make sure we hadn't dreamed it. We were only children then, and didn't know what we were asking. My parents had pulled us past all reasonable boundaries and into an unknown jungle, their rules and roads growing hazier as we went. My sister and I never smoked anything after that, but the next time my brother picked up a spliff, he was never able to put it back down.

Afterward, I went outside to the lawn and lay my ear flat onto the grass. I had stepped past an invisible threshold into another life, and I could hear it talking to me. I pressed my ear into the earth and the earth softened. My dreadlocks grew roots into the dirt, anchoring me there, each lock entwining with the deep roots of the trees, their voices reaching upward and growing into me.

8

Chicken Merry Hawk

DAD WAS HOME WITH US FOR the summer break of 1992, growing godlike in this new bliss, wild and infectious. When he was this way, I pressed my skin into his colossus, greedy for this warmth, the sun tilting on its axis to shine for me. *Stay. Stay,* I wanted to say. His recording contract was for two years, but the record label could only grant the band visas for six months at a time, so for two Novembers in a row, he left us. Once our summer was over and school began, he would be gone again to Japan for half a year to finish his album. I hoarded away those afternoons we spent with him learning to play cricket, when he showed us how to run down and arc our arms into a perfect bowl, how to swing the heavy bat, how to aim for a perfect six. Every day he was a new Dad, a more carefree version of himself waking up to greet us. He told us the same ten jokes of his childhood and dazzled us with his tree-climbing skills, throwing down ripe mangoes and apples, singing "Catch this, catch this," until our bellies burned with glee.

That hallowed July, we shared a stage with him for the first time. We'd written a song together, in the Bombay mango shade. We three wrote the lyrics, and Dad the music, a song about saving the environment that we performed for modest crowds at the Montego Bay Cultural Arts Centre. My heart was full as Dad glanced over at us and glowed, playing along on his guitar. This was his Zion. Music for him, I understood then, was not only prayer, but a way to be loved. His bandmates were only temporary stand-ins for this sense of belonging, and for a sweet few months, as we played in our family band that summer under one harmony, he saw himself, himself, himself. Here, too, lived his devotion to making the perfect Rasta family; the hope that he would never be an outcast again. And for one glorious moment that summer, we outstretched our arms each day, closed our eyes together under an afternoon shower, and sang in thanks for Jah's blessings. When we opened our eyes, my father was gone again across the sea.

Every morning of the new school year began with my father's voice crooning out to us from our CD player, honey over our heads, warm and familiar while we got ready for school. As he sang, we sang, warbling along to every ooh-we-ooh and sha-na-na, every golden word. He was a superstar to me, and I wore this pride at school like armor, the magnificence of having an extraordinary father becoming my own magnificence. I had just turned eight, and began every other sentence with, "Well, my father is in Japan . . ." Sure, a few students at Catherine Hall had parents who went to America, but I was the only one with a famous father in Japan.

While my father was away, we went downtown to Ika Tafara's shop to call him every weekend. Ika was my father's closest Rasta bredren and was revered by many Rastas in Mobay for being a survivor of the Coral Gardens Massacre, an incident that sparked one of the most gruesome periods of government brutality in Jamaican history, a period that my father sometimes offered in snatches when he lectured us against Babylon, showing us the long history of its violent reign. When Howell's commune was burned to the ground, the vision of a unified Rastafari movement was demolished, and Rastas, who continued shepherding peace and love, became public targets for unprovoked civilian and police beatings, and widespread discrimination. They were often arrested for walking along the beachside areas being developed for tourists, because their appearance was viewed as an eyesore, and the government, while courting foreign investors, tried to ban Rastas from using Montego Bay's coastal roads. Their families turned them away, just as my grandmother had done to my father that rainy afternoon, and most Rastafari became nomadic and reclusive, choosing to live peacefully among themselves in small encampments scattered all over the island. My father was only a baby in 1963 when Ika lived in one of these farming encampments in Coral Gardens, a neighborhood in Mobay that rested on former plantation grounds the government and local landlords had been trying to reclaim for hotel development. When the Rastas refused to cede the farmland to Babylon, the police arrived to evict them with a shower of bullets, killing three Rastas. Despite calls for retaliation from a fringe group of Rastas, the majority of Rasta bredren in Mobay refused to engage in any violence, upholding their pacificist beliefs and calling for unity. Undeterred, a small band of six Rasta outliers armed themselves and fought back, and two police officers were killed in the crossfire. In violent retribution, Alexander Bustamante, the white prime minister at the time, targeted Rastafari island-wide, ordering the military to "Bring in all Rastas, dead or alive." Years later, I would learn the rest of this brutal history on my own, horrified as the details unfurled before me. For one long weekend in April 1963, beginning on the day that Rastas call "Bad Friday," the Jamaican army went on a rampage, raiding and destroying several Rasta encampments all over western Jamaica. The police force had been target-training with pictures of Rastafari for years, so when Bustamante finally gave them the power to drag Rastas away at gunpoint, many Rasta bredren did not make it back home. The police captured hundreds of Rastas and forcibly shaved their precepts and cut their dreadlocks. They jailed, tortured, and injured as many as 150 Rastafari, and killed an unknown number of Rasta bredren. Soon after this, "Babylon" came to permanently replace the word for "police" in Jamaican patois. I was never taught one word of this in school; the massacre has been all but erased from Jamaican history, with very few among us aware of these atrocities, but the term for police being "Babylon" remains.

Ika didn't talk about the Coral Gardens Massacre much, but sometimes I would watch his face settle into an austere quiet and wonder where he had gone. I liked Ika best of all my father's bredren because he was kind and naturally jovial, greeting us with jokes, lifting my brother up over his head. He and his wife Isha had no children, even though they had tried, I later learned. My siblings and I were always happy to slip into their embraces, thrilled with how cheerfully they lit a fire to our rambunctious spirits. Eventually his shop became a second home to us, especially when my father was gone. Tafara Products was also the place I spent the most time among other Rastafari. By the time I was born, there were only a few Rasta settlements left, dispersed and far-flung across the parishes. But when Ika opened the store in the late eighties, it soon became a collective meeting place for the small group of Rastas who lived in Mobay to smoke ganja, play drums, and reason among themselves.

Stepping inside Ika's shop was to part the musky brocade of another world. Rough-hewn and heavy with the smell of black African soaps and incense, Tafara Products was a militant haberdashery of Rastafari goods, and had shelves stacked with African history books, plus a cavalry of Haile Selassie iconography in every hallowed position, stamped dark on every painting, postcard, and photograph. Always watching. Keeping militant guard were posters of Bob Marley smoking a giant spliff, Malcom X holding a machine gun, and Marcus Garvey looking stern in his feathered helmet. This is where my parents bought most of their clothes, where they found our giant map of Africa. The shop was an oasis in the midst of Babylon. Everything smelled earthy and hempy, and so did we long after we left.

Each weekend we entered the shop's smaller side room to gather around the telephone and speak to our father in Japan.

"Budgie," Dad's voice said, crackling and far away. "It's so good to hear you, Princess."

My heart wrenched with longing, hearing him. He had a rasp in his voice that told me he just finished singing.

"What time is it there?" I asked. It was always the first thing I asked him. My father chuckled. He told me that it was already the next day there, and I marveled at that.

"The three of the I them famous," he told me, and I could hear him smiling. The Tokyo music scene had fallen in love with the photo of three Rasta children and their marigold garden, he told me. "Every night when we perform, they project the I them faces up on the big screen." I tried to imagine it, my face projected on a giant screen in the future, a world away. I couldn't wait to brag about it at school.

Before I handed the phone back to my mother, my father said, "I man have another big surprise for you." He shared with me even sweeter news that we were getting our first car.

Back home we jumped around the living room, kicking the air to

Dad's music and dancing. Blessings were upon us, stretching past the fences like Mom's pumpkin crops. "We're rich!" my brother said. I imagined myself in the back seat of my shiny new car, tinted windows rolled up with the AC blasting, waving regally at the passersby outside. When my father's next letters came, we went straight for the pictures. There it was, the first photo in the stack. A picture of our new car. We all squealed. In the photo Dad stood next to a brand-new dark-green Isuzu Gemini, with his hand on the open driver's door, smiling like the dawn. Mom rang out her high laugh, the sound rising and looping around our roof like birds.

There was nothing before us or behind, my mother's joy hanging on the clothesline plain for everyone to see. Her laughter never left, even when she seemed a little more exhausted with every sun-bleached day, where she hand-washed and hung, raked and tended, tidied and cooked, then washed again. Most nights after our homework was done, Mom stretched out heavy on the couch and closed her eyes while she helped us get ready for our first Kwanzaa. One evening, she called us over to her as she rested. With a calm smile she looked over and told us we were going to have another brother or sister. My siblings and I screeched in excitement at the news, then screamed even louder when Mom told us we could help choose a name from the African naming book.

In the weeks that followed, we lived under the star sign of YES. Life was a sweet manna that we opened our mouths and guzzled freely. We came alive on the weekends as Kwanzaa drew closer, and the Bombay mangoes grew bigger than all our fists put together. We all piled into one hammock to feast on mangoes, all of us sprawling like lizards, fat with riches, pregnant with amber trickling down our arms. We danced in the rain, turning our shower curtain into a waterslide, turning our waterslide into a warm pool of mud. Giggling, we burrowed our bodies in black mud, layering our arms and torsos thick until we were covered to our necks with it. Mom laughed and spurred us on. When the air crackled and smelled like smoking rum, we knew the canefields below us were burning to make sugar, and black ash would soon rain down on us. My siblings and I would jump in the air and catch black leaves like wings, laughing and pressing them to dust in our hands. There was no sweeter season in my life. I could live till the end of my days here, rewinding this memory like an old videotape. Ash on my face, under that falling sky, my hands outstretched to the heavens, accepting.

When we walked into Ika's shop for the Kwanzaa celebration that December, I felt for the first time like I belonged. About thirty Rasta bredren and their families had come from all over Mobay to give thanks. I played the congo drum and sang of Black upliftment with other Rasta children. We recited Marcus Garvey like scripture, and we ate veggie chunks and callaloo without salt and pretended to like it. Walking among them, I almost felt chosen. My parents were two young stars within the group; all the bredren and sistren showered praise on my mother, and though he was still across the sea, the sound of my father's voice sang out through the store's speakers and into its spacious backyard.

The other Rasta children were shy like us. There were about twenty of us there, peeking from behind our mothers' hems. We edged around each other with giant saucer eyes, all our teeth soft and twisted from a lack of calcium, all our limbs whittled to sticks without vitamin B_{12} in our Ital diets. But soon enough we abandoned caution and were racing around the shop's overgrown yard. The gathering slowly segregated. The Rasta bredren went outside and the Rasta women stayed inside the shop, cradling babies, serving plates of Ital food. Calm and attentive, their faces weary, the women were all dressed similarly; unadorned, with heads covered, long skirts and dresses made with African prints. None of them joined the bredren drumming and reasoning outside in the yard except to bring plates of food, and even then, none of the women I saw breeched the circle to speak.

The Rasta bredren strutted like peacocks, wearing giant tams and coiled cones of dreadlocks orbiting their heads, mighty bushes of wiry beards, and calloused hands pulling on their precepts. Some were in jeans, some in dashikis, some with hair wrapped, some flowing free. Some of them did not wear shoes. They'd walked barefoot on a thousand streets then walked into Ika's shop with horned and mangled feet as if it were the most ordinary thing in the world. When I asked my mother about this, she told me that some Rastas believed shoes were the invention of Babylon and that Rastafari should walk natural upon Jah's earth. When I asked her how come they had ridden in a car to get here, she chuckled. Years later, when I got up the nerve to ask my father why he wore leather but did not eat meat, he scolded me for impertinence. The more Rastas I met, the more I realized there was no singular or accepted gospel among Rastafari bredren. Each man crafted his own credo, paved his own road. Some Rastas, I learned decades later, did, in fact, refuse to travel in motor vehicles or operate Babylon's machinery. Some did not touch Babylon's money, except with gloves or a plastic bag. And some, my siblings and I learned, after speaking to the other Rasta children, did not send their children to school. Each man simply authored and interpreted his own livity according to which of the sects and tenets most called out to him. Some were stricter than my father, some more lenient. And though I could not speak to the condition of any other bredren's private household, almost all Rastafari believe in upholding peace and harmony in public, viewing themselves as Jah's anointed defenders, uniting Black people in the struggle against Babylon.

As I observed the group of Rasta bredren from afar, watching their calm, austere faces as they reasoned, how sometimes they gestured to the boys to join them in the circle, I felt envy. For it would be two and a half decades before I would learn all the varying tenets that brought them together, when I sat down to write and looked it up myself. It was then I learned that there are three main sects of Rastafari. The Mansion of Nyabinghi is the oldest, and the one from which all the other sects were born. Nyabinghi is militantly Pan-Africanist, believing in Haile Selassie as the reincarnation of God on earth, in Black unification, liberation, and repatriation to Ethiopia. The Twelve Tribes of Israel is the most liberal Rastafari sect, welcoming wayward uptown Jamaican youth and white foreigners as members; they eat meat and believe in Jesus Christ. The Bobo Shanti, the newest sect of the three, live closed off from society as a self-sufficient group, adhering to Jewish Mosaic Laws from the Old Testament, including observing Sabbath, and special separation laws for menstruating women. I had lived under some semblance of many of these rules for most of my life, but did not know which of these names to call myself. Though my father considered himself most closely aligned with the Mansion of Nyabinghi, he never officially became a member of any of the three sects, and over the course of our lives, would draw his own rules and inspirations from all three, creating his own kind of order; his own Mansion.

Some of the Rasta women who had gathered inside were much younger than my mother, including a teenage girl named Josephine, who was the new wife of a Rasta bredren named Samuel, a taxi driver who my mom used to charter. Samuel was older—forty years old, I later learned—and Josephine was seventeen, just out of high school. Which made her only nine years older than me. Her face was slim and dark as a river stone, and from a distance I could see her eyes, wide and questioning, as she spoke with my mother. I nudged closer and listened as Josephine asked my mother for advice on what she should expect as a Rastawoman in her marriage. Her words were hushed as she asked about extramarital relations and polygamy in Rastafari, which was a common practice among Rasta bredren, no matter the sect. Much of what they discussed went over my head, but my mind bristled as I listened, a strange feeling edging up in me as they spoke. Josephine's voice was a little sheepish as she told my mother that Samuel made her sleep in a different room when she menstruated and forbade her from entering the kitchen or cooking during her monthly cycle because she was "unclean." My mother expressed dismay at hearing this, touching Josephine's arm in solace as she said, "My children's father don't bother with that old 'unclean' foolishness no more. But, sistren, let me tell you—" Just then Josephine spied me, and my mother shooed me away, saying this was "big people business." Usually I would whine and ask to stay, but this time I didn't object; there was something in the air that felt deflated, a portent static in the room that unsettled me.

Before I turned back to run into the chattering yard, I observed the Rasta sistren. All their faces were drawn and exhausted, their hands burned and calloused from housework like my mother's were. Almost every sistren held a baby and a toddler on her arms; some were pregnant like my mother. Some were so busy minding children that they could barely talk among themselves. Unlike the bredren's circle, there were no wails of "Jah Rastafari!" erupting from their midst. There were no spiritual revelations here. Only women taking turns running back to the kitchen, diligently attending to their children and to their men. Their wants pursed and shapeless, their white tie-heads coming undone. Just then, the frayed whisper of a ghost breath caught me. Like a flash of a white wing, a pale figure of a woman, vaguely familiar, fluttered in the curtains against the wall. A thought, hovering just beyond my reach, slowly sucking the air out of the room. I shuddered, then shook the specter away, turning to bolt as quickly as I could back into the festivities. It would be a long time before the thought ambled perilously from the bushes of my mind again. But the next time it did, I would have no choice but to heed it.

It was 1993, and the new year stretched over us like a hungry yawn. My dreadlocks were now at my shoulders, though they still seemed an alien part of me. I watched Mom's belly growing as she stood at the stove making our food. Sometimes I stayed up to watch her stomach as she slept. An eel glided across her belly, as her skin stretched and moved. The ultrasound said it was a boy, and Lij kept gloating about getting another brother. "Doctors can be wrong," Mom told us. "They don't know always the truth."

As she grew rounder, our time on the phone with Dad grew shorter, until eventually the entire phone call was just between my parents. During one of these long calls I followed Isha into the back of their storeroom and saw that there was now another telephone there. I made sure no one was looking, then I slowly picked up the second telephone and pressed it to my ear.

"Well," Mom said, her voice pained and low, "this baby is already coming, Djani. Nothing we can do bout it now."

My father took a breath.

"Oh Jah," he said. "Trouble never blow shell though, eeh." His voice was hoarse. "And now Juju go behind I man back, sign new contract for more royalties and nuh seh one word to the I."

"Mmm-nnn!" Mom exclaimed. I stifled my breathing as I listened, trying to understand what my father was saying about Juju Hewitt, the keyboard player in his band.

"He is a damn backbiter," Dad continued. "Trying to rob I and I. From we was a yute him a snake."

"Mmm-hmm, true true. I remember," my mother said. My father had been playing music with Juju since their teen days. His first band,

Future Wind, was managed by Juju's father, who had tricked my father out of his royalties.

"He is a bloodsucker. A johncrow. Born from iniquity," Dad said, his words burning raw. "Trying to tief from I and I? *I and I?!*" His voice was unspooling now, rising.

"The band is called Djani and the Public Works. Djani! Djani!" My father was spitting fire so quickly now, Mom had no time to react.

"I man go get a gun and shoot Juju inna him bomboclaat—!!!" I ripped the phone receiver from my ear and clicked it back into its cradle.

His anger scorched a strange anguish in me. I had never heard my father curse like this before, and the shock of the badword struck me down. My heart raced, my face grew hot. I knew listening in had been wrong, and it felt wrong. But he felt wrong too. Even his voice had been different. It was as if I had lifted a heavy mask and saw my father naked for the first time. This was not the same peaceful man who had taken the stage with us, leading our family band and beaming as we all sang together. That father was holy; he was mighty. I couldn't recognize the man on the phone, just some disfigured creature, his voice monstrous. It terrified me. Even as I tried to ignore that pang of fear and remember my father again as he was, the feeling lingered with me from that day into the next, odd and foreboding.

In May, a month before the baby was born, my father appeared alone at the gate in a taxi, with only the suitcases he left with. As the car door opened, his mood slithered ahead of him. He hugged us tersely with his face drawn tight, the scar on his forehead catching the light. A dark and noxious cloud hung overhead. The band had broken up. He had returned from Japan with a lone box of already pressed CDs—all he had to show for the second trip. There was no car. He had paid his keyboardist Juju Hewitt for a space on a Japanese shipping container for both of their cars, but only Juju's car came over from Japan. My father's voice, roaring out death threats against Juju on the phone, rang again in my ear when I saw him. I bristled at the thought of it. For the rest of the year he would try to get his car on a new shipping container, but it was too expensive. We never saw the dark-green Isuzu Gemini in person, and it would be nearly a decade before I sat in the back seat of a car my father could call his own. Soon there were only days and weeks of rain.

That June, Shari was born. A sister, not a brother. Mom was right, the doctors did not always know. She was Shari Makeda, *Distinguished female ruler*. Mom pet-named Shari "Sri," the spiritual title of a yogi guru she believed was reincarnated in our baby sister. I took one look at Shari's frothy smile and knew we were now complete. I was eight, Lij was six, and Ife four. There were only the four of us siblings in the world, our bloodlines stitched exactly so, one to the other, one to the other, marking us only. Lij didn't even mind that he had another sister. Not when every Rasta bredren in Ika's shop told him it was blessings from Jah, being the only boy in the family.

With another Sinclair daughter born, my father's paranoia only darkened, his gaze shrinking our world like bars of struck-iron. He had returned to us shell-shocked, reentering our lives a wounded soldier. Each week he seemed thinner and older. Barely touching his guitar. "Somebody mussa obeah the I," I overheard him telling my mother, his voice grim as he recounted losing the recording contract, believing he had been cursed. One afternoon, two months after his return, he told me and my siblings that we needed to be purified. Under the dark brew of possession, I watched my father stalk the yard, yanking up cerasee leaves, bitter roots, and black vines, which my mother blended into a pungent goop poured into three big glasses. I started retching before the mossy liquid even reached my lips, and immediately started pleading to my father, to no avail. "I and I need to guard ourselves from iniquity," he told me and my siblings, ignoring our gagging and cries. "A weakheart is ripe for the worms of Babylon. So drink."

He loomed over us eagle-eyed for what seemed like hours, as we bawled and struggled to swallow the bitter potion. We were there until night fell, surrounded by stains of our own green-black vomit. Until my father believed we had finally been cleansed. "The I them have to be vigilant," he said when it was over, his voice like a whip. Being double-crossed by Juju again only made him more obsessively distrusting, not just of the world outside the gate, but of the world outside our door. "If the I them let yuh guard down, Babylon will tek advantage of yuh," he warned. Our joy made us heedless. Easy prey for the wicked world out there. So, there were to be no more nature walks, and we were not allowed to leave the yard. There was no more running around the bush, no more dancing in the rain. No more jumping and catching sugarcane ash. Our star sign of YES became a stop sign of NO, as he reeled us in tighter and locked us under his stare, always with the constant warning, "Chicken merry, hawk deh near."

Soon, he didn't even allow us around other Rastafari people anymore. He trusted no one, not even them, with our livity. Our purity was now his purveyance, only. We would never celebrate another Kwanzaa at Tafara Products again. Would never run among other Rasta children. With each month came a new revocation, a new rule, and I began to see that he had kept the promise he made before he left for Japan the first time, after all. Everything *had* changed. His second return marked the beginning of a life of strict discipline and unquestioned devotion I would later come to think of as the Mansion of Djani. In our household rose a new gospel, a new church, a new Sinclair sect.

9
Hydra

For months I waited for my father's storm clouds to lift, for that johncrow to stop circling, but it lingered, marking us. I was now nine years old, and as if it had been some hazy dream all along, Japan and its heady promise grew ever distant. My father returned to playing shows for tourists at the hotels again, his head slumping heavier with each passing week. There was no looking back. We lived under a vast albatross hanging around the necks of my parents. Whatever mood cracked its thunder across my father's face, our mother's energy allowed us to glean the meaning. Eventually my siblings and I learned to read them as skillfully as we read everything else. Sweets and bitters, sweets and bitters. Their forces pushed and pulled, pushed and pulled.

If Mom wanted to let us loose like bright sparrows upon the world, our father wished to squeeze us back into our eggs, overgrown and silent in his nest, never ready to be hatched under his watchful eye. "The I them need discipline," he told us. The first thing he did when he came home was rifle through the refrigerator and discard everything he found objectionable—our cow cheese and condensed milk, our chee-chips and frosted flakes. "Stop polluting your temple with Babylon crap," he told us. Then had come the putrid green potion, which still rose like bile in my throat whenever I thought of it. More and more we were kept apart from the world, kept away from Babylon's plague, so as to preserve our purity. We never saw our aunties or cousins, we kept no outside friends. No one was good enough for the sect of Sinclair, and there would be no other influence in our lives except for him. He became obsessed with our livity, and our moral architecture, making us watch the speeches of Louis Farrakhan and memorize the details of why Mumia Abu-Jamal should be freed, every weekend.

Now the slightest skyward laugh or hint of play set him off. "I man sick of the ramping and gallivanting," he scolded. "And your mother just put the baby to sleep, Rasta." We would be quiet for as long as we could, whispering furtively around the trees and wishing Shari was old enough to play with us. Eventually we would become boisterous again, forgetting our father's rainstorm and lapping the sunshine of the world within us, just as Mom had taught us to do. I couldn't make sense of his sudden desire to bend us into children we were not. It was a shock to me, how unsteadily our world teetered, how quickly my father had become the hurricane. I never quite got my bearing, trying to adjust to the pain of our world diminishing, and the uncertainty of what new censure might be coming next. Though I tried to keep some sense of normalcy for my younger siblings, so much was outside of my grasp to control. No matter how close we clung together, the unpredictability of our new life eventually fostered a distrust of any kind of joy or period of calm, which then hardened into a wariness of outsiders we four would spend our lives struggling to shake.

When he wasn't playing hotel gigs, my father threw himself into yardwork. As he did with most things, he took it to its extreme. He hacked at the overgrown grasses with his black machete, chopping up and down the yard in the hot sun, slashing away at the weeds with a vigor one could easily mistake for anger. He scowled while he worked, sweating through his clothes, his long dreadlocks tied back in a ponytail, his face screwed tight in attention, his forehead scar gleaming. Yardwork as penance. If he heard us ramping he would skulk outside and grab his rusty rake from the laundry area and tell us to rake the yard. "Those who don't work, don't deserve to eat," he said, continuing, "work maketh the man," his voice clear as a lash, burning hot at our backs. Somewhere inside the house, my mother breastfed Shari and rocked into her quiet place. Dad was pushing, but Mom was nowhere to pull us back.

My father had always made speeches about many things I didn't yet understand, and this was one of them. I thought about his words. Work maketh the man. If we didn't work, we didn't deserve to eat. I was only nine years old then. Lij and Ife were seven and five years old, both antsy and lively as lightning. They looked to me, waiting, as I held the rake. Its handle was loose, its cheap wood weakened by rain. A sudden glimmer entered my mind. Pointing to the fallen mango leaves scattered across the lawn and the yard below, I asked which of them could make the biggest leaf pile in the yard. And off they both ran, little legs pedaling around the yard, laughing and grabbing dry leaves with their hands and tossing them into a pile. I smiled to myself, belly full with the thrill of outrunning his anthracite gaze—my father and the rest of the trinity blindfolded somewhere out of sight. And soon enough, our work was done.

Work maketh the man, my father said, but as he needled his attention in on me it seemed that the lifework of a Rastaman was making a Rastawoman. I never forgot the young woman we had met at Kwanzaa, the muted fright on her face as she questioned my mother about this life, or the unsettled air in the room. But I had never once considered drawing a direct line from her—or any Rasta sistren—to myself. I was so young then, and still fiercely believed in the father I knew; he was not like some other Rasta bredren. His mood would lift eventually, and he would return to me again.

One hawkish afternoon my father watched me and my brother climbing the Bombay mango tree. From the terrace overlooking the lawn, he called me over to him. When I approached him his gaze pinned me down. "How tall are you now?" he asked. He stood next to me and measured. I was above his shoulders. My father frowned, eyes scouring me up and down, as if in growing taller, I had done something wrong. I was only nine years old, still years away from puberty, but he inspected me like fruit on the verge of rot. "Go change outta those tights," he said, pointing to the black yard-tights I wore every weekend around the house.

"I man don't want my daughters dressing like no Jezebel," he told my mother later, in the kitchen. "No girl-child of mine go wear pants again," he said. Without objection, my mother ransacked the drawers of the family dresser and threw out every pair of pants and shorts my sisters and I owned. Now we would only wear clothes approved by my father: skirts and dresses tailor-made from Kente cloth. Our hems were to fall below our knees, our chest and midriff covered at all times. Pierced ears, jewelry, nail polish, and makeup were forbidden. All those arbiters of vanity, those garish trappings of Babylon. "And once you reach the right age," my father told me, looking into a future I could not envision, "the I will wrap your locks in a tie-head like your mother." I was startled to hear him say it. I had been naïve, in not expecting that this was the life my father had imagined for me. But I was even more startled by the uneasiness his new rules stirred in me.

My dreadlocks were now well past my shoulders, which pleased my father. Proof that our new livity was righteous. That Jah was still watching over us. My hair had grown matted, flecks of lint and old matter knotted down the length of each dreadlock, a nest containing every place I had laid my head. It hadn't been brushed in two years. Dad caught me pushing my fingers through the thicket of roots in the bathroom mirror once, as I tried to twist the crown of my hair into shape.

"Stop that," he told me, frowning at my vanity. "Hair fi grow. Naturally and natural only. Like Jah intended."

"Yes, Daddy," I said, and left my hair alone.

Living as Jah intended was a constant astonishment; joy and terror flipped easily on the same worn coin. I was now in the fifth grade at Catherine Hall, and the stares and taunts, though they never truly stopped, had slowly petered out. Monique was a year ahead of me in sixth grade. Her hair was a long and winding black river, which she wore in two braids snaking down her back. One of her parents was Indian, which made her popular with all the boys at school. And whomever was popular with the boys was also popular with the girls, so I decided I would be her friend. My father always warned me about "friend and company," instructing me to shun all outsiders, who were all the children of Babylon, as if they carried plague. For most of my school days my brother and I were inseparable, so I never saw the sense in making friends with anyone else. But as he grew older, Lij found more thrill with the ragamuffin boys he scampered around school with, kicking and play-fighting like wolves. I wanted to be a howling wolf like them, but now every day it seemed that

Rastafari closed its cage tighter over my world, shrinking me small in an ever smaller place. A churlish envy stung me like nettle, then grew in me a yearning for the cherished and forbidden.

I found Monique in the crush of students in the canteen and slid next to her on the hot metal bench. She didn't object. She had very dark brown skin, smooth as a pebble, and dimples. The canteen tables shone silver, lined in neat rows, and buzzing with students. I looked ahead and listened as she ate her beef patty and chatted with some other girls. Every time she spoke, she flicked one shiny braid over her shoulder. Envy pinged in me as I tried not to touch my own brittle dreadlocks, scratching at my shoulders. I saw Monique looking at my hair anyway. All morning I tried to imagine what sixth graders talked about, as I had no idea, and finally after some time when neither of us spoke, I asked her if she liked spelling. "No, it's boring," she said. I lied and said I agreed. She must have known it was a lie, since only weeks before all of Catherine Hall lined up to watch me in the final of the spelling bee competition, but if Monique remembered, she didn't say. Soon enough we were laughing and chatting amidst the humming crowd. I told her I won the All-Island Maths competition and traveled to Kingston to collect my award from fancy politicians. My face had appeared on the front page of the paper. She told me what boys liked her and how she had a crush on Anthony, a skinny, unremarkable boy from her sixth-grade class who recited one tired and nasty rhyme about concentration and penetration. Suddenly I had a crush on Anthony too.

Back home I chittered to my parents about making a new friend, a girl two years older than me, in sixth grade. My father sat still and listened as I recounted my day and sang songs of my new friend. Far-off clouds gathered in his face as I spoke. He pulled on his long beard and told me I was at school to excel, not to make friends.

"Friend and company will lead you astray," he said. "The same people laugh in yuh face ah the same people who stab yuh behind yuh back."

I tried to defend Monique and our thin friendship. Beauty was irrefutable evidence of moral good to me back then, like in all the Disney cartoons my siblings and I gulped down like nectar. But my father's eyes had gone dark, poised to storm for something outside of me entirely. His nose flared as his voice rose.

"Don't trust no baldhead," my father said to me. "You overstand?"

I listened, breath-caught, and told him yes. All I would ever need were the five other people who lived in this house, he said. And I, frightened disciple, believed him, then. "All I and I need is one another," he said, eyes piercing into me. I nodded.

"Remember what I man seh. Stay away—"

"Stay away from friend and company," I repeated.

But at school I didn't stay away. My sisters were still too young to be my confidants, and I'd had no real friends my age. Kept indoors at home, I grew curious in my loneliness, wanting to be near other girls, to learn of their strange lives, and live vicariously through them. Instead of heeding my father's words, I shrouded those growing parts of myself, amassing a trove of all the versions of me he would not like. I found Monique wherever she went, or maybe she found me, and day after day I braided myself around her sticky tring-gum secrets, where boys and budding breasts hardened like candy. Monique was the blush and I was the brain, a dusk rose and its greenling thorn. We laughed our way through lunchtime, our faces shining high in the luring heat.

I came to realize that what my father wanted, on his return from Japan, was the perfect daughter. And when a Rastaman said *daughter*, he meant both his wife *and* his child, as my father called my mother his "dawta" when speaking to his Rasta bredren, who also called their partners their dawtas. For the men of Rastafari, the perfect daughter was everything a woman was supposed to be. The perfect daughter was whittled from Jah's mighty oak, cultivating her holy silence. She spoke only when spoken to. The perfect daughter was humble and had no care for vanity. She had no needs, yet nursed the needs of others, breastfeeding an army of Jah's mighty warriors. The perfect daughter sat under the apple shade and waited to be called, her mind empty and emptying. She followed no god but her father, until he was replaced with her husband. The perfect daughter was nothing but a vessel for the man's seed, unblemished clay waiting for Jah's fingerprint.

"You're old enough now to help out in the kitchen," my father told me, making quick work of whittling me. "The I need to learn from your mother. Watch how she carries herself." I watched my mother and found in her long silences something potent waiting to be said, like the anxious moment before thunder. But no matter how much I longed for it, she never thundered. She never spoke her mind or disagreed with my father. She smoked and breastfed Shari, she smoked and spared me from the tedium of kitchen work, she smoked and woke up before dawn to cook all our meals and hand-wash our clothes, folding them away afterward, like her thoughts, in the back of the chest of drawers, untouched.

She was the perfect daughter.

Perhaps it was true what my father said. That I lacked discipline, the way any nine-year-old lacks discipline—I didn't always listen, I was skeptical. I doubted his gospel. I was curious. I touched the flame simply because it was burning. Because discipline always seemed to me the pin that held the butterfly in the display case. *Work maketh the man.* Day after day, I swung over those words, and saw ahead of me a life withering slowly under all his multiplying decrees. Day after day my heart bucked up against it. I was never going to be the perfect daughter. A grin of mischief opened ever so slyly inside me, a seedling of a voice that said no.

Even as Rastafari wound its chicken wire around my girlhood alone, my brother and I were inseparable at home. Though he was two years younger than me, my thoughts flowed through his mind and his thoughts poured out through mine. Whenever our father was gone to work we resumed our ramping, Lij challenging me to see who was brighter, who could run around the yard the quickest, scheming to put lizards on the other's head. We had no idea that our own ramshackle Zion wouldn't last, neither of us read the bones thrown down in the yard.

Lij had been chasing me across the lawn, wielding a giant mantis to stick in my hair. Giggling, I zipped left and ran sideways into the house to lose him. But there he was again. I could no longer outrun him. Laughing, I turned to face him with my mouth hanging open, but his empty palm was already there. His running motion drove the full force of his body into my jaw, which slammed hard against the bathroom wall. I felt my front tooth crumble to chalk in my mouth.

Lij screamed and grabbed my hand as I grabbed my mouth. Blood rushed over my tongue as I slid it across my gums. There, I felt a sharp unfinished crag in the place where one of my front teeth used to be.

Bits of tooth silted in a tasteless mass in my mouth. When my mother appeared, that's when the tears came. "Let me see it!" she said to me, cradling my face. "Oh Jah! Oh, sweetie. Oh Jah," Mom said as she looked into my mouth, and into my future.

"I didn't mean it," Lij said, tugging on my dress. "Saf, I didn't mean it."

Mom mixed some warm salt water and helped me rinse my mouth in the bathroom sink. When I spat, crumbles of tooth came out and I watched them disappear down the drain. A part of me made from the mud of us was now gone and I would never get it back. I slid my tongue across my teeth again and wept, braying as loud as my mouth would allow.

"Please, Saf," Lij said to me. "I'm sorry." But I could not speak to him yet. I pushed him away, hard.

There would be nothing perfect about me ever again. When my father walked through the door, this is how he found me. With my head in my mother's lap, howling little animal howls every time my tongue felt the broken and empty space of my gone tooth. I couldn't see through my tears. He looked over me, touching my back, and asked what happened. The tears joined into rivulets down my cheek.

"She broke her front tooth," Mom said, caressing my head.

"Lij pushed me into the wall," I stuttered out. I felt the wind whistle against my speech, cold striking raw against the open nerve.

My father kissed his teeth in annoyance and disappeared into the bedroom where my brother had been moping since I pushed him away from me. As my father shouted at my brother about too much ramping, the volume of his voice took the air out of me. Lij kept whimpering that it was an accident. His voice breaking. And now, I was whimpering too.

"I man not goin tell yuh again, Fyah," my father said from beyond the wall. "Stop follow back ah yuh sister them," he said. I couldn't hear my brother's response then. Couldn't read his mind.

"Leave. Woman. Frocktail. Alone," my father shouted at him again. Lij mewled out in agreement, weakly, from his corner in the room. My heart withered to hear it.

When my father came back into the living room he looked me over, checking for a parasite.

"What yuh still crying for?" he asked. I sniffled at him, my face wet. He told me to sit up, so I sat up, still whimpering. I looked in the mirror and half my tooth was gone. That version of myself, the one I liked, washed away.

"Yuh not in pain. Yuh not dying," my father said. "So stop the cow bawling, now."

I tried to stop. I made no more sounds, but the tears still ran warm salt streams down my cheeks. He glared at me, and I shrunk back.

"All of this bawling is just vanity," he told me.

And with that he turned away from me in disgust.

My parents couldn't afford to fix my tooth. They didn't have insurance and their dentist-friend, who was my brother's football coach, told them it didn't make sense to cap my front tooth until I was older, because my mouth was still growing. I wanted to protest, but what did it matter. My distress over my tooth was only vanity, my father said, and vanity was a mark of Babylon. I suspect he liked me broken. My mouth was a barricade between me and the crawl of adolescence, a broke-glass fence around my body. I stopped smiling completely. I held my hand across my mouth whenever I spoke. I forgave my brother for what happened, but I could no longer hear his thoughts. Gone was his heart beating inside my heart. Lij had suddenly grown shark skin. Now the truth loomed like the holy trinity right over my head—what he was being groomed to become had nothing at all to do with me. We would have mourned it then, if we could have seen it, our oneself being severed at the root.

I hardened now, becoming impenetrable as a pearl around a grain of sand. I sat clench-mouthed at school and spoke without opening my lips too wide. Though I'd often moved shy in the world since I had grown dreadlocks, in my classes I always shined. But now shyness slid into me in the classroom, and I grew even more doubtful of myself in the world. At home in bed, I felt my vibrance diminishing and felt its loss as a burning ache. When I spoke to Monique, her eyes darted into my mouth, and my hand flicked up instinctively to hide it. Sometimes I saw her in the distance talking to someone else, and when she laughed, I was certain she was laughing at me. Despair bloomed inside me, painful and mine only.

At the end of the school year, Catherine Hall threw a carnival. Balloons and clowns crowded the school, vendors crunched in with cotton candy and peanut brittle and their bright pandemonium of wares. My mother joined us at the school carnival with Shari, rosy as an apple and weighing down her arm. One of the attractions was riding on a mule, and after some begging, my mother paid for me and Ife to ride it. I smoothed the pleats of my dress, handsewn from brown and black African fabric, and got atop the mule sidesaddle. As the mule vendor pulled us around the parking lot, a photographer appeared and snapped our picture; I shivered away and shut my mouth tight. The next day the local newspaper would print our picture in a half-page spread, my face gloomy above the caption: TWO RASTA GIRLS RIDING A MULE.

Loud music blasted throughout the hallways and the canteen at school, while all around me bodies danced to celebrate the start of summer. I wandered the empty corridors alone. I passed the sixth-grade classroom, where someone had shuttered almost all the windows. I pried one open to look. Inside the sweaty room were girls grinding their behinds against the boys as dancehall music blasted from a battered radio someone had plugged into the wall. Some girls had their eyes closed, while the boys gripped them tight, all of them writhing. Their movements rhythmic and trancelike. This was the Babylon I had been warned about. The unwoken slack and sinfully common. But I looked on through that slat in the window and didn't turn away. Monique was there, too, wining on Anthony in the dark, her eyes half-closed in what looked like bliss. She looked up. Her eyes caught mine and I slammed the window and hurried away, my face hot.

My classroom was empty. I sat at my old desk and looked over the class rankings, trying not to think about what I had seen. I was in the top three again, and I let my eyes linger long across the letters of my name, the song of it. A shadow hovered in the doorway. I looked up and it was Anthony. Scrawny boy with reddish-brown eyes, hair like black peppercorns shaken all over his head. His eyes accompanied a smile that seemed to always be hiding something. His khaki uniform was stained with sweat at the armpits. In his hand he held a folded piece of paper.

"Yo, Rasta girl," he said, affecting a Black American accent I thought was so cool.

"Hey," I said, covering my tooth with my cupped palm.

He walked over to me and handed me the folded notepaper.

Before I opened it, he said, "Monique wanna know why you keep following her around, man." His eyes pressed into me, waiting.

"I'm not," I said, digging my fingernails into my palm.

"She don't like you," he said, eyes narrowing. "She don't want no Rasta for a friend."

"Oh, okay." I looked down. My throat was burning hot. I would not look at him.

"Okay, cool. So just stop," he said, walking back out. As he turned, his eyes were leaving their oily mark on me, laughing.

Just before he was out of sight, he turned again to the window outside the classroom and blurted out, "Jah Rastafari!" then cackled loudly, running away. Outside I could hear a thousand unseen people snickering too.

I turned away from them and unfolded the note.

I don't want to be your friend. Please leave me alone. It was signed, *Thank you, Monique* in beautiful flowery handwriting. A bright hurt unfurled in me and I nursed it against my throbbing head, my eyes burning. Dad had warned me about friend and company, but in my weakness I hadn't listened. He was right again. Babylon was a nest of vipers, writhing. I wanted so badly to lay my face against them, to nurture this hurt. I wanted to press my finger into some deeper wound to feel a kind of pain that might overwhelm everything else I now felt. This thing that lived in me and grew daunting as I grew, my lonely hydra.

I left the classroom and went down the steps to find my family, ignoring the hisses coming from the students in the shuttered sixth-grade classroom as I walked by. I held my head up, held it straight. Down the steps and around to the front offices, I saw an upturned piece of plywood on the ground next to me, something smashed and abandoned in the din of the carnival. Jutting out of it was a long rusted nail. Ahead of me in the distance were my mother and siblings. They could not see me, so I turned away from them. The bottom of my shoe scraped thin against the ground, a pair of flimsy crepe rubber-soled sneakers my mother had bought for me at the market. A dark need leafed in me, waking. I lifted my left foot over the rusty nail, and with full force I stepped down as hard I could, feeling the nail tear through my shoe, then rip through my skin and flesh. The wood was now attached to my foot and moved when I moved. I clenched my teeth tight against my own scream and stepped down harder.

10

Age of Wonder

EVERYONE BELIEVED THE NAIL WAS AN accident, and I let them believe it. My mother had scooped me up and sprinted me to the school nurse for a tetanus shot. I saw the size of the syringe and broke into a frantic gallop for the door, but the nurses locked me in. Panicked, I scampered under the desk, hugging my knees. When my mother and the nurses tried to drag me out, I made my body limp. "Please, Safiya," Mom pleaded with me. "You'll get lockjaw if you don't." It took my mother, two nurses, and two teachers to drag me out from under the desk as I scratched, flung pens and notebooks, eyes peeling wild, my head wrestling from side to side, begging as they clasped me down to the nurse's bed. When the needle finally went in I barely felt it prick.

Waking from the fog of the tetanus shot on bedrest, I cherished the slight throb in my foot where the nail had punctured me. When no one was looking, I pushed my finger into the bandage on my foot where the wound still hurt. I slid my tongue over the jagged point of my broken tooth and flinched. I spent hours trying to salvage a self from the scrapheap of rejection, as the note from Monique kept unfolding in my mind. From my window I watched my siblings sailing daydreams in the yard, and longed to feel a part of them again. I stayed in bed reading for the next few days while Mom brought me bowls of miso soup and massaged my body chakras with her warm hands. From my perch I overheard my father lambasting the principal for leaving deadly weapons lying about the school, only breathing free once I heard him leave for work. The trilling of Lij and Ife grew outside again in his absence, while Shari slept frothy next to me in her crib. Mom came in and sat with me on my bed, her face a ponderous mirror. She studied me for a long time in the daylight, then touched the crown of my dreadlocks.

"Anywhere you go, I'm going too," she said.

Her kind face was a mercy. It told me, with her warm eyes searching, that she already knew, somehow, about the nail.

She moved to the end of the bed now and placed my feet in her lap. Rubbing her hands together until they were warm, she made a bronze fire in her palms, then touched them tender to my throbbing foot.

"When I was in high school, they teased me too," she said. She rubbed the warmth of her hands together and touched them once more to me. "They called me 'dundus' because of my red skin and red hair," she said. "They laughed at me and your auntie Audrey because we had holes in our shoes. Girls would hold their nose and seh we smelled like fish."

She almost never talked about this part of her life. Sharing none of her suffering, she kept these stories bottled away. But now she saw me slipping away to something heavy, and she was here to pull me back. I fixed my gaze like a hook in her as she spoke.

"These are growing pains we all face," she said. "But you will always have me."

She reached out to me now and pulled me in.

I ran my fingers along the nub of Mom's sixth finger, which was a comfort. Beyond the partition of the bedroom, Lij and Ife chatted breathlessly as they watched television. It had been so long since it was just the two of us, in a quiet space like this. I hadn't realized until now how much I craved it.

She reached into her canvas handbag and pulled out a book called *Poems of a Child's World*. "I bought this for you," she said, and handed it to me. I turned the book over in my hands, held its weight against me like an anchor.

My mother could read my dark moods like a poem. Whenever gloom or fury overtook me, she recited "If" by Rudyard Kipling in my ear. Her voice was clear and musical as she spoke the familiar words to me now. She began reciting poems in high school, and the habit grew with her.

Part of me thought she kept these poems polished in her memory just to calm me down, to lift me up.

"Something about poetry always soothed the ills of the world for me," she said, now turning the crisp pages of the book between her fingers. She pointed out the poets she loved in high school. Blake, Keats, Shelley. "Maybe you will like them too." She smiled.

Above us an Anansi spider wove silk as she spoke.

"I was a dead-left child, abandoned." Her voice was thin and faraway. I gazed into the unspoken distance of where she was now gazing. "My world was small and bleak. But poetry made it seem wide and wild and warmer."

Her face lit up as she laughed and told me that that was alliteration. I asked her what alliteration was and she explained it to me.

I crowded in greedy. Each word she tossed I caught, and watched it come alive in my hands.

"Poetry is the best of what I have come to love about this world," my mother said.

My skin prickled. I longed to be cocooned in this, to be rooted here indefinitely in the tenderness of her telling. In time, I was laughing along with her, my hand in her hands, the wound in my foot now a faint throb. A new world was slowly opening its lacquered shell to me, its radiance beckoning. Here, on bedrest, nursing my visible and invisible wounds, what my mother pressed into my hands that day was gold.

Long after my mother left me to read the book by myself, I thought about what she had said. How poetry could cast a light on a meager world and make it boundless. How pain could be transformed into something beautiful. Monique's words may have crafted my hurt, but words could also unmake it. While flipping through *Poems of a Child's World*, she had turned to a poem called "The Tyger" by William Blake. "This is one of my favorites," she said. Now I turned to that page again and read.

> *Tyger Tyger, burning bright,*
> *In the forests of the night;*
> *What immortal hand or eye,*
> *Could frame thy fearful symmetry?*

As I read each line, a neon tiger, prowling, emerged from the jungle of my imagination, and its brilliance burned Monique's note to ash. I could see it so clearly, this beast striped fluorescent, lighting the lush thicket of vines, pulling and pulling me in. I was bewitched.

> *In what distant deeps or skies.*
> *Burnt the fire of thine eyes?*

I sounded the lines out aloud, feeling the rhymes growing delicious on my tongue. Later I went to the *Encyclopaedia Britannica* and looked up William Blake. I couldn't believe it. He died nearly 170 years before me, but his words grew a thriving forest in my head. A thought, I understood then, and its incendiary mind, could outlive itself. A well-made word could outspan carbon, and bone, and halved uranium. Until now, I imagined the world divided in two halves: the world of the spiritual, of my parents: Jah and livity, vibrations, energies, and chakras. And then, there was a world of things I could measure and understand, visible and knowable. Now, I felt there was another world just out of reach. A gossamer wing flashed against the bedroom window. I took out my journal and wrote my first lines of poetry in vines of cursive. Wings in the sunlight, wings against my dress. I pulled wing after luminous wing from my mouth. Watching them flutter alive with each word, my hands a vibrant garden. The poem was called "The Butterfly," the first to pull itself from the soft veil between all worlds, a seam to slip through to any place, any time. I knew then that as long as I had a word that leapt aflame in my mind, I would always be living in an age of wonder.

11
Moth in Amber

THE NEW TENANTS MOVED IN RIGHT next to us, renting the once-locked downstairs room of Ms. Gordon's house like rummagers overtaking a living thing overnight. Some weeks before, Ms. Gordon had returned home to visit family and slipped a long look down her glasses at me and my siblings, her dark eyes squinting. "Hmm" was all she said as she studied our dreadlocks, thick and long and unkempt. The last time she saw me, my hair was combed and plaited in two perfect pigtails. "Hmm," she said again as she glanced down at Lij with his thorny dreads, smiling his wolf-boy's smile. "Hmm" was all she said to herself, as she peeked into every corner of the yard, overturned every stone and leaf, exhaling a sharp upturned "Hmm" as she looked at the new crops we had grown, healthy sugarcane and pumpkin in our haphazard garden. Ms. Gordon held her hands behind her back, looking down her glasses as a detective would a magnifying glass. "Hmm," Ms. Gordon said a week later, her cold judgment cast down in stone, as she turned to look at us one last time before leaving for Foreign again.

A week after that, a young baldhead couple moved in right under our noses, hired to tend to the yard and watch over Ms. Gordon's part of the house. Like ants upon a living moth, they appeared from some dark nowhere and overwhelmed us with their strange pink lotion smells, their meat-breath, and their blaring dancehall music. Dad called out for Jah, called down thunder and lightning on their heads every night. My siblings and I didn't have to be told to stay away from them. The baldheads were smiling and cordial but gawked at our dreadlocks and food, gaped at our well-worn system of living, and had immense trouble pronouncing our names. The baldhead woman kept calling Shari "Sha-Sha," every time she saw my baby sister, cooing in a baby voice. "Hi, Sha-Sha! Come here, Sha-Sha," she said to Shari every day like a pet, until my baby sister, in one of her first spoken sentences, railed up like a lion cub and screamed, "Mi nuh name Sha-Sha!" Then we knew that it was time to leave. As was their way, my parents left no time for goodbyes. We departed for school one day from our home in Bogue, and when we got back we lived in a new house on the other side of Montego Bay. Mom had done all the packing herself, loading all our memories and our lost selves helter-skelter into the pickup truck loaned by one of my father's friends. When we arrived at our new home, we found ourselves in a government housing scheme surrounded by a neighborhood full of gawking baldheads called Farm Heights.

There we learned to adapt to scarcity as we had learned everything else. Since my father had returned from Japan two years before, our household was leaner. Our house at Farm Heights was a modest two bed-room, where Lij, Ife, and I shared one room. Ife and I slept side by side on one bed, while Lij had his own mattress. We ate rice and stew peas with dumplings nearly every day and stayed in on the weekends. There was a flushed cherry tree in the front yard and a bursting June plum tree in the backyard, which regularly filled our bellies. Outside there was a sloping hill that my siblings and I ran down to bowl when we played cricket, so as far as we were concerned, we had everything.

This was the first year I resigned myself to sorrow's permanence, a silent egg that lay in my hollow and stayed, a knotted cough in the throat I could feel but could not expel. By the time I was ten I'd already grown tall and gangly, and my body became something no longer my own. With every new birthday, I shed the old self, emerging bruised with the skin of the unknown. I became that curious creature who discovered her creases and bends, her new growths and thickening hair, her eager wants. As I approached eleven, I began waiting for the blood to come. "Any day now it's coming," my mother said, recounting the girls who'd gotten it at my age, sounding my death knell. I went to the bathroom every day with racked anxiety, watching the tissue for its red mark of doom, remember-ing with terror Josephine's worried face, how she was forced to sleep in a separate room when she menstruated because her husband thought she was unclean. I wanted to be pure. I wanted to be clean. How cruel to be growing into a body I no longer knew, girlhood terrifying with its many unknowables. Shame, too, grew slowly with me now, as I noticed for the first time not only a river swelling between me and my father, but that he was the one who fed its tributaries.

All year high school had loomed a shadow of uncertainty over me. I had passed my Common Entrance Exams with flying colors, and by the summer of 1995, the school choices seemed to have already been fated—all the brightest girls either went to Montego Bay High School or Mount Alvernia High School, both of which were all-girls schools.

As the first child of four, everything I did was new territory for my parents. Both all-girls high schools cost money my parents didn't have. One afternoon, my mother held up the newspaper in excitement, showing us the Classified page. "Look at this, Djani," she said, reading the ad out loud. There was a new private high school opening up in Montego Bay, offering two scholarships for "gifted and underprivileged" students to attend. Students would have to apply, and those chosen would then go to an interview. My heart sank. All the other girls in the sixth grade in Mobay were preparing to go to Mount Alvernia or Mobay High, but here I was faced with a new unknown.

I pushed out my lips when they told me to prepare for this scholarship interview. "So does this mean that if I want to go to any school in my life, I'm always going to have to get a scholarship?"

The question fell out brazenly, each word burning my tongue. I knew, as every Jamaican child knows, that no sentence directed to your parents should begin with the word "So." My father's eyes widened slowly, torched with a rage I could see coming and that told me to cower.

"*Have* to get a scholarship?" my father spat. "*Have* to get a scholarship?" he said again, his face twisted in disgust. "So yuh think yuh better than scholarship, eeh? You think I and I made ah money?" My mother glared at me but said nothing.

My father stood up now and closed his attention on me. I hung my head and tried to look away from him. "Eeh?" He glowered over me. "You think the I and yuh mother made ah money?" I could feel his heat on my face.

"No, Daddy," I said. He was raked up on his legs, looming over me.

"Gyal, you facety and out-order," he cursed. "Who do you think you are?" He bent and shook the kitchen table furiously, rattling it loud against the floor. I jumped back in fright.

"Yuh lucky I man don't box you right off this table," he said, teeth gritted. "Don't ever question I man and your mother again."

"Yes, Daddy," I whimpered.

"Gyal, get outta my sight." My lower lip quivered as I scuttled away. I hid in the bedroom for the rest of the day, while my father quarreled about me and my insolence with my mother. I burned with an indignant anger at first, my knees drawn up as I pouted in bed, not seeing what was so bad about my question, but when I heard my parents discussing the shrinking family budget and our growing family expenses, a creeping guilt flooded me and I went to the bathroom and wept, wishing I could take it back. My thoughtless question would be fuel for angry outbursts for weeks to come.

For weeks to come, I dwelled on that red feeling in my stomach when my father had turned his words on me and called me "gyal" for the first time. My father only used regal honorifics for the women in his life. Empress. Princess. Budgie. Dawta. The word "gyal" was an insult in Rasta vernacular and was never used for a girl or woman who was loved and respected. Calling someone a "gyal" was a marker of her unworthiness, used with the intent to hurt and belittle. When he called me "gyal" in the froth of his anger, the insult was my fledgling womanhood. My looming impurity. For weeks I felt that word like a knife between my legs. *Gyal.* A dirty word. Pinning me to that moment.

When my mother told me I was one of the finalists for the scholarship, I was not surprised. I had alchemized my father's rage into my best effort at winning this scholarship, resolved to be so excellent, my parents would never have to worry again. My father would know I was truly sorry then. I was chosen among hundreds of Mobay's underprivileged applicants for the chance to attend St. James College, a private school founded by rich white Jamaicans, where the tuition was $35,000 a term, exorbitantly more than we could afford. The school was not gender-segregated, but that didn't matter. My parents knew that this was tuition paid, uniforms made, one less child to worry about; a burden lifted. All finalists would be interviewed by the school's founders and a final decision would be made in a few weeks, in time for the new school year in September. As I prepared for my interview, my stomach lurched again at the wide unknown. All my initial reluctance at needing a scholarship had given way to my competitive need to be the best. Dad's lasting gift to me.

When we got to the air-conditioned lobby in the office building, we were met by a short white woman who introduced herself as Mrs. Newnham. I shrunk shy in the face of her warm hello. She was the first white woman I had seen up close and with whom I had had a conversation. I had seen the white tourists on Bottom Road and observed them from afar as spectacles, orbiting visitors who smelled like suntan lotion, with hair raked in silly canerows and beads, aliens who walked half-naked down our busy streets, half-dressed on vacation among Jamaican people on their way to work, to school, to the bank. There were two worlds in Montego Bay passing each other by wordlessly, seen and unseen; the Jamaica these white people inhabited was not the same one I did. Mrs. Newnham was also the first white Jamaican I'd met who really sounded like a Jamaican—albeit a Kingstonian one, who pronounced everything with a pinched mouth, until "Jamaican" sounded *Juhmaicun.*

I gradually felt my worries melt away. Mrs. Newnham didn't seem to be cold or mean, as I imagined all white people to be, the evil bloodsuckers my father warned me about when he cursed about Queen Eliza-bat. I watched her curiously as she talked with my mother. She wore round glasses with thick frames that obscured most of her soft face and wore her hair in short black curls. Next to her I felt rough-hewn, my clothes cut from Kente cloth and handsewn by my mother, my hair in its wild dreadlocked state, dangling branches in my face. She asked me to come with her, gesturing toward another room with a closed door. My mother squeezed my hand reassuringly and gave me a big smile as I went with Mrs. Newnham. Through the door, I turned and saw my mother's face still smiling. She raised one confident fist, giving me power.

The room was cold and blinked at me with ten insistent eyes. At a table in the center of the room sat five men, most of them white, smiling and waiting for me. Mrs. Newnham winked at me as she left again through the door. I could feel the men looking me up and down, my dreadlocks falling into my face, my cheeks hot. I had never been all alone with so many white people before.

They greeted me then went around the room introducing themselves. They all had gold watches on and school rings with large ruby insignias on them that glistened as they spoke. One white man asked what I did in my spare time.

I told them I loved to read and write poetry, and that my favorite poem was "The Tyger" by William Blake.

"Oh, do you know that one?" The white man turned to ask the man who sat next to him.

Before they could ask another question, I began to recite. "'Tyger, tyger, burning bright, in the forest of the night,'" I looked at each of them as I spoke. "'What immortal hand or eye, could frame thy fearful symmetry?'" I continued. The words gave me electric power. They leaned back in their seats, staring at me, and looked back and forth at one another.

"My god, you speak so well," another white man said. "You speak so well," they all said, several times. I was unsure how else I was supposed to speak.

As the interview wound down, I told them I liked to read the newspaper. "Really?" they said, and chuckled in disbelief. The kindest white man at the table, the one with a long nose and twinkling blue eyes, asked me to tell him about something in the news, sports, or current affairs. I stopped to think. I wanted to make sure my answer was untouchable, an answer they would remember the next day. I knew everybody had been talking about West Indian cricketer Brian Lara's record-breaking summer and that was the most expected answer.

"I've been following the Donald Panton scandal," I said, barely missing a beat. Two of the men fell back in their chairs in surprise. Donald Panton was the *other* big story that summer—a prominent Kingston businessman who was now under investigation for financial fraud. Here was my audience, I thought.

Their eyebrows raised as I described what I knew about the scandal.

"You are one bright young girl," the kind white man said, still leaned back in his chair, eyeing me as if I had performed a miracle or sleight of hand, though he was still unsure of which.

Just as soon as it began, the interview was over, and the committee came out with me, crowding my mother and congratulating her, asking her what her secret was to raising children. "If I had a dime for every time somebody asked me that"—my mother laughed—"I would be rich."

Before we even left the building, Mrs. Newnham told us they didn't need time to deliberate, that I was awarded a scholarship to go to St. James College. My mother hugged me, breathless and grateful, and thanked Mrs. Newnham and the committee. Outside the building, she jumped and squealed. She embraced me again, her neck in my neck as time stretched endless into some far-off world where we are still embracing even now. Beyond the hazy light of the veiled world lives this moment of my life diverging—I went one way, and the other girl, the girl I never became, went the other, with all her mysterious possibilities, all her unknown and possible worlds.

"Donald Panton?" my mother said. She squinted at me incredulously as we left with our good news.

"What do you even *know* about that, Safiya?" she asked.

"Everything," I said.

I was three weeks away from my eleventh birthday when I walked up the staircase of the private high school where I would spend the next five years. I didn't know what to expect. The converted estate was a rolling space filled with orange trees and one massive poinciana tree bursting with blooms. Its long pods rattled the roof of the old Lada taxi that my mother hired to take me the first day. She kissed me on the cheek and waved goodbye, as I jumped out hoping no one saw me arrive. I was the first one there. I ambled up the steps and found my classroom, which was a bedroom converted to look like a classroom. From the seventh-grade window I watched the driveway where shiny SUVs crunched the gravel as they pulled up and one white girl after another poured out in crisp white shirts and ties and short blue pleated skirts. Every time another white girl pirouetted out of a car, my stomach lurched. These were to be my classmates. I had never spoken to a white person my age before, much less sat next to them. What were they like? I stood tall and straight as a ruler when the first white girl walked into the classroom. "Hey," she said nonchalantly, and walked past me to claim a desk.

"Hey," I responded, trying to echo her casual attitude.

"I'm Shannon," she said. She looked almost identical to the kind white man from the scholarship committee. Like him, she had brown hair, a long nose, and light blue eyes that twinkled. Her accent was very much like Mrs. Newnham's—a distinct upper-class Jamaican accent, her mouth closed around the words like a June plum.

"I'm Safiya," I said, covering my broken front tooth and trying to sound like a more constructed version of myself. I could see her looking at my dreadlocks, thick and falling into my face, covering my eyes.

A silence spread between us, overgrowing the air and making me worrisome. I had so many questions for a white Jamaican. Top of my mind was, "My father says you're the devil, is that true?" But I thought better of asking that.

After thinking some time about what to say next, I asked Shannon, "Do you eat dumpling?" She stared at me, then rolled her eyes.

"Of course I eat dumplings," she said. "What kind of dumb question is that?" She squinted at me. My heart sank. I had no idea if white Jamaicans also ate what I ate. I thought they ate fancier food from Foreign. So now I knew.

As we stood there, more girls filed in. A blond girl, another blond girl. As they came in, they greeted one another. Most of them already knew each other; they had gone to a private prep school together. I saw Shannon whispering and snickering to them about what I asked. I decided I would ask them a smarter question, one that had never failed to carry me yet.

I walked over to where the three white girls huddled and introduced myself again. Then I asked, "Do you know how to spell Czechoslovakia?"

They all stared at me, then laughter shattered the air.

"Are you serious?" Shannon asked me.

I nodded firmly.

"Oh my god, duh. Of course I can spell it. I mean, that's not even a country anymore," she said. Then she turned back to the other two girls, laughing.

I considered this. Considered my beloved hand-me-down encyclopedia, pictured my old self lying on the grass at Bogue, where the sky seemed so big, and the world was hers, handsome as a relic stuck in amber.

No one had told me, I wanted to say to them. No one had told me any of this.

II
MEDUSA

*Do you not see how necessary
a world of pains and troubles is
to school an intelligence
and make it a soul?*
—JOHN KEATS

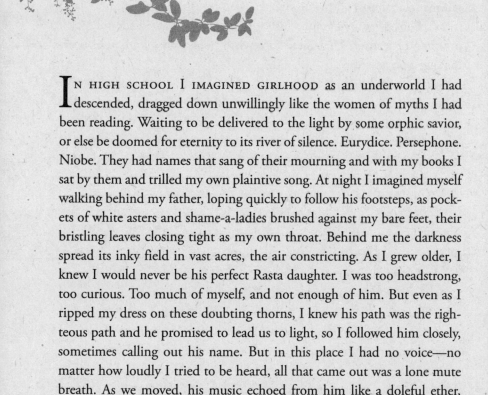

12

My Eurydice

IN HIGH SCHOOL I IMAGINED GIRLHOOD as an underworld I had descended, dragged down unwillingly like the women of myths I had been reading. Waiting to be delivered to the light by some orphic savior, or else be doomed for eternity to its river of silence. Eurydice. Persephone. Niobe. They had names that sang of their mourning and with my books I sat by them and trilled my own plaintive song. At night I imagined myself walking behind my father, loping quickly to follow his footsteps, as pockets of white asters and shame-a-ladies brushed against my bare feet, their bristling leaves closing tight as my own throat. Behind me the darkness spread its inky field in vast acres, the air constricting. As I grew older, I knew I would never be his perfect Rasta daughter. I was too headstrong, too curious. Too much of myself, and not enough of him. But even as I ripped my dress on these doubting thorns, I knew his path was the righteous path and he promised to lead us to light, so I followed him closely, sometimes calling out his name. But in this place I had no voice—no matter how loudly I tried to be heard, all that came out was a lone mute breath. As we moved, his music echoed from him like a doleful ether, pulling me forward. He sang out for his losses, his livity, his god. Soon his song became my song, my sisters' song, my mother's song. And when I reached out, I could not touch him, I was not clean; I was not worthy. Still. I crept along the river, dark as glass, trying to remember myself. *Who am I?* I wanted to say. *Who am I to you now?* But his gaze was fixed forward on a future I could not see, as I scuttled along behind him, my bare toes sludged black with mud. I had to follow. Where he went, I went, his thoughts molding my thoughts, until I became the perfect shadow.

Most school mornings, I woke with an anxious pit in my stomach before I got dressed and ready to go to St. James College. I had to travel the farthest and so woke the earliest; the long drive toward the wealthier neighborhoods on Montego Bay's coast was a persistent reminder that my family's dream of upward mobility had thudded to earth like a rotten mango. Almost all my classmates lived less than a ten-minute drive from school, swanning around lush verandas in their gated communities, preening beneath vast satellited roofs with pools and guesthouses overlooking a private sea.

The school building and property was a mauled remnant of British colonialism, an old "Great House" passed down from enslavers related to one of the school's founders. Gone shabby and overgrown, it was a house whose ghosts still loitered the classrooms, most of which were converted from the main bedrooms, and some from former servants' quarters, with permanently locked closets and scratches at the windows. An eerie quiet always brewed just beyond our voices, a pallor of the past's hand-me-down burdens.

We were the inaugural class, the first experiment. There were eight of us in seventh grade, all girls, including one other scholarship student, plucked from some other government housing scheme, the two of us an exercise in charity, chosen to give St. James College some kind of cultural character. We moved in between the visible and invisible lines that separated us, fixed under the omen of our names. Two of my classmates were white Jamaicans who still lived in sprawling mansions on former plantations. Others were children of American and Canadian expats who vacationed abroad several times a year, and who spoke in chirpy and unfamiliar American pop-culture vernacular, girls whose parents packed lunches with American snacks I had never seen, girls whose perfumed and toy-blond mothers picked them up promptly every evening with just-polished red nails, pale fingers drumming along the steering wheel of their luxury cars. They had all gone to the same private prep school together, had all rode the same horses, growing up in a sequestered paradise built by their parents on the untouchable land of their gated neighborhood, where they played tennis and lunched at the yacht club together, and when it was time for high school, their parents had formed a board and built them a private high school so they wouldn't have to rub shoulders with the rest of the island in our many public schools. The bond between them was as unspoken and unbreakable as the barrier between us. I had not yet grown accustomed to being around people like this, the army of short white girls in pleated skirts, filing into school loud and self-assured, laughing with each other. They moved in this world, in all worlds, with bliss and delight. They all unbuttoned their school shirts two or three buttons down, folding their collars into a deep V to show their bosoms, while I, still bosomless, kept my shirt buttoned up to my throat, wearing my tie knotted tight around my neck like a boy. Since my dumpling gaffe on the first day of school, I observed them as if they had just landed on my shores, studying their strange manners and references, parsing out the upswing of their voices on the end of their sentences. I wished for that freedom.

"Did anyone see *Party of Five* last night? It was so good," Lizzy said, her blue braces sparkling in the sunlight coming through our classroom window. They had formed a circle in the middle of the classroom, faces flush and certain. The last few months I'd grown into a sea sponge, listening ever closely, as their inscrutable conversation washed over me in waves.

"No, I was too busy watching reruns of *My So-Called Life* instead," Shannon said. "I cannot *believe* they canceled that show. Jordan Catalano was my whole world!" She sighed with her eyes closed, her mouth also full of braces, metal twinkling as she spoke. I glanced over at Cassandra, the other scholarship student, who had arrived while they were talking. She rolled her eyes and looked out the window, both of us sitting silent and confused while our classmates continued shrilling about people and things we knew nothing of.

"Jared Leto is sooo hot," Shannon's cousin Heather said, throwing her head skyward to shake down a waterfall of yellow hair, her pink throat exposed. The other girls cooed. "Sooo hot."

"That show just *gets* me," Shannon said, and the other blond girls nodded along. "I was thinking of getting my hair cut like Angela," Shannon said. Who was Angela? I flipped the pages of my textbook as I pretended not to listen, but ingested everything.

Along with tuition and uniforms, my scholarship to St. James College came with new books. Two weeks before school started, I glided into the bookstore on a sunbeam, buzzing as I picked out my textbooks, pressing my face inside to smell their pages, glossy new worlds waiting for me. This was what I imagined Christmas must be like, cradling my new books.

One evening my mother approached me as I sat reading. "Bonjour, mademoiselle! What you reading?" she asked, doing a little shimmy. I'd been learning French and she loved practicing each novel word with me, running my grammar and conjugations on a loop until I perfected them. Dinner was over, and I sat at the empty dining table reading *Men and Gods*, a book on Greek myths Mrs. Newnham had assigned. My siblings were bolting around our shared bedroom, shrieking with the crickets. It was becoming harder to find my own space to read in our crowded house, and each day I craved more time with myself, more time to slip into that warm and lonesome home of quietude.

Choking smoke rose from the lit mosquito coil as my mother and I sat talking. "I was just reading this Greek myth about a woman called Persephone," I told her. "She lives in the underworld for half the year, and when she is gone down there her mother misses her so much that they have months of winter, and when she's back with her mother they have months of summer."

Like sudden thunder, my father's voice boomed out to us from the living room. "The Greeks stole dem mythology from the Egyptians," he said. He had been listening to us from the couch while doing his daily newspaper crossword and now walked in to join us.

"It's good yuh reading other things for school and widening your horizons," he said to me, "but the I should always know where Babylon propaganda comes from." The light between my mother and me ebbed as he hovered over the table. He glanced over my textbook of Greek myths and pointed.

"They stole the Egyptian myths, changed all the Egyptian gods' names, and erased our history. All of this originated in Africa," he said, still gesturing to my book.

"Yes, it's true," Mom said, nodding, then took a half-smoked spliff from behind her ear and lit it. Her ganja smoke and the smoke from the mosquito coil formed a potent cloud around me, making me heavy-headed.

"The world didn't begin with the Greeks," Dad told me. "That's what Babylon wants you to think. That's why they don't teach you about the universities of Timbuktu and the great achievements of Africans. Why they don't teach you about Hannibal, who was a great Black man, but instead they teach you about Alexander the Greek."

"You mean Alexander the Great?" I asked. Outside the crickets were screeching a ruckus in the dark, and the cool night air sifted through the slats of our open window.

"I man don't recognize him as nothing Great, he is Alexander the *Greek.* He was no great man to I and I. Babylon want you to think he was great, but he did nothing but bring war and destruction to Africa."

"Yes, Daddy," I said, making a note to look up both Hannibal and Al-exander the Great Greek later. In the new house, Haile Selassie's portrait had now moved to a prized shelf on the whatnot in my parents' bedroom, but when my father looked into me, the emperor's eyes and his merged seamlessly into one perishing gaze.

Our school was small, thirty-five students in total, so it was nearly im-possible for me to hide, even when I longed to disappear. My dreadlocks announced me dramatically wherever I went, a black fleece covering me and my broken tooth. Some mornings I arrived at school early enough to walk around alone in the backyard outside, dew moistening my socks as I strolled the fragrant orange trees that guarded the half acre of land. Then I'd walk around the side of the school to the entrance, and stand under the old poinciana tree, its trunk big enough to house me. When the tree was in full blossom, its branches cast a green shadow over the school entrance, orange flames bursting in sticky blooms, a beckoning sign of my own girlhood passing. In class I could see the tree from my window. I dreamed of it and it dreamed of me, and I tried to put its scorching dance into words.

One morning the quiet of my walk was broken by fingers snapping impatiently, and someone rasping my name from above. It was Mrs. Pinnock, the science teacher, calling me up to the terrace that overlooked the school's backyard. Mrs. Pinnock had a way of instantly turning the air in a room sour. She never called on me in class, even when my hand was up to give the answer.

"Sinclair, why were you down there alone? You are a young girl," she said, shaking her index finger at me before I could answer. "You should not be wandering around the school grounds alone before the teachers arrive, you know better than that," she said.

"I didn't know I wasn't allowed to, Miss." I concentrated on her shoes as she spoke; she wore the ubiquitous sheer nylons and polished block heels of Jamaican teachers, the same ones my grandmother wore. After promising not to walk the grounds alone again, I turned to walk to my classroom.

Then Mrs. Pinnock outstretched her hand like a barricade, blocking me. My chest bumped against the bone of her wrist, and I jumped back and looked at her.

She grimaced. "Can you please brush your . . . hair?" she said to me. "You can't be just walking around here looking like a mop. We still need to have some standards for the students of this school." I would not let her see me react, though my shame grew an aching knot in my throat.

I gathered my quivering voice. "Miss, my father says I am not allowed to brush my hair. Miss," I said, trying to sweep my locks away from my face and off my head forever, but they sprung right back, incorrigible.

"Your father?"

"Yes, Miss." Her face turned sour. Like most churchgoing Jamaicans, she had most likely been weaned on those old folktales that warned that a Rasta bredren was an evil Blackheart Man, coming to snatch and murder her in the night. All that old fear now gathered into true disdain, barely veiled.

"Well, at least catch it up in a scrunchie or something," she said, gesturing at my head.

"Okay, Miss." Once more I lifted my hands to move my dreadlocks away from my eyes, and Mrs. Pinnock suddenly grabbed ahold of my wrist.

"Eh eh!" she gasped, winding her head back to look at me. "But ah wha' dis on your hand?"

There were deep brown henna patterns and intricate laced details framing each of my hands. A family friend from America had visited us and diligently stained my hands and feet with her homemade henna while she and my mom smoked. I had loved the ritual of it, sitting in a circle of wise women talking, my ears perking up, catching the seeds of their conversation.

"It's henna, Miss," I told Mrs. Pinnock.

"Henna? What is henna?" she asked. Her voice was already accusatory.

"It's a kind of dye that you put—" I was trying to explain.

"Go and wash it off," she said, finally letting go of me, waving me away before I could finish.

I hadn't moved, so she looked back at me, nostrils widening. "It won't come off, Miss," I tried to tell her. "It stains the skin for a few weeks."

"What you mean it won't come off?" She dug her fingers into the brown henna patterns and kept rubbing until I winced and pulled my hand away.

"So it's a tattoo?" she said, her voice louder. "This is not allowed at school."

"It's not a tattoo, Miss," I insisted, my voice quivering now. All that I held bound in me was coming untied.

"Then *go* to the *bathroom* and *wash* it *off*," she said, articulating each word slowly, then pointing to the girls' bathroom down the hall. "And come back to the teachers' lounge and show me."

"But, Miss—"

"Go now!" she said.

I walked down the narrow hallway as if I moved through molasses. My palms and feet were sweating as I walked past my seventh-grade classroom, my head hung so low I could see into the lonely catacombs of myself and the silent girl sinking into darkness. I scrubbed my hands

raw until my skin burned, turning red in between the henna designs. I
rinsed again in vain, closing my eyes as I dried them. Back I waded down
the hallway to Mrs. Pinnock in the teachers' lounge to show her that the
henna truly could not come off. She kissed her teeth, grabbed my hands,
and held them out to the other teachers.

"You see this?" she said to them, gesturing to my hands. "Now these
people just taking all kind of liberties." By the way she hissed *these people*,
there was no mistaking who she meant. The teachers all nodded silently,
dark eyes staring at me.

"You're off with a stern warning this time," Mrs. Pinnock said. "Another one and you'll have detention."

"Yes, Miss," I said, choking back tears as I left the room.

At morning assembly we all lined up in the lobby according to our grades
as Mrs. Pinnock made a public announcement to the school. "A student
came to school today with something called 'henna' on her hands." I
looked at the floor as the sun and a bevy of eyes shined immediately on
me. "No tattoos or permanent markings are allowed on our students at
St. James College. Any student seen with any kind of tattoo at school
after today will get detention or suspension. Do you understand?"

Head bowed, back bent, I trudged to class while shaking the long
yarn of my dreadlocks down over my face.

At lunchtime the rich girls often decided to forego the lunchroom and
eat under the shade of the trees in the front yard instead. Whatever they
decided was a class decree, so we would all follow them downstairs, out
into the noon sun, spreading out our blue pleated skirts in the grass, then
ate and talked until the bell rang. Many of them would buy pizza and beef
patties and warm coco bread from the tiny tuck shop that Miss Norma
ran out of the converted kitchen, and with burning eyes I watched them
eat the food I was forbidden. Some classmates would unzip their name-
brand lunch bags bought in shiny American stores and eat fancy chips
and cookies, crackers with cheese dips, and chocolate pudding and bright
Fruit Roll-Ups. While I instead unpeeled my cheap nylon lunch bag to
eat a sweaty lettuce and cheese sandwich, peeled orange, with a bag of
imitation chips my mom had bought from a Chinese grocery store. Some

mornings my siblings and I left home with an empty fridge and emptier lunch bags, and my mother would tell us not to worry; she would bring us food at lunchtime. We shuffled out the door with grumble and doubt. But sure enough, every lunchtime she would appear on the horizon with Shari on her arm, walking up the gravel walkway, her long skirt swaying as she moved, to present me food—grilled cheese from a hotel kitchen, Ital chunks from a Rasta tuck shop, a veggie patty from downtown. I never knew how she was able to buy these lunches, when our kitchen and our pockets went bare as Dad waited for a paycheck, or how she made it in time to three different schools' lunch hours, and I never asked. Sometimes I even sulked at what she offered. But she always came, and I was always fed.

After Mrs. Pinnock's announcement about my henna, I sat subdued with my classmates at lunchtime. There was nothing to say and no friend to say it to. My world was a string of dismissals clinking against each other into one long, ugly necklace, and that necklace and its ugliness defined me. No one questioned my silence, my bent hideousness. I might have camouflaged my body right into the fungi-ridden bark and not have realized it. After Shannon finished her lunch she declared to the group that she was going to climb the young mango tree, which perked me up because I didn't know anyone else in my class liked to climb trees.

I watched her as she clambered up into the lowest branch, her pleated skirt ballooning and exposing her legs and black boy shorts underneath. I moved closer to the mango tree, looking up as she climbed several branches higher.

"I think it's cool by the way," Shannon's voice called out to me from above. "Your hands. I always wanted to try henna."

The glare of the sun caught my eyes as I looked up at her. "Thanks," I said, holding my palms outstretched in the wind, looking at the henna patterns, my hands still sore from scrubbing. I leaned against the trunk as casually as I could. Shannon swung her legs down to a lower limb, and my stomach bucked when I realized she was clambering down closer to talk to me.

"I don't know what's the big deal," Shannon said. "Katherine has a whole tattoo on her ankle and no one said anything about it. Teachers here are such prudes," she said, rolling her eyes.

Katherine was Heather's older sister, and I had heard much bragging of her ankle tattoo, which was still scandalous to us seventh graders. Katherine was Mrs. Pinnock's favorite; she always complimented her blond hair or her blue eyes. I felt a pang of realization just then. Though Shannon had been the one to point it out, I knew she couldn't really see the truth of it—there were two different systems of punishment at St. James College: one for me, and another one for girls like her.

Shannon climbed closer, her gaze fixed on my locks.

"So is henna part of your . . . religion?" she asked.

I shook my head. She asked me if I could wear nail polish. No, I said. She asked another question hooked into a question about Rastafari, and another, to which the answer was no, always no, I was not allowed. But she kept going, as if she were trying to reveal something clever about Rastafari to me. Why was henna allowed, but nail polish wasn't? Why do you only wear skirts and dresses? Why can't you wear pants? Why can't you wear makeup? Why can't you pierce your ears? Why can't you shave? What were the rules? Who made them?

My father, I wanted to tell her. My father did. And now it seemed I couldn't escape him. All my excitement at talking with Shannon was dampened by the vision of myself as a perfect daughter of Rastafari, what she wore, how she looked. My humility. My purity. My silence. It seemed that Rastafari overtook every moment in my life, every conversation, every hope at friendship.

My necklace of shame weighed heavier and heavier, and my face grew hot under the spotlight of her questioning. I watched the other girls float off in the distance.

"But what about your brother?" Undeterred, Shannon was in my ear again. "Does he have his own rules too?" She was on the lowest branch now, her pale legs swinging down near my head.

I shook my head. "He doesn't cut his hair, and we're not supposed to eat meat. But other than that, he's fine."

"So only you and your sisters have these rules to follow?"

"Yep," I said, picking at the bark. "And my mom."

It might have been easier to tell her, if I'd had the words for it then, that every Rastaman was the godhead in his household, that every word my father spoke was gospel. There was no foundational text or unifying tenets, no holy house except the Mansion of Djani. That living in a Rasta household was like being at a constant church, except the scripture was as variable as the sky, my father both the god of the sea and the god of the sun.

"Well, what happens if you don't follow his rules?"

"I get in trouble."

Shannon winced and shook her head.

I didn't tell her what "trouble" meant in the Sinclair household, nor could I have imagined what it would come to mean, eventually. That one day I would wake under a ruptured sky and not recognize my home. That I would look into the frayed face of my future and choose to run. But it didn't matter. Not yet. Because I followed the rules.

I leaned back against the trunk of the mango tree, smoothing down the pleated hem of my uniform skirt, which had been tailored to be longer than any other girl's at school. A curved line of black ants trailed up to the white blossoms where Shannon sat, her skirt ballooning in the wind, exposing her pale thighs underneath. I longed to climb up into the tree like that, to feel the wind at my thighs again. But I was too old now to climb trees, my father said.

"What's it like up there?" I wanted to ask her, but instead I said nothing. Loping along the underworld silently. A perfect shadow.

I sat quiet on the taxi ride home, ignoring my chattering siblings, thinking about my talk with Shannon at lunch, reliving the way Mrs. Pinnock had looked at my dreadlocks, how I wanted so much to be anywhere else. When I emerged from the fog my mother was there in the doorway of home, as she always was. I watched her eyes widen as I told her about being scolded for the henna at school, and that Heather's older sister, Katherine, had a tattoo on her ankle and never got in trouble for it. My sadness was catching, and I watched it darken my mother's face in a wave of guilt, then anger, and just like that, it metamorphosed into something else. As if she had always known some ugly secret about the world and now watched her daughter encounter it for the first time. She kissed my forehead, rubbing my hands with her warmth. Then she got up, pacing back and forth, saying, "It's not right. It's not right," again and again. I had hardly ever seen my mother agitated, but this bothered her. My siblings, who had been listening, agreed indignantly that it wasn't right.

"How can she not know what henna is? It's so ignorant," Mom kept saying in disbelief. Then after a little while she sat down and told me that I would meet many people like Mrs. Pinnock in life, but the trick was to let their words and actions wash over me.

I tried to disentangle myself from the blue hour that beckoned, but all I felt was anger.

I watched the clock for my father to come home, remembering to recount every detail that would stoke his fire and brimstone, wanting him to call down Jah's lightning on that baldhead Mrs. Pinnock. That night, like any given night in Farm Heights, our power went out without warning, which meant Mom reached for our kerosene lamp and some candles, and we all lay in the dim firelight playing word games in feverish rounds until we fell asleep. We huddled like this in the flickering light until we heard my father at the door.

Mom and I launched into a testimony of what happened at school, with Lij and Ife joining in excitedly. My father listened, pulling on his precept silently like a wise man. When we were finished my mother said, "I'm going to speak with Mrs. Newnham tomorrow." I beamed and looked to my father, waiting for the familiar fire to pour like lava off his tongue.

His face looked especially weary in the glow of the candlelight. He held our world up on his shoulders, but I never once thought about what he was carrying. In the two and a half years since he got back from Japan his joy was rarer, and days were hushed with disappointment or torched with anger as he watched his career wither. He flicked his locks over his shoulder and said to me, "Ah so dem baldheads stay, Budgie. They don't know nuttin bout this Rasta trodition. Brainwashed Christian eejiat dem." I nodded and smiled, ready for the big bangarang that would come next. I imagined my father lashing Mrs. Pinnock with his sermon of righteousness, making her cower small small under his sharp black gaze.

But then he shook his head and said, "Makini, you can't go up there and make no big commotion."

My mother said nothing. She stilled, as if one of the candle flames went out.

"But, Daddy—" I said.

"You need to keep your head down, do your work, and don't cause no trouble," he said, stopping me in my tracks.

"I'm not causing any trouble. She was the one—"

"You're on a scholarship," he said. "They paying for the I to be there. Don't make no fuss at the people them school," he said again.

I looked at Mom, and her eyes were half-closed. I had not seen her take it out, but she had already lit a tiny spliff butt and was blowing the thinnest smoke into the air. By now I had begun to trace her pattern of smoking. My mother never spoke up or challenged my father, not once. But like clockwork, whenever she disagreed with him, in lieu of voicing her opinion, she pulled out a spliff, her eyes narrowing to slits instead. As he spoke, she said nothing else. She took a candle and got up and left, closing the door behind her.

"You hear me?" Dad said. He held his hands in the loops of his waist while the buckle of his new red belt, a gift from a Canadian friend, reflected the dim lamplight.

"Yes, Daddy," I said. I could hear faint sounds of clanging coming from the kitchen; my mother washing the dishes in the dark. Like her, I had expected his brimstone for the baldheads who had wronged me. I wanted him to defend me on this path he had cut through the jungle for us. Instead, he moved cautious and smiling in the face of Babylon, and saved all his fire for us.

My father came and lay next to me in the bed. He was good at ignoring my sour mood, or eclipsing it entirely.

"Now tell me again about school," he said. Since I began at St. James College, I'd been regaling him with which of my classmates' fathers was a businessman and what kind of car each classmate's mother drove. He seemed to relish these stories about the other parents, so I hoarded every morsel to report back to him. I might have found it hypocritical if it hadn't served as a potent tonic. It made him feel irie, so I treasured it. Anything that lifted him meant the whole house lifted too. As I spoke, his eyes closed sleepy and satisfied, as if I were a conduit for his relayed success.

"Heather's father owns Margaritaville," I began. I'd perfected these stories like an art, watching my father's face shift and light up with each impressive detail.

"He owns all of it?" he asked me, with a faraway voice.

"I think so . . ." I said. I wasn't sure if that was true, but I knew the grander the parent's success, the more spirited he seemed. Over time I'd woven him a grand myth of their world, because it fueled his belief in reaching the summit, deepened his faith that somehow his livity in Rastafari would change our lives.

"My daughter goes to school with the owner of Margaritaville," he said, his voice drawn out with honey, sweet with pride, if Rasta could feel proud.

The power was still out when I looked over and watched his eyes close shut into a stony sleep, his dreadlocks draped down around his hands, resting on his belted waist like wayward rivers, black and branching. I loved him like this. The lamplight shone off the shiny scar on his forehead, the moon-calm of his sleeping face fixed in a smile. When he was happy, we were invincible. I was almost twelve and didn't yet think of happiness as a disappearing myth. I craved these velvet hours, wishing we could stay this way, despite Babylon. After a while, I got up and left him to sleep. But if I had known this would be the last time my father and I would lay so tenderly next to each other, I might have stayed there forever, stepping no farther across that river, never having to know what would happen next.

13

The Red Belt

FROM THE CRAMPED HOUSE ON TENTH Street, we could no longer see the sea. This was our first rented house after we'd left our paradise of Bogue, and the ghost rhythm of the far waves lapsed in my mind, haunting most acutely when the days scorched hot. The sun burned hotter without the sea breeze behind it, living as we were this far inland, surrounded by cardboard cutout houses, each one a dusty-yellow copy of the other, walls pressed in tight, my family sweating under the gaze of neighbors peering from fence to fence. My father raged, disgusted, mocked them as butus at the dinner table, then smiled liquescent and waved politely, even engaged them in mindless conversation when he saw them outside. He was an astute politician. He seemed to care immensely about what people thought of him, and as I grew older, the more his contradictions became plain. He despised Babylon, while yearning for its trappings. And when he did not defend me against Mrs. Pinnock, it struck me how much grace he offered these meat-eating strangers, and how little for us. With him, nothing was ever certain nowadays, not even love. As the months stretched on, his moods soured to new depths, strained by the unpredictability of a musician's living, chasing gig after gig. But at twelve, I was still young enough to keep approaching him, a kicked dog slinking back, doing as my mother did. She was the unchanging rock he crashed upon, sparing us as much of his storm as she could, as we watched her moods closely to know when it was safe to come back to Dad again.

It seemed worth the worry when he smiled at me and called me by a name he had chosen. *Budgie*, he would say, singing out the nickname he gave me when I was born. "When you were a baby, you cooed like a budgerigar. Such a calming, beautiful sound, like my favorite bird." Sometimes I forgot that he had grown up in the country, running down the rambling miles of green hills that he said looked like the English countryside. There, he had known the color and song of every bird, could point out the finch from the grassquit, the warbler from the thrush. So rarely did he speak of that old country, that old self, a pond by the lake that he found music in, that I wanted to stay at that pond, with that boy, watching a budgerigar flit from branch to branch of his cottonwood tree. When he sang for his Budgie, I cooed and went to him.

In these warm moments my siblings and I crowded in like crows around the settee, pecking at my father's feet, beaming even as he rehashed jokes about his boyhood friends, imitating their voices and mannerisms, the bulging guts and greasy skin of "meat-eaters." I never considered that perhaps he told the same jokes because they were all he had, all the good he held on to from his old life, a well-worn coin in his pocket.

Looming just out of view was the danger that our blissful moment might fill with rain. Some days Dad's dream of the fish-filled pond under the cottonwood tree would suddenly bleed into a memory of someone named Aunt Nicey, a relative we had never met, and only heard of on these moody occasions when my father's face went dark as if she herself had flipped the light switch. We learned to hate Aunt Nicey, for when she rolled into our frame like a thunderstorm, all the birdsong went out of my father's world.

"I never knew my father" is how the story of Aunt Nicey began, unfailingly. My father's eyes no longer sun-bright under those verdant pools. "I never knew my father," he said again, in a trance. "Not his face, not even his name." We sat still and watched him, rooted. "Nobody wanted me," he continued, unpeeling his youth in scraps. "My aunt Nicey used to feed me hot porridge as a boy. Scalding. And when it burned my tongue, I would cry, then she would pick me up and beat me for crying at the hot porridge." He didn't wait for our response. Though we all sat there at the settee trying to anchor him to this living world, he was already gone.

"I was born without a family," he said, as if his own life was a miracle that slapped itself crying into existence. "Aunt Nicey," Nicey Reid, was my father's maternal grandmother. She disavowed his existence so much that she forbade him from calling her "grandmother." We all knew well that my grandmother gave birth to my father when she was fourteen, a misfortune that Aunt Nicey could only see as a mistake.

My grandmother was a star student who became the village cautionary tale—the good Christian girl who they all blamed, claiming she spread her legs the first time a grown man whispered in her ear, throwing a promising life in scholarship down the river, with my father its leftover warning. He was a bruise on the face of the Reid household, where people still openly mourned the island's loss of the British monarchy, thrown from house to house, a bastard doomed to be burned, beaten, and mistreated as all unwanted things were. This was the Christian way. This was Aunt Nicey's way. My father was born in the throes of Jamaica's rebellion, the island's Black citizens now orphaned by the circumstance of being Caribbean, mothered by nothing but our own dream of independence. Free to author any future they wanted, some Jamaicans still chose the cramped confines of the past, dusting and preserving those old colonial rooms, while some like my father razed all that came before them, setting fire to the curtains of the master's house.

"You children don't even know how good you have it," he said now, speaking to no one in particular in the now stifling room.

"My own aunt Nicey threw me into a barbed wire fence when I was boy," he said, jabbing violently at his scar, a shiny keloid knot the size of a small beetle on his forehead to prove it. Ife and I gasped, clutching our arms around each other. His scar had been so much a part of him that we never once considered the violence of its origin. As Dad spoke, his scar darkened and pulsed, branching into the trio of veins erupting from his forehead. "*This* is where my head gashed open," he said to us, pressing his finger to it. "And almost every single day I spen' in Aunt Nicey's house as a boy, she curse me for the hospital bill."

I could almost see the smoke coming off him, whiffs of sulphur, as if lightning was about to strike our settee and make him bellow out Jah's name in recognition. We listened and nodded and said nothing, afraid that if we moved even an inch in any direction, his fire might be set upon us too.

"And your grandmother seh nothing when she come back and see what they do to me," he said, kissing his teeth. He spoke to us very little of our grandmother; he never referred to her by any name other than "your grandmother." He never spoke of her without reminding us of her Mistake.

"She is a weakheart, Rasta," he said, his mouth forming into a scowl, voice booming. "She is a coward." He was pulling on his precept now, emerging from his youth and back into himself. There we sat, silent and sweating, picking at our toes, unsure of how to look at him now, unsure of what would happen next. We'd been with him in the sunlight, under his cottonwood tree, watching the old birds at the fishpond, and in a flash, a black comet had fallen and singed us to bone. Whatever fueled his memory burned hot in him and would never cease.

"I never knew my father," he said again, quieter now, as if he was waiting.

We were the family he had made for himself. But we were just children. I was barely twelve, and my siblings even younger. In our cloistered isolation, every moment of instability seemed normal. Like the afternoon my parents gave us spliffs to smoke, they had established this strange sect of Sinclair for so long they could not see when unhealthy boundaries had been crossed. We had nothing to give my father now except our fear and confusion. Finally, I thought to reach out my hand to touch his hand, but it was too late.

"Laugh and the world laughs with you," he said, his voice cool and snarling, as he pointed at each of us. "Cry and you cry alone."

Then, like a mask had been switched, a manic smile flashed mirror-wide across his teeth, glinting razor-straight and sharp, cutting into me as he rose from the couch and left us.

My father grew more severe and soured as the year wore on that rainy season, and the rut of our financial woes deepened. It was October, and the June plums were in bloom. The drowsy lull of those late evenings on Tenth Street were charged with the hypnotic rattle and clink of dice and game pieces as my parents played game after game of backgammon until the evening news came on. Once the seven o'clock chime struck, my siblings and I scattered to our rooms on cue, trying to disappear. Whatever clouds had been brewing in him all day—late paycheck, overdue light bill, landlord asking for last month's rent—would break into a hurricane as he listened to the daily news report. Turning the volume all the way up, he would spit obscenities and bark retorts at the newscaster, calling every politician a "tiefing bloodsucker" or an "agent of Babylon," and even the downtrodden with their houses flooded he called "damn butus" and "ignorant baldheads." Now, this was the only song he sang for us every night, while the five of us cowered. And, when the seven o'clock news finished, he'd turn right over to the other local channel to watch an identical news report a second time at eight.

This was what thirty-four with four children looked like. Three years after his return from Japan, with a growing family and no record deal. Our days grew leaner, one or two fewer dumplings on our plates each time, often eaten with nothing but a thick sauce made from coconut milk, or shredded callaloo sautéed for breakfast and again for dinner, and though we complained to Mom when he was out of earshot, there was nothing to do but eat what we had because we were hungry. Some days my mother's plate had little or no food at all, so content was she to dish us all of the pot and leave the scrapings for herself, even though she was still breastfeeding Shari, who was nearly four. "Jah will provide," Dad would say when food was short, and Mom would walk out into the yard and find something astonishing for us to feast on. Ripe June plums and cherries, bursting with golden pulp on the tree, from which she made cherry juice or sweet June plum stew to feed us, miracle hours of thickened sugar we licked from our hands and asked for more.

My father was never going to be a carpenter or a banker or a taximan, he always said. He sang for Jah and would see no other path forward, so had no choice but going back to singing cabaret in the west coast hotels, covering the same ten Bob Marley songs he'd perfected into a golden spear, thrown treacherous into the crowd of tourists eating steak dinners and drinking themselves into a blind oblivion. With us at home, he could still be king. All sights and sounds were his, all words were his. If he rose blissfully, all of us were to be blissful, too, no matter our feelings. He had never washed a dish or plate, never turned on a stove, never touched a broom. My mother placed every meal before him as soon as he beckoned for them, and his Ital diet was our diet. The television remote and every channel we watched were his. His song the only song. And so it followed that our punishment was his alone.

His ruthless moods and lectures were always our penance. Some random mornings he would wake in a suffocation, dark and downcast, and we knew there would be no sunlight in our world that day. He had an argument with a record producer or a ruined rehearsal with his hotel band, or maybe he needed an early paycheck to cover our rent. We never knew the cause. Whatever it was, the day's curtains were drawn, and not a sound was to be made by anyone. There we would sit, my siblings, my mother, and I, dour and gloom-struck, choked in a smog of his fury, none of us allowed to speak.

We came to dread those hours, like we dreaded the news report, for in these days we no longer knew how to read his weather. Now, not even my mother could pinpoint what triggered his humors and mercies. When he laughed, he wanted us to laugh with him; when he cried, we would cry even more. Young as we were, we all learned to walk on eggshells. Every evening before he left for work he required attention. He thrived on procession and ritual. My mother was to iron his clothes, which she had hand-washed the day before, then laid out for him. After boiling enough water she would wash his dreadlocks, pouring warm anointments over his bowed head at the bathroom sink, the both of them moving in silence as she scrubbed his knotted roots. Next she would towel his hair dry, then oil each lock as he sat eating the fruit she had cut for him or drinking the tea she had steeped in his Japanese bowl, barely a muscle moved. I imagined a servant, just out of frame, fanning a palm frond back and forth.

Soon I, too, was appointed into this ritual procession. My job was to help make bootleg copies of his album, *Rocking You*. "Because the I is so meticulous," he told me, "I man only trust you with this, Budgie. The I make them better than the printing shop." It felt good to stand in his sunshine then, as the one he chose to assemble these bootlegs he sold to tourists after his performances for extra cash. He didn't own the rights to his first album and was denied masters or copies from the record label, so he bought a disk burner and created unauthorized versions of himself. Those evenings when he beckoned for me, calling out, "Budgie. Come and help me now, Princess," I would pause my homework and go to him, because my hands were his.

Those evenings when our father left for work, my siblings and I breathed free, three screeching animals, unpenned. My brother had a few friends in the neighborhood, but my sisters and I were forbidden to keep baldhead friends or go beyond the gate. Friend and company were the stewards of Babylon and couldn't be trusted. We weren't allowed to sleep over at our aunties' houses. Over the years, one cousin had been approved to come to our house, where he could be supervised under my parents' watchful eye. My siblings and I all accepted this as normal, even as we spent an unnatural amount of time shut in at home and severed from an ordinary life. As the years went on, our persistent isolation became an integral part of the sect of Sinclair, and one that warped my value in traditional friendships, which I once saw as disposable as the rented homes we left behind. Back then, we four believed we needed nothing but each other, and eventually my sisters and I learned to love keeping to ourselves. We had been in the Sinclair bubble for so long, this seclusion became second nature. We had not yet begun to yearn for what else was beyond the fence.

Unlike at Bogue, we could count all the trees in our yard on one hand, but even here in our shrinking dominion we wanted to taste everything. Ife was usually the marshal of our curiosity, so moved was she to experience this world by eating it. Often, we would find two deep fingerprints in the butter where she feasted, we caught her licking the knobs and hems of forbidden things, and once at Bogue she even bit into a millipede, smiling with the biggest bug-black, yellow-shelled teeth, while we all gasped. On one sweaty afternoon we found ourselves alone at home, free to ramble about the yard. Starting in the backyard, we swung from the clothesline, lassoing our arms and legs around every tree limb, and hacked into any bush we could find. We crawled through the damp crabgrass, following Ife's lead, biting into leaves, plucking the long stems of fountain grass to taste its sugary dew. We galloped from tree to bush, biting into the dark June plum leaf, tasting the waxy hibiscus leaf, sucking the velvet petal, licking the dusty golden stamens. There was still pleasure in this scorched world if you knew where to find it.

We crawled until the sun was falling, my siblings and I glistening with sweat as we approached the cherry tree, which was so laden with unripe fruit that some branches drooped to the earth, scraping the grass. Each green cherry hung hard and bright like a little world.

"Do you think we can still eat them if they're green?" I asked Ife.

"I've eaten them green before," Ife said. "And it tastes so much better."

We considered this. Ife had eaten them green and had survived, and Lij and I watched her now as she bit into one.

"Mmm," she said, chewing and sucking its seed.

Lij and I followed suit. It was crisp and tart, a bright tangy juice filling my mouth. I shook my head side to side in delight.

"Ife, you're a genius!" I said, and Lij agreed, already reaching for another cherry.

Soon we were jumping and snatching green cherries out of the tree two and three at a time, filling our mouths and laughing.

"Let's take some for Mommy and Daddy," Ife said, and we began to shake the tree like locusts. I held out my T-shirt like a basket in front of me and filled it with fruit.

"This is the life," I said, long after we lost count of how many we had eaten. We three stretched out and sighed, bellies full under the burnt sky.

It was not yet dark when our father hopped out of the taxi at the gate, though the light had almost gone. He was supposed to be working at a hotel hours away in Negril, so returning this early was a bad sign. Perhaps his show at the hotel had been canceled. He wore the same bleak screwface he used when he was on the phone with a hotel manager.

We stood up from the cherry tree, slipped our shoes back on, and ran up to greet him. We were sticky and smelled of crabgrass and green cherry juice. Mom was not yet home to defray or interpret the particular riddle of his face, but by the way he slammed the car door we should have known he wasn't to be bothered. We approached him shyly and hailed him.

"Hi, Daddy—" we chirped, meeting him on the way to the front door.

"Why unnu still outside?" he snapped. "Yuh nuh see it dark? Get inside and go bathe now," he said, swatting us away.

We'd all gotten up the steps and into the house, when our father turned on the living room light and examined the state of us. Twigs in our dreadlocks, sweat and dirt on our foreheads, green stains down our shirts. He looked us over, then pointed to Lij's shorts bulging with cherries.

"Fyah, whaddat in your pocket?" he asked.

"Uhm. Some . . . some cherries, Daddy," Lij said.

"Try one, Daddy!" Ife said.

I watched his face closely as my siblings spoke and knew his spirit's candle had already been knocked over. His brow furrowed into a shadow centuries deep, his scar prehistoric.

"What yuh mean, cherry?" he said to us, cocking his head sideways. "There is no cherry. The cherries are green."

"Well . . . we tried some today," Lij said, taking a green cherry from his pocket and holding it out to our father. "They actually taste good!"

My father's face slipped into that deadly smile that did not reach his eyes. He pulled on his precept, looking at us, then his eyes narrowed.

"Empty your pockets, boy," he said, grabbing my brother by his shirt-neck. Ife and I gasped.

"But, Daddy—" Lij whispered, holding out both hands now, full of green cherries.

My father chuckled and shook his head. We were lined up before him, our heads drooping, sunflowers without sun.

"Don't move," he said, and walked out the door, down to the yard.

"We in trouble now," I said to Lij and Ife as we waited in the living room, our arms and legs now itching, our nerves uprooted.

"But why?" Ife whimpered. Her eyes were wide and already glistening with tears. "What did we do, Saf?"

I had no answer for her. She was only eight, and I could not explain to her then how I already knew all his light had gone out. We were in his burning world now.

I heard my father curse from the front yard. "Ah wha the bombo-claat!" he shouted out, using a bad word usually reserved for the thieving record label execs and the hotel managers and Juju Hewitt. His voice was ragged, unfamiliar. Its terrible roar shook me, and Ife started sniffling. His footsteps pounded back up to the front door, which he slammed behind him. The walls shook in their frames. He pointed at us, sniper sight, and cursed out again.

"The I them took every green cherry offah the tree, Rasta. Every single cherry," he said. Voice dropping, his face held a reptilian calm as he spoke. I could not look at him.

"Yuh understand seh green cherry make you sick? Eh?"

"No, Daddy," we said, one pitiful voice.

"No? So you think I man have money for doctor or hospital bill?" All calm evaporated, his face contorting as he raged, his voice booming.

"No, Daddy," we said, throats quavering.

He glared at us and we were small, so small he could crush us under heel. He began unbuckling the belt he was wearing as he spoke. We had never seen him do this before. It was the new red leather belt that had been gifted to him by a Canadian friend only a few months before, still shiny and stiff with disuse. We looked across each other's faces with confusion, soon mown down by fear as he pulled the red belt out from the loops of his khaki pants. Dad had given us many rabid lectures, and had spanked us by hand a few times when we were younger, but this was new. Our next moments were still uncertain.

"Fruits fi eat when dem ripe," he said, wrapping the belt in a loop around his fist. "Let every fruit ripen on Jah tree."

"Daddy, we didn't think—" I said, but couldn't finish. I moved in closer to my siblings helplessly, as close as I could get to them, wet with my own fear and shivering against their bodies, their bodies shivering feebly against mine.

"The I them too unruly!" he roared, suddenly circling round behind us. He whipped the red belt down with stinging force across our three backs. We screamed, and Ife crouched to the ground, her hands clamped over her head. Everything was sideways then; a hard crush of roof and rubble crashing down on us, our little kingdom shattering.

"Sorry, Daddy," Ife was saying over and over. "Sorry, Daddy, I'm sorry, Daddy."

Lij and I joined her. "Sorry, Daddy!" we pleaded.

It was useless. My father dragged Ife up and planted her next to me and Lij again, where we stood unmoving like soldiers in a line.

"Hold out your hand," he said to Ife.

"Please," she said, shaking her head and wriggling away from him. "Please, Daddy!" she cried out.

"Don't 'please' me," he said, and he spun her around and clapped the red belt hard across her palm. *Thwap*. The full stroke of his arm tore through the air. Thick leather lashed her skin, her small arms. *Thwap*. She screamed, pleaded. He thrashed her three times, five times. A gasp leapt through me as he swung. *Thwap thwap thwap*. My sister was wailing and pleading. Next to me Lij was mewling quietly, while I tried to catch my own breath. All three of us had tears and snot running down our faces now, bodies shaking, breathing heavy. We looked at the man wielding the red belt and we didn't know him.

When he let Ife go, he told her to sit down on the settee. She closed her eyes and cried, her animal wail filling the whole house.

My father's eyes had gone dark, almost blank, something releasing each time he struck us.

"Hold out your hand," he said now to Lij, who held his palms out and clenched his eyes shut.

Thwap. The red belt struck my brother's palms and wrist. My brother made only a soft moaning sound, trying to be strong. *Thwap*. *Thwap*.

"Waste not, want not," my father said, flinging the belt hard against my brother's small hands with all his might. Lij closed his eyes and moaned painfully and deep, keeping his face still. My father grabbed my brother, flipped him around, and whipped the belt down his buttocks so many times he finally bawled out, howling to the roof. Stray green cherries fell to the floor from his pockets as my father beat him. I closed my eyes and shook. When he was finished, he sent Lij over to Ife on the settee.

"Hold out your hand," he said to me, and I did, trying to steel myself. My father's voice was calm, his hand steady.

"Yuh too unruly," he said, as the red belt came down on my hand with a force that made my shirt flutter up. *Thwap*. The sting of the leather seared underneath my skin, and I cried out, as the strap of the belt marked red lines on my wrist. The pain was worse than I had anticipated.

He flung the thick leather belt at my hands.

"Yuh should know better," he said. "Instead, yuh leading them astray."

Thwap. *Thwap*. *Thwap*. The world was upside down. I cried and pleaded, not to him but to something beyond him, anything that might make it stop. I remembered too late what he had told me about hunting. He knew the name and feather pattern of every bird because he'd also made a practice of killing them. He loved his birds as much as he loved shooting them from the trees with his slingshot. I was so busy being the budgerigar that I hadn't noticed the stone.

Down came the red belt until I could see nothing beyond this moment but his face snarled, his teeth bared, his red eyes wide and wild.

In the aftermath, my siblings and I sat together in silence huddled like crows on one bed in our shared bedroom, losing the hours that followed in an ugly blur. The hiss of crickets prickled the night air. Our faces stained white with our own salt. I can't say we keened and held each other chest to chest then, wishing to become one strong man between us. I can't say we confided in our mother when she returned, that she in turn spoke soft condolements. I can't say we pressed aloe vera into the welts and bruises that littered our hands and buttocks, our tongues still raw from the tart juice of the green cherries. Or even that we went to school the next day and clamped our mouths shut on our secret thorn. Instead, we simply deserted the bruised husks of ourselves, walked out of them entirely, abandoning that small child asking why over and over as the flame of the day extinguished.

That was the last day my father wore that belt. When the beating was over, he walked into his bedroom and drove a nail into the wall above his bed. There, next to the portrait of Haile Selassie, he hung the red belt, waiting for the next time his spirit bid him pull it down.

14

False Idol

THE NEXT MORNING I AWOKE IN a tumbledown haze to the sound of my sister Ife singing, and began combing the day's blue for meaning. The sting of the lashes had faded, but the memory of my sister's cries would stay, branding me anew every time my mind skipped over them. Now her voice warbled quietly as I lay and let its gentle wave carry me, drifting back to the coastline where we were born, thinking about the morning three decades ago, when my grandmother Isabel awoke and spent her last hours bleeding to death, with only the lapping sea as her witness. Where earlier, under the same perishing sky, my young mother awoke, pushed her feet into tattered shoes, and walked to school, not knowing she was motherless until a man on a bicycle slid his hands into her underwear, throwing her to the ground when she resisted. Where a decade before that, two parishes away in the country, my grandmother Sweet P awoke a teenage pariah, singing a church hymn to calm her shell-shocked solitude.

Now this blue morning, under the bruised sky of our bloodline, my sister Ife awoke singing that same hymn to soothe herself, wrapped in the consoling arms of my mother. Here in the gathering numbness was our matrilineal mark: Each of us turned to stone overnight. Thrown, ripple after ripple, into the same strange sea. Delivered by some grief the night before. Here, the women of my family all met under one sign, stamped by what confining fates we had been handed. A girl had no choice in the family that made her. No choice in the many names that followed her, wet-lipped and braying in the street. She was Psssst. And Jubi. And Catty. Mampy. Matey. Wifey. Dawlin. B. And Heffa. My Size. Empress. Brownine. Fluffy. Fatty. Slimmaz. Mawga Gyal. And Babes. Sweets. Chu Chups. And Ting. Machine. Mumma. Sketel. Rasta Gyal. Jezebel. And Daughter.

Born under the same relentless sun, we were kindred. Pinned by the weight of our inheritance, the crucible of Black womanhood I had not yet passed through. Even then, waking with the welt of it under Ife's song, I could not know what strife still lay in wait for my sisters and me. After she finished singing, I stayed in bed unmoving, eyeing a cocoon in a jar on our bedside table, where a once jewel-green caterpillar had hardened into a brown thorn overnight, and was now as unrecognizable and unmoving as a dead thing. It was hard to believe anything beautiful could come next.

By ninth grade the girls in my class had formed an unwilling ministry, each girl constructing her own private self, pressing alms into the palms of the saint of the hairy armpit, god of the slick mucus glistening the seat of our underwear, twined in holy communion with the ripe, red danger of ourselves. My blood had not yet come. Thirteen, and still the last of my class uninitiated, every so often my mother sang out "Any day now, any day now" in my ear like a warning bell. I dreaded the thousands of days that would unfold from me after this. After Mrs. Pinnock had cautioned me, I no longer walked the yard but waited out my early mornings indoors instead, exploring the high shelves of the library adjoining our new ninth-grade classroom, waiting for the girls to file in loud and electric, sharing the parts of their lives unavailable to me, parts I resolved never to share with anyone. This is usually how Cassandra found me, at my desk with a book or walking between the four tall rows of shelves with those dusty and unloved volumes I wished to steal away.

Cassandra was one of the other scholarship students, a year older than me like everybody else, and shorter than me like everybody else. She was pretty, with reddish-brown hair and skin like a ripe-yellow mango, always staring with big wide eyes that sometimes looked green. It was an unspoken truth between us that she knew the same wolf-howls of harassment

I knew, knew it better in fact because she walked downtown and took the public taxi by herself, neither of which my father would ever allow. Yet she walked as if she had never felt the world pin its heavy weight on her back, her laughter often appearing before her. She was chosen for St. James College based on her need rather than her merit, and seemed to take this fact heartily, gleefully daydreaming in the back of the class and rarely opening her mouth except to laugh at whatever might tickle her.

Cassandra sauntered in with her schoolbag slung carefree over one shoulder, her tie hanging loose around the collar of her school shirt, unbuttoned and creased to her bosom like the other girls. "I'll freak you right I will, I'll freak you right I will . . ." she sung, bobbing her head with relish as she sidled into a seat next to me.

"Wazzup?" she asked, mimicking a Black American twang. I was studying for our upcoming French exam and was in no mood to entertain her this morning.

"Hey, Cassandra," I said. In fact, her family called her Cassie, and she had been known as "Cassie" for about ten minutes when we'd met on the first day of school. Then the rich girls arrived and promptly informed us that there was already a student named "Cassie"—and so she would have to go by Cassandra. The "original" Cassie was the blessed and blameless Cassie Thomas, who was beatific and honey-whispered, lovely even with a mouth full of metal, a biracial princess on whom all the teachers doted. She was the only other student in class whose grades were as high as mine, which only mustered in me a deep mutual respect and none of my usual competitiveness, because she was impossible to dislike.

I tried ignoring Cassandra now, glancing out the corner of my eye at her head bobbing as she sang and watched me closely.

"So yuh do anything fun this weekend?" she said, nudging me with her shoulder.

"Not a thing," I said. "Nothing at all." It had been three weeks since the red belt came down on my hands, but the pain of my siblings' wails still rang out in my ears.

"How come you nuh go out after school? Or do anything?" Cassandra asked me, stretching her legs out in front of her.

"My father doesn't allow me," I said.

"Not even on your own street?"

"No."

"Outside the gate?"

"No."

"Man, Rasta strick, eeh?" She was shaking her head as if she couldn't imagine a world in which she was forbidden to walk outside the gate. But it was not strange to me; it was all I'd ever known. For so long my father drummed into our heads that our purity would be tainted by playing with the children outside, I eventually came to believe it. Now not even seeing them chittering on the road could tempt me outside the yard.

We could have been friends, Cassandra and I, trading our secrets like one whispered sin between us, but she became the second place Cassandra on the first day of class, and showed no interest in being anything except the "other" Cassie. Being extraordinary was one of my father's markers that our livity was righteous. He warned us away from anyone he deemed unexceptional. "Those kind of people will never get anywhere," he said, "and friend and company will ruin your life." So, I could never share with her what kept me awake at night; how inevitable it seemed to my father that I would fall to ruin. How every move I made seemed to cast a pearly string down a spiderweb, growing vast around me, a web of which I was somehow both the architect and the victim, ensnared.

"Really and truly," Cassandra laughed out, snapping me back to her window-wide eyes. "I would just go out anyway and take the punishment later." She shook her head and shimmied. "Is pure cute boys on my street, can I tell you? My father always cussing me up and down, getting mad ah wah!" She laughed.

"I would be too scared to upset my father, though," I said, thinking of my father's face, iron-wrought and dangerous, smiting me down. "You not afraid?" I asked her, blood rushing my cheeks.

"No sah. I just watch and wait for the green. I can always tell when my daddy gettin upset because his eyes change like the sky. When him sad his eyes look gray, and when him angry his eyes look green. I can even tell when rain ah come just by seeing his eyes them," she said.

So, there were many ways to read a father's face I was learning.

"Bwoy, they were fire-green when he thump me down the other day, for talking to taximan. Big big man, big as him. When I tell you I had to run!" She chuckled, eyes widening. My eyes widened, too, as I listened. Then after a pause, she said, "Wha bout you? Your father ever—"

"No," I snapped, and looked away from her.

"He never beat you?"

"Never," I said again. My palms stung anew as I studied the floor, the mast of myself sinking beneath it. I was ashamed of my father then, for he had made me ordinary. By beating us he was no different than the butus and baldheads he railed against. He made my wounds commonplace, just another young girl wanting to absent herself from the world. I didn't want to be here in this classroom, with the needling memory of my palms stinging, commiserating with Cassandra about how we were beaten by our fathers. Not while Cassie Thomas squealed and flung her wrists around her daddy's neck every afternoon when he rolled down the school driveway to collect her, carrying her toy dog on his lap.

"Well, you lucky, then!" Cassandra said. "Everybody mi know get beaten. Bad. I think my father getting fed up with me now, can I tell you? One of these days him fit fi kill me," she laughed, smoothing the pleats of her skirt. "But soon my mother will send for me. Soon soon."

She never talked about her mother, except in the abstract mention of her being faraway somewhere in Foreign. In truth, I might've counted her as the lucky one then, but I would never tell her that.

"You ever been to Foreign?" she asked me now, her eyes brightening.

"No, not yet," I said. I'd heard and relived the one story of my father being in America as a young teen so many times over, I could imagine the snow and the waxy red apples and a yellow taxi cab with only one person riding in it. My father and my auntie Audrey were the only people I'd known who had ever left Jamaica. I thought often of my mother's story, of going to the American Embassy in Kingston to apply for a visa and being denied, turned away publicly by a red-faced white man already calling out "next."

"I've never been to 'Merica neither," Cassandra said. "But soon soon. And can I tell you? I cannot wait."

The other girls started gliding in now, weightless, already turning the air of the room silken. I looked away from Cassandra to watch Shannon and Cassie Thomas and Heather talk about their weekends; how they went swimming at Doctor's Cave, the members-only beach that only few could afford. These girls were British and American citizens who went shopping in Miami whenever they felt like it. Had never thought of a visa. Or a red belt. They stepped in and out of our world whenever they felt like it. They stepped outside every gate, laughing in that blinding way that said they already knew who they were going to be, the road bricked and polished ahead of them.

Cassandra had still been talking to me but I could no longer hear her. She knew, and I knew, as I watched the other girls from afar, that if I came upon a forked road in between these two Cassies, exactly which way I would choose to go. And I would have clawed her eyes out to get there. She shrugged and left my side, slinking into her desk at the back of the classroom.

In the middle of the day halfway through the school year we moved to a new house in the same government housing scheme, our second rented house since Bogue, this time only five streets over from our last. The new house on Fifth Street was smaller again, with no yard and no dining room, and with two bedrooms that we shared among the six of us. My siblings and I mourned the loss of the outdoors like a limb. Any lingering interest we might have harbored for meeting neighbors or remembering the names of the children on our street was annihilated, for we never knew when we would move again. We four had each other, and that was enough.

On Fifth Street the houses stood wall to wall, close enough to see into the rooms next door, to hear what music they were playing, smell their meat cooking. Our neighbor Oneil had a scowl for a face and spent most of his days shirtless, blasting the lewdest dancehall music. Most mornings began with the blunt sounds of his fists hammering at his girlfriend's face, followed by her high-pitched wailing for him to stop. I plugged my ears, making a point to turn away from his waves if I ever saw him outside on the high concrete steps at the back of the house. I wished for him to fall off those steps, break his neck. For Oneil was how Babylon looked to me—a shirtless scowl and a blade hungry for blood, spreading nothing but ugliness in this world. My father went out of his way to hail Oneil, most days having long conversations about news and football. I could not bear to hear it. A noxious tide overcame me when I tried to understand how he laughed with a man who represented everything he spent his days warning us away from.

I told my mother I didn't think it was right, and that we should do something, and she agreed. But if she did anything at all beyond agreeing, I never saw it. One Saturday morning, mere hours after we had to blast our music loud enough to drown out the blood-curdling shrieks for help, my father took another long jaunt outdoors to chat with Oneil. When he returned, zippering up his smile as he left Oneil on the back steps, I finally asked him what had been sitting heavy as a beast on my heart. My father had never laid even a fingernail scratch on my mother, and would never, for striking a Rastawoman was against his livity.

"Daddy," I said, "why you always talking to Oneil like that?"

"What you mean?" he said. "I man being neighborly." His brows were already knitting in that unbecoming way, his scar pronouncing itself.

"But he is a bad man. He beats his girlfriend," I said, picking at the hem of my dress. "I hate to hear it. I don't think it's right."

"I man don't think it's right neither," he said, his eyes boring into me. "But what that got to do with the I?"

Very faintly, my heart started kicking, which it always did whenever I initiated a conversation with my father that involved my opinion.

After taking a breath, I said, "So you should tell him to stop."

He chuckled, gray-faced, smiling the red smile that cut into me, announcing the agony that came next.

"That's none of I and I business," he said. A static noise buzzed in my ear.

"But I think—"

"I man don't care what you think," he said. "Oneil is a big man, and what goes on in his house is his business."

"But, Daddy—" The noise was louder now, thickening in my head like a field of crickets.

"Listen to me," he said. A blade-edge of dread nicked at my throat. "I am the man of the house, and you are just a girl. What I man do and who

I man talk to is my business. What goes on in *this* house is my business. Don't ever question the I."

He was still talking now, but I had grown numb, my ears jungled, the noise so loud that his words went through me like ghosts. I had left my dumb husk there next to him on the settee, nodding and pliable, while I slipped away and down into the damp shadow of her, now growing scorching and impatient, pacing the catacombs of myself, my hands over my ears, biding my time.

The first five days of Cassandra's absence, I thought nothing of it, cherishing the early-morning quiet and reading *A Midsummer Night's Dream* under its sutured gaze. I thought she'd finally decided to skip school, which she was always threatening to do. By the end of the second week those early mornings shrilled louder in her silence, as I waited for Cassandra's voice outside the classroom door and it never came. Soon it was three weeks since she'd been to class, and I was surprised to find that I missed her. As the school days widened in her absence, none of the other girls in the class seemed especially concerned.

"It's been such a long time since we saw Cassandra," I said to Heather and Shannon at the end of the second week, and after an exchanged glance between them, they shrugged.

We all knew the dangers, had all grown up being told. Every single day she awoke, a girl might go missing, disappeared while walking along the overgrown roads those early mornings or snatched from a taxi on her way to school. Never to be seen again. My family had no telephone, so there was no way to reach out to anyone, even if I had Cassandra's number. Maybe she'd finally gone to Foreign with her mother, like she always said. I imagined her there, laughing in a shopping mall and drinking ice-cold Coca-Cola from a fountain.

When we neared the end of the school year, it was the silence from the teachers and principal in her absence that seemed most unusual to me.

"Boy! I really can't believe Cassandra has been gone so long and nobody knows why," I said to my classmates one afternoon. "I really hope she's okay." Two months had passed since I last saw her.

In a private huddle near the classroom doorway I could see the white girls whispering, glancing back at me every so often.

"Should we just tell her?" I heard Heather say. Seemingly resigned to something, they broke their huddle and approached me, faces red and heavy.

"Cassandra isn't coming back," Heather said.

"How do you know?" I asked her. She glanced at Shannon.

"Our parents told us," Shannon said. Of course. Their parents, who were on the school board, who were the architects of this experiment.

"What happened to her?" I asked.

All seven of the other girls in my class molded a curdled stillness around the question. It hung there in air.

"Because," Shannon said finally, "she's pregnant." A stone struck me in my chest right then. My own blood had not even come yet. I hadn't even considered—couldn't even imagine—that one of us could be *pregnant*. The sound of the word collapsed in my body like a ruined bell. This was the omen that hung over me every time my father saw my growing body, every time I asked if I could wear a pair of jeans and he struck down the question. And now here it was in front of me, another fourteen-year-old girl's undoing.

I stared wide-eyed at Shannon, my hand clasped over my mouth.

"Oh my god," I said. "Pregnant?" The word sunk its barb in my tongue.

"Yep," Heather sighed. "They expelled her."

"I can't believe . . . Cassandra would . . . it's such a shame," I said. Everyone agreed it was such a shame. We took turns sighing and shaking our heads for some time, until eventually we all turned back to our books and studying for final exams.

Ashamed is what I wanted to say. I was ashamed that Cassandra was devoured by the fate of her own web. That she hadn't been as wily as I thought she was, hadn't snipped or retwisted those threads that authored the downfall of girls like her. Girls like us.

Back home that evening, dazed from the news, I waited until night fell and my father left for work to tell my mother about Cassandra.

"Jeezam peace!" my mother said, and held her head in her hands.

"Isn't that shameful?" I said. She shook her head and sighed.

"Listen to me," she said. She took my hands and held them firm, pressing her palms into mine. "Do not tell your father one word about this, you hear me?"

I nodded.

"If he hears about this, that will be the end of it. I don't even know what he will do. This is just between us, you hear me?"

"Yes," I said.

And that was it. I never spoke Cassandra's name in my house again. Never saw or heard from her again. Soon it was as if she had never been with us at all. Those early school mornings came and went, and I opened my palms to let her go, blowing away to nothing in the breeze.

Weeks after the pregnancy news had passed, I lay brooding and awake in my bed at night, thinking of Cassandra's mistake, of my grandmother's. How a shame that was never mine could haunt me like a bloodhound. I thought again of Eurydice, my mythic familiar, and promised myself I would never be ordinary. If I was born the doomed girl, then I was determined to burn that myth, be the bard dreaming up my own salvation. I would rewrite the history of the women before me. In our final days at the house on Tenth Street, I'd watched the brown hull of that cocoon rive open in its jar, saw its wet orange and black wings nudge and emerge, as my siblings and I sighed in awe. We had wanted to hold on to that awe when it was not ours to keep. We kept that butterfly in that jar until its wings grew moist, flapping slowly, incapable. By the time we decided to let it out of its cage, there was no flight left in it. One day, I promised myself, I would let myself out of this cage, and fly.

As I lay there restless and overthinking in the witching hour, I heard my father come through the front door. I listened to him place his guitar down in his bedroom, undress and walk out to the living room, heard him turn on the television. A faint sound of soft, mindless guitar-rock tinkered from the living room, then women laughing. I heard a soft moan, then the sound went lower. My mind hitching on a dark notion, I glanced over at my siblings in their beds, their mouths open, cloaked in sleep. I crawled on all fours down the short corridor to the living room, where the television light flickered blue and pink on the walls. I hid behind the settee where my father sat unmoving and watched. Glowing blue on the screen were Black women, naked and gyrating, flesh for flesh, twirling around a pole in slick patent leather spike heels, red-lipsticked and shiny-wigged, touching the softest parts of themselves.

Something severed between us just then. But I couldn't look away. Curious and greedy, a globe growing heavy and warm inside me, I knew then that everything my father had told me was a lie. A man's invention. Only weeks before he had dressed me down, made me small small. "You're just a girl," he had said. But just like Haile Selassie, he, too, was only a man. Plain as the purple glare on his face, the truth, hasty and pitiful, now revealed its innermost parts to me—a Rastaman was not ascetic or untouchable or particularly saintly. He was just another creature boiling under the tropic heat, collapsing under his carnal and banal desires, like every other man. My father watched the screen silent and stone-faced as the women kept undressing, laughing and touching, kissing and opening. Slowly his silence crackled into anger as he watched, and he kissed his teeth so loud it blasted my heart thinking he'd seen me. But like a howl in the darkness, my father raged out loud to himself alone.

He huffed and pounded the settee with his fist.

"This could be I and I daughters doing this, Rasta," he said. A part of me screamed to crawl away from this, to turn away now. To escape the snare of the future ruin he had been imagining, avoid the upturned mirror of seeing him see a derelict version of myself.

"My daughters will never do this, Rasta," he hissed again to himself, pounding his fist into his leg. The screen's blue glare transformed the sneer of his face, but still he kept watching them. Not switching off, not turning away. He watched. I stayed crouched there, my eyes transfixed by his disheveled face, watching him, watching.

15

Book of Esther

MY MOTHER SAT WITH OUR FOREIGN visitor, a Japanese woman named Reina, under a shaded blue umbrella on the beach. Both women sat on towels in the sand, their legs outstretched, watching my siblings and me splashing in the sea, both smiling. From the sea's distance, their warm faces made a handsome twin, both with dark hair cascading down their backs; my mother's dreadlocks, which she so rarely let loose in public, and Reina's dark waves, knitting together in a sunny blur. Reina was my father's Japanese friend, someone he told us he'd met on his first trip to Tokyo. She was earnest and agreeable, her face soft and sculpted into a permanent smile. We first met her three years before, a few months after my father's final return from Japan, when she appeared at the gate with such an avalanche of Japanese toys and gadgets that my siblings and I were too drunk with glee to question. But now, as I drifted out in the neon-pink donut float she bought for our beach trip, the questions appeared like yellow butterflyfish, nibbling at me.

Reina had appeared on our doorstep at Bogue like so many other female friends of my father—half-remembered and slippery in my mind. There was "Mama Lee," Leah from Brooklyn, who had the same amber skin as my mother and hair as slick as her tongue. There was Halima, the light-skinned Black American who had painted the henna on my hands and slept next to us in our tiny bedroom overnight. There was Auntie Crista, skin bright as custard, with straight black hair, a rich Jamaican businesswoman who was my father's ex-girlfriend from his days as the lead

singer of Future Wind. There was June, a former beauty queen with russet skin and cascading hair who was also introduced as a friend from my
father's youth, and whose children my mother now taught at the private
prep school on the hill. And then there was Reina, who he met around the
same time he started writing some of those love songs on *Rocking You* that
he mailed across the ocean for his family to listen to. You could have lined
them all up and called them cousins of Esther, women who were deriva-
tives of my mother's gentle face, soft eyes downturned, her throat turned
up to the sky, laughing. My mother spent her waking hours caring for the
five of us. She never went out for anything other than grocery shopping or
household errands. Most of her sisters had now gone to Foreign. I never
met any girlfriends that my mother made on her own, or any friends from
her youth; all the women in her life were ones my father had introduced
to her, each one arriving cheerful and pliable on our doorstep.

I drank the sun like a potion and watched them, my mother laughing
with my father's Japanese friend. The sea dried salt on my face, briny on
my lips. My siblings and I had always liked Reina. She had planned and
bankrolled this lavish beach day for us, paid for the chartered taxi to Doctor's Cave beach, bought us all new neon floaties and Lilos, new bathing
suits and trunks. As I floated out, I kept my eye on my sisters, who were
squealing and splashing where crystalline water lapped the sand. None of
us had ever stepped foot on this beach before, and we were overfull with
thanks for Reina's blessings. Ife and Shari flapped their neon-orange arm
floaties in blissful commotion as they bubbled in the shallow, while my
brother waded over to me every five minutes to ask when he could have
his turn floating in the inflated pink donut. "When I'm done," I said.

Doctor's Cave was exclusive and exclusively for the wealthy. On
our homebound Saturday afternoons I tried to picture its white sands
in the lonely coast of my mind; I heard so much about its sea-trampo-
line pleasures from my classmates each Monday morning. I now scanned
the crowd to see if any of them were here, lazing somewhere among the
throng of tourists, pink and indistinguishable. The beach was full of
blinding rows of white people who smelled like suntan lotion, round
men in Speedos and women whose thin hair had been raked into braids
and beads, many of them turning shades of red. Every wary eye turned
to gaze as we entered the beach. Not only were we the only people here

with dreadlocks, my family was among the few Black Jamaicans enjoying this members-only beach club this Saturday morning. Most every other Black face belonged to the security guards, the waiting umbrella men, the buzzing waiters, the cashiers, and the lifeguard with the wandering eye. Turning away from the alien scene, I looked out toward the buoy, closed my eyes against the sun, and tried to feel at home.

At lunchtime we emerged wrinkled and ready to eat our fill of the forbidden—pizza, pineapple sodas, and melting ice cream cones—in a tangle under the umbrella in the sand. We stayed until closing time and rode back at sunset in another chartered taxi, ready to dash about the yard once we touched home. By then we'd moved to our fourth rented house, in a community called Porto Bello, which was even farther from the sea and closer to the country. Here we had space enough to become ourselves again—a big green yard in the front and a shadowy backyard overtaken by a carpet of millipedes and molting breadfruit leaves, overlooked by a veranda.

In the months that had passed since I snooped on my father watching television, the more I had grown disillusioned with his lessons of purity, and the more my questions about him swarmed. Questions that only grew louder during the week of Reina's visit. One afternoon I watched my father stroll the yard alone with her, pulling on his precept and gesturing occasionally at the surrounding hills, his arms outstretched ahead of him like an invitation for a future I could not imagine. But perhaps she did try to imagine it. More than once I registered a ponderous thought rippling across Reina's face as she pored over our locks, silently observed my siblings and me chatting, as if we were all part of the larger proposal. One night as we ran into the kitchen for dinner, I watched her beaming at us again, bewitched.

"It's just amazing how happy they are with how little you have," she said to my mother, who nodded and smiled back at her with something like pride.

I thought about what Reina said, tried to see myself in her words, and it was not pride I felt then, but something smaller. I turned away from the two of them and walked back to my room, doubt gathering like mosquitoes above my head.

Reina arranged to stay in a hotel for the entire week, returning to the resort's gated property every evening. And every night after my father nodded goodbye to us and slung his guitar over his shoulder to go off to work, I lay in bed with a book and waited to hear the familiar sounds of his return. I watched the nights bleed into the coming dawn and descended the ladder of my imagination, spending each blue hour listening in vain for a front gate that never opened, for footsteps that never came, finding only the crickets shrieking in his absence.

After she left the second time, we never saw Reina again. Just like all my father's other vanished female friends, we were never told why. Nor did we ask. We had long come to expect the impermanence of friend and company. Much in the same way we stopped decorating the bedroom walls of the many houses we moved between, my siblings and I now expected all outsiders to be transient, all our relationships with Babylon transactional. Over time we grew barnacled and kelped, accustomed to riding the chaotic surf of our parents' shifting whims. And over time, I began to notice subtle swells of agency in my mother, emerging like riptides beneath us.

She began teaching her S.P.I.C. classes more widely, first at the main bookshop in Montego Bay, where she captivated scores of children whose parents hoped they would "get bright" by being in the presence of the brown Rasta lady. We would accompany her on Saturdays to the bookshop and help lead the call and response games of her workshops, anticipating the sweet treasure at the end of each session when my mother, foregoing her salary entirely, accepted payment in the form of us picking out whatever books we wanted from the store's shelves.

During the weekdays my mother began teaching S.P.I.C. classes at Reading Prep, the new sister school to St. James College, built by the same white Jamaicans and American expats. Just up the hill from my high school, it provided a redoubled haven for the younger siblings of my wealthy schoolmates and the offspring of upwardly mobile Jamaicans. As part of my mother's teaching contract, my two sisters attended Reading Prep for free in lieu of her getting a salary, though she received a small gesture of two hundred Jamaican dollars a week, which paid for the battered taxi that transported all of us between school and home. The principal of

Reading Prep had taken a liking to my mother and allowed her to use the empty classrooms after school to privately tutor students with her S.P.I.C. workshops. These workshops, at the height of their popularity, earned my mother her own handsome income for the first time in her life, and I could see her changing then, under the freedom of her own power, doing what she liked best in the world. At work she found female friends of her own, with whom she laughed louder and more often, and with whom I overheard her sharing the private particularities of her own dreams and fears, for perhaps the first time since I was born.

In high school the condition of a girl's body was always on trial—who was hairy, who was pudgy, who smelled like ketchup, who had no boobs, who was too skinny to have a period. My classmates all believed that my blood had not yet come because I didn't eat meat and looked underweight. We all knew, or would all soon learn, that by thirteen or fourteen our bodies no longer belonged to us, our hind parts and innards were now some communal meeting place for review and commentary. We knew who all the schoolboys thought was sexy and why. We knew the details of JonBenét's underwear and the contents of her tiny stomach. We knew, because every day American newscasters and comedians reminded us, that the seminal shame belonged not to the president but to Monica Lewinsky, whom Heather came to school and decreed was a slut. "What kind of girl says she was sad he wouldn't let her finish?" she asked. Yes, what kind of girl, we agreed. Though I didn't even understand what the question of finishing meant.

At home, with the US president's sex scandal dominating the news, my father fixated nightly, shouting his opinions from the backgammon board that was usually open between my parents after dinner.

"Babylon waan demonize a man for being a man," he said, and shook his head, as I sat squirming through the evening news with him. "See, this is just proof of nature," he said, pointing at the looping newsreels of Bill Clinton.

"This is proof that men not supposed to be monogamous." Then he threw his rattling dice across the backgammon board, his face lit by the television's blue light. I sat and listened at a kettle's boil. My heart fumed at what I could not say. I looked over at my mother, and I knew what he said upset her, because she got up and shrunk away with a spliff in her hands, staring out into the night-sounds that beckoned from our front door. She didn't confront him. She never did. Instead she said nothing, her face fixed in disgust. I rose in a huff and stormed away from him.

One Saturday morning, weeks later, I stood up from the toilet in my father's bathroom and saw the faintest pink droplets blooming in the tissue. I was fourteen. A light breeze carried through the window and I could hear my father strumming in his bedroom just outside the bathroom door. This was it, I thought. A sick wave of terror and relief came over me. I walked out the door. My mother was gone downtown and his was the first face I saw when I stepped past the threshold. I never forgot the young woman we met at Kwanzaa all those years ago, her frightened look as she spoke about her menses. I knew there were Rasta bredren, like her husband, who made their women sequester and sleep in different rooms when this happened. That there were men who believed we were unclean. My father, I hoped, was not one of those men. He never bound my mother's hand or her body by those rules. And since his body was already a part of mine, I thought nothing at all of telling him.

"Daddy, I think I started menstruating," I said. I walked over to his bed where he sat with his guitar.

His door must have slammed shut in the wind, for I jumped back when I gazed upon my father's face. He held his palm up to stop me, as if to caution me from coming any closer.

"Don't ever talk to the I about that stuff," he said. "Talk to your mother bout that." I wanted so badly to believe he was not one of those men. But now his expression said it all. His face was too familiar as he spoke, his mouth downturned into scorn.

My legs went cold, and I realized I had been wading in a wide river all this time. Its water had been growing so slowly between us that I did not realize it was now taking me under. My body came from your body, I wanted to say, but he was already a fading figure on the other side of the bank. I waded away to the far side of myself and walked away from him.

Soon enough, all that was unsaid between my father and me began to harden into something else entirely, slowly turning bitter on the vine.

There were some days that passed without a word exchanged between us. One weekend evening my father rented a car to take the family to meet a new friend of his who lived deep in a country town named Awful Gully. Her name was Primrose, a seamstress with bright yellow skin whose thin hands shook under the gaze of four Rasta children and their mother when she offered us lemonade and fruit from the heavy branches in her yard. She looked to be about ten years younger than my mother, about ten years older than me. My mother brought along some material for her to sew into curtains for our house, and work skirts, just as my father encouraged, saying he hoped a friendship might spark between them.

After they chatted for a while about measurements, we finally left the bright yards of cotton and gabardine with the dressmaker, and I thought nothing more of it until the weekend afternoon months later when my father asked Lij and me to take a walk with him up the hill from our house. It was noon and the sun scorched high, but my brother and I felt ourselves lucky to be summoned for some time with our father, so rarely did he ever ask us kindly to do something with him in those days. As we started our climb up the long gravel road, we were careful to skirt the black thicket of wormwood that Ife, Shari, and our new puppy Rusty had all emerged from poisoned weeks before, their faces swollen beyond recognition. The higher we went, the thornier and more petrified the trees appeared, bent and witchy in dry gravel under the perishing sun. When we got to the top, the hill opened unto a narrow clearing from which we could see all of Montego Bay, sprawled and crawling beneath us. My father put one leg on a big rock near the grassy cliffside. I put my leg on the big rock as my father did, wiping the sweat from my brow and parachuting my shirt in and out to find some wind. Lij put his leg on the big rock, just the same.

My father had been quiet since we got to the top, listening to us and laughing. Now he looked out at the view and pulled on his precept.

"You guys make me so irie," he began. His voice was smooth and soft, like a song. "I man always so joyful to hear how well the I them doing in school. I man want you to keep that up, keep setting the example for you two sisters them," he said.

"Yes, Daddy," we said. His kind words fanned a cool breeze over our heads. We glowed then, feeling blessed.

"I man brought the I them up here because I wanted to reason with you two about something."

Lij and I braced our elbows on our knees and nodded eagerly.

"Since you two are the oldest, I and I thought it was best to get your vibration on this."

"Okay," we said. Never had he spoken so tentatively, so politely, looked at us eye level to eye level.

"You remember Primrose?" he said.

"Yes?" we said.

"What do you think of her?"

"She's okay," I said. "She's nice. And, she can sew."

"Yeah, she's nice," Lij said. My father smiled and pulled on his precept again as we spoke, then looked out into the city. He took a breath.

"What do you think about her being your second mother?" he asked.

I took my knee off the rock and stood up straight. So did my brother. A black thunderclap of clouds must have appeared overhead, and maybe it was already raining, for I could barely hear or see ahead of me. Lij and I looked at each other, two screwfaces warped into a ferocious scowl.

"No," I said.

"No," my brother said, shaking our father's little afternoon incantation, the pleasure of this walk, right out of our heads. We were a pack of ready claws and fangs. We would have ripped the sky on that hill to scraps just to shield our mother from hearing any of this.

I took a step back and looked my father straight in the eye like a lionheart. "We already have a mother."

And that was it. Lij and I both puckered into a sulk that said this matter was utterly and completely closed.

My father nodded solemnly and said not one thing more. Lij and I pouted as we walked the winding way back home in silence. My father's face was drawn tight in resignation and a blank, unfamiliar quiet, as he followed behind us. If this eventually morphed into anger as we drew closer to home, I do not know. We never turned back to look at him—I couldn't look—and though Lij and I never discussed what was said, we didn't have to. We already knew, had already sworn wordlessly to each other, that once we crossed the threshold of that gate back into our yard, running away from my father and into the arms of our mother, we would leave the poisoned trace of his question in the wormwood thicket on the hill where it belonged, where it would always remain.

We never spoke of it again, not even when we were alone. Not even that unassuming day a week later, when we heard a rustling uproar coming from our parents' bedroom. My siblings and I were reading when our father burst into our bedroom in a panic, begging us to help him. His eyes peeled wide as he heaved against the doorframe. He told us that our mother was running away and we needed to get her to come back. My brother and I glanced at each other then, heart-struck with worry. He must have planted the poisoned question in her ear anyway.

"What do you mean?" I asked, looking to my father's twisted face.

"She gone!" he said. "She on the road now, out the gate! Oh Jah!" He was disheveled. I had never heard his voice quiver like this. His contorted face, his dreadlocks flying askew, his wild eyes glistening.

We were shocked into stillness as he wailed. What he described seemed unimaginable.

"Please!" he shouted at us again. "She running away from us! You need to come tell her to stay."

His voice cracked, and we knew it was serious. The four of us gasped and scurried to the driveway, the ground pounding with my heart. True enough, my mother was outside the gate, marching away in her pink housedress, clutching a Lada bag full of clothes. My sisters, seeing her there out on the road, already walking away from us, started to cry.

"Mommy, please come back!" they screamed out as we rushed up the short driveway to the gate, and she turned to look at the four of us for the first time. Her face was torqued and torched, collapsed in an expression of fury I had never seen, one I didn't even know she could muster. I fell back on my heel, seeing the pained expression burning there across her face. She looked down at us and shook her head no, her face so wrenched in rage it was nearly unrecognizable. She kissed her teeth and turned away from my father, gazing back down the road that led out of the neighborhood.

My father got on his knees and clasped his hands into a prayer. "Please please please, Oh Jah Oh Jah. Please, Esther," he cried.

"Please come back, Mommy!" Lij cried, clutching Shari's hand. Rusty rounded my brother's ankles and yelped at the commotion. My sisters wailed, snot and tears slick on their faces.

I was stuck in place. Watching my mother there, with her humble bag of possessions, wading beyond the shock of the scene, I didn't know what to feel. I knew the earth was moving beneath us. That it would smash apart and swallow me without her. *Well, let it*, I thought. I was willing to torch my world if it meant her freedom. This was power. Power I never knew she had. Seeing my father collapsing into himself, I felt conjured, reborn.

But I also felt a pang of pity for her, standing there torn in a crumpled housedress with her hair and knees uncovered, and it broke something in me to know that it was Rastafari and its invisible fences that kept her at the gate. Her modesty. Her circumstance. She couldn't drive a car, and had no taxi money, having spent her month's salary on the four of us already. There was no friend who could come to her rescue. Her closest sister and confidante was thousands of miles away in Foreign and would not be coming back. She had finally found the strength to walk out, but had nothing but a plastic bag of her earthly belongings, having already forfeited all her resources, every last cent, for us. For him. I was weeping then as I watched her, her face contorted with rage and hurt, alone on the street with her arms crossed, helpless, as she pulled her housedress closed around her chest. I promised myself that woman would never be me.

"Mom!" I screamed out to her now, joining the sputtering cries of my siblings. "Please don't leave us!"

Don't leave me.

I cried out for her to come back, even though part of me still wanted her to have the strength I longed for myself. To leave him. Escape this place. To nurse whatever feeling had dragged her in her housedress out of the gate with nothing but a Lada bag.

Don't look back, I thought.

She gazed down at the path out of the neighborhood, then looked back at the four of us crying out for her. She clutched her stomach then, as if she had been yanked on a tether, and her hardened, incendiary expression melted into concern. She gripped her bowed forehead and took another long look down the road, as if she was taking one last breath, then, shoulders slumped, started walking back toward the gate.

16

Not Hollywood

M<small>Y MOTHER CAME BACK TO US</small> and promptly receded into the walls of peeling wallpaper, soundlessly. The woman who walked out through the gate had flashed up in a bright flare and disappeared. Now terror lay dormant in our household, waiting to erupt. Its burnt blood-charge skulked the air at every turn, some cataclysm lying in wait to make our family, as we had known it, extinct. It had been five years since my father returned empty-handed from Japan, and two years since the red belt had come off his waist for good. What began with the broken record deal and the belt began to worsen after my mother's attempt to leave, and would only continue to darken over the weeks and months to come. My father began blaming us for his stalling career. Often, we were two or three months behind on rent, hastened by his habit of picking fights with entertainment coordinators, subsequently losing a hotel gig or two a year. Whatever hurt him made him in turn hurt us. And what hurt him most, the one disappointment he would never recover from, was the loss of his lifelong dream—the same dream he sang out to us all those years ago at Bogue—of being a respected and celebrated musician. He chased the artist's life, and would not compromise with a regular job, which he saw as beneath him. He lived a Rastaman's life, and would not concede any of his tenets, even though imported tofu and vegan meat substitutes were the most expensive items in the supermarket. All of this only further packed the pressure keg of frustration, and now anything at all seemed poised to set him to explode.

Beatings became a fact of life, like dirt and air, and they arrived without warning, without reason. There was no pattern, except the chaos of my father's interior life. Any conversation or news report from Babylon could trigger a lashing from the red belt. Any petty squabble between my siblings and me would rain down thrashings at his hand. For he was judge, jury, and executioner of every moment, divining without counsel who was wrong, who was lying, who deserved to be beaten. Who was a weakheart. Of the four us, Shari was spared violence—my mother held her close, attaching herself to Shari like a shield, breastfeeding my sister until she was seven—for who could beat a child still suckling at her mother's breast? It should have driven us all apart, my siblings and I—resentments at being beaten for someone else's misdemeanors. It should have fostered the in-fighting and the wild finger-pointing of shell-shocked children, but instead it brought us together, turning us most fixedly against him in revolt, until we stopped calling him "Daddy" among ourselves altogether, uniting instead against a man we simply referred to as "He" and "Him."

When he was gone the house breathed free. In his absence my mother jolted to life again and did her best rebuilding work, weaving her cocoon around us. His overnight stays at hotels became more frequent, and it was there, in his gone hours, that we began to grow into ourselves. It was all an intricate dance we were learning, the delicate work of unremembering the bruise of the night before. After breakfast Mom would smirk conspiratorially, then press play on the CD player while my siblings and I gazed sly-eyed and expectantly at each other, waiting for the familiar crash of guitars and the banshee wail of Dolores O'Riordan's voice exploding from our speakers. We loved this, so Mom loved it, too, setting a match to every morning by blasting the Cranberries at full volume, loud enough, no doubt, to be heard down the entire street, while all of us jumped around and screamed "This is not Hollywood!" full-throated with the music shaking the room. For a breath of a moment, we could forget. Our bellows meant the morning was impenetrable, belonging to me and Lij and Ife and Shari and Mom. I wanted to believe I could live here. Wailing in unison at the top of our lungs, feeling some semblance of freedom, some belief. That the sunlight glittering through the rattling windows was ours, the Anansi spider shifting down its silver web was ours, and the croaking lizard racing toward the Anansi was ours too. And each morning I left the house armored and upright, ready for the arrows of the girls.

When the spell wore off, I came to dread waking. I feared both my time at home under my father's gaze and my time at school under the glare of the girls. Nothing I did would ever sate either. The first time I walked under the arched gateway of my classmate Lizzy's estate I knew that no one at school would ever be allowed to see where I lived. Her house was a gated fortress on a hill, with a sprawling yard and a massive pool overlooking the city. It was a mansion with more rooms than family members, each filled with a heady colonial design, four-poster mahogany beds mossed in white mosquito netting, strange masks on the wall, laid with thick rugs and fine vases I made sure not to touch. I left the Mobay I knew and stepped into another place, another time, where Black women laid out feasts at the dinner table and cleaned up after us, while Lizzy's mother called down from the top-floor balcony in her neat British accent, asking whether we wanted to go jet skiing tomorrow or to the country house. The "country house" was an inherited great house built on a former plantation, serene and plentiful, with hovering help and a kitchen with a stone table so colossal it seemed more suited for a king's banquet than a girls' sleepover. There was even a broken waterwheel still visible on the grounds, where mules and the enslaved once toiled to make rum and sugar.

Driving back home after that weekend it was impossible to not see myself through her family's eyes. I couldn't tell her that my sisters and I still shared one room, or that my siblings still shared a bed. That sometimes I was unsure of dinner, unsure of my father, unsure of the future. I couldn't tell her that my next-door neighbors beat their granddaughter so severely that the whole street could hear her screeching and begging for her life. That her animal wails made my brother cry and made my father nod in approval. I couldn't say that our house was not ours, that we had never owned a place that was ours. And would never. That everything was small, much smaller than I had ever dreamed. That I wanted most of all to be mighty.

My scarcity began to eclipse my sense of wonder; all that beauty I had been nourished on at Bogue, burned away to ash. I slowly started to feel that perhaps my fate had been fixed, that eventually I would have no choice but to accept the future my father had written for me. Until a school trip to Cuba began a minor but crucial shift in the forward trajectory of the girl I was becoming, the one I still followed, pulling her silken thread to the underworld of myself. It all began with a pair of pants. Though it now seems trivial to the point of incredulity, in my household, pants were not just another item of clothing for the women in my family. A woman wearing pants was a sign of ruin to a Rastaman, a lewd gesture in the face of His Majesty. "Any dawta wearing pants is nothing but a Jezebel," my father would tell me, preaching from the gospel of the Mansion of Djani. So I made this my crusade. Every weekend I would beg for pants instead of skirts, and one Saturday, after swatting me down for years, my mother finally smiled and said, "Sweet P and I have a plan."

Our school had arranged a class trip to Havana, which my grandmother was helping to pay for. She and my mother devised an elaborate pitch to convince my father to let me wear pants. They explained that if the plane to Havana crashed while I was wearing a skirt, my sprawled legs and underwear would be exposed to the leering eyes of Babylon in the wreckage. I would be disgraced. But if I traveled in jeans pants instead, my dignity would be preserved even in the event of my death.

And that was enough for him.

I'd never seen my mother wear pants, but the thought of it must have thrilled her, too, for when I walked out of the dressing room to show her my first pair of jeans, she tittered with joy as she wheeled me around and complimented my height and my legs, telling me I was beautiful. She could always make the impossible happen, because for the first time since I read Monique's note—*I don't want to be your friend*—in my empty classroom, I felt that beauty was possible again.

In the humid hotel bathroom in Havana I slipped on my new jeans shorts and admired my legs in the mirror for the first time. The shorts were a rough denim that fell just above my knee, not sexy or particularly stylish, but to me they made the morning shine brighter. This was my first glimpse of the girl I could someday be, away from the glare of

Rastafari, and I cherished that more than anything. I strutted into break-fast with a wind in my step, joining the other girls. They took no notice of me, their morning conversation unspooling uninterrupted as we ate. There was no fanfare, no parade for me. I fidgeted in the wicker chair and shrunk. When our teachers began to corral us onto the bus for our first planned tour, Shannon rose yawning. She complained that the wicker had left marks in her thighs, and she turned around to show the other girls the red crisscross pattern of the wicker imprinted in her white skin.

"Well, my thighs don't have any marks," I said to her, turning around to show my legs.

She rolled her eyes. "Of course not. Because your shorts are ridicu-lously long. I've never even seen shorts as prudish as those." She laughed and Heather laughed along with her, and even Cassie Thomas and the twins agreed. They all walked toward the bus with thighs and buttocks sunlit and affirmed. I closed my mouth again and withered, longing un-expectedly for home.

The girls made me small and that made my parents no taller. Soon my disappointments became their failures, making our household a cyclone of personal catastrophes. Even my mother, who charmed everyone, had failed to charm them. She had been hired by Mrs. Newnham to teach S.P.I.C., and the first day she walked into my classroom I buzzed with pride, ready to show off with her. But when my mother stood before them at the blackboard and held up a picture of a stately American build-ing and called it the White House, all the white girls in my class snick-ered. My mother's face fell and looked to me for help. I gripped my desk and scowled, shushing them. I told them that she was right, it *was* the White House.

"Are you kidding?" Lizzy turned to me and said, flicking her blond hair. "That's not the White House, that's Congress." Then all the rich girls started laughing.

I glanced at my mother, deflated in her long skirt, her hair frizzing at the crown where she had piled her auburn dreadlocks into a bun. She put the picture down and looked out at all the red-faced girls giggling at their desks. Then she slapped her forehead and started laughing along too. "Of course, you're right!" she said. "How silly of me." Then she carried on, with a smile.

I dug my fingernails into my palms as the tittering died down, wishing my nails were at their necks instead.

Afterward, my mother and I never talked about that day in the classroom. It was the Sinclair way. We pushed our heavy boulders up the same punishing hill, passing each other and pretending we were alone in our misery. We each carried our weight in silence until it consumed us, collapsing, as all things must, into a black hole. One Saturday afternoon I decided to let that boulder go. Let it crush me if it must. My mother had gone shopping without me and returned with an unflattering pair of new sneakers. I looked them over and twisted my face into a pout. I hated PE almost as much as I hated casual Fridays, and these hideous grandma sneakers my mother pulled out of the bag and handed over to me would get me laughed out of school next week.

I handed back the sneakers. "I don't really like them," I told her.

Her face fell. My father, who was in earshot behind us on the couch, sprang up to face me.

"A wha' yuh just say to your mother?" he asked. Shari, who was playing with her toys on the living room floor, looked up, frightened by his sudden bark.

"I just . . . I just told her that I didn't like the shoes, Daddy," I said.

"Did you say thank you?"

"No, Daddy." My mother's face looked gray, her mouth drawn into a tight line. I was fourteen and had not considered what it might have taken for her to buy these shoes, and my thoughtless dismissal must have hurt her. I had not seen her this pinched with anger since the day she walked out the gate. Every disavowal was a reminder of her shortcomings, walking daily, as we all did, in the shadow of colonial wealth.

"I man getting sick and tired of yuh attitude," my father scolded. He looked from my mother's pained face to mine and glared. Since I began wearing pants, he eyed me with a new disgust. He must have felt me slipping further away from him, each day pulled under the influence of Babylon. Weeks before, he had woken from a dream and recoiled at the sight of me. "I man know who you are," he said. He spat it at me like a curse. "Yuh think yuh too good for the I. When yuh get older you gwine see I man pon the street, drive pas' in yuh fancy car, splash dirty water inna mi face, and act like you don't know me." My mouth hung open, shocked to hear this. I could offer no defense to such a strange pronouncement.

"All I said was that I didn't like them," I reasoned. My voice was loud—too loud—with fear. His dream, and its terrible specter of my future self, must have been the sign he had been waiting to act on. Without another word, my father walked into his room and hiked out with the red belt. Mom told Shari to go into our shared bedroom and close the door.

"Are you working?" my father asked me, gripping the belt.

"No, Daddy." I looked away now from his snarl back to my mother, who was still holding the rejected shoes, her face downturned.

"Are you working?" he asked again.

"No, Daddy. But I—" Before I could finish, the belt came whipping across my chest. I screamed as it stung my skin.

"Yuh think yuh too good?" he asked, whipping me again. I buckled as the belt slashed across my back.

"No!" I screamed. The belt tore at my skin, stinging through my shirt.

His hands rose again to the ceiling and came hammering down on me. I tried to brace the lashes with my hands. I couldn't see my mother, but I knew she was behind me, somewhere in the archway, somewhere out of sight. I willed her to come to my rescue as I cried out.

"I man sick of yuh," my father yelled, whipping the belt into my back. I shrieked out guttural animal sounds.

"So yuh think yuh too good for us?" he barked. I could hear him but I could no longer see through the blur of my tears. My ears were ringing as I fell to my knees and pressed my palms unto the floor to hold myself up. His hands arced in the air again and came down with a force that was meant to undo me.

"Daddy, please stop," I cried. Tears and snot ran their salty mucus into my mouth, down my shirt, slicking the floor.

I couldn't breathe.

I knew Lij and Ife were in the bedroom, listening behind the closed door. Whenever one of us got beaten, we all wept and frayed behind the door, but stayed out of sight to save ourselves.

He left no time in between each lash, whipping again and again, slapping my back, my neck, my legs. I bawled out, trying to look for anyone, anything at all that could help me.

"Help!" I screamed until my throat tore, imagining the entire neighborhood hearing my wailing pleas, knowing that every week the girl next door's screams echoed into our yard when her grandparents beat her, but none of us ever went to help her.

As the belt came down again, I pushed up from my knees and ran toward my room. Before I got to the bedroom my mother moved into the doorway and held out her hand to block me. I didn't recognize her face in that moment. Something intangible had ruptured. She pushed me back into my father, her eyes dark, her mouth still drawn in a gray line. It was a different person who pushed me back into the belt, a mother I had never met, some woman who stepped out from an inverted world and who hated me. She was hurt and so she let him hurt me. An unearthly sound left my body.

My brother rounded the corner then and screamed. His face was stained with tears, his mouth open.

"Please stop!" Lij screeched. I wailed out for him as he wailed out for me. I begged my father to stop, as Lij cried out. "Please leave her alone," he begged, his twelve-year-old voice breaking.

"Get back from here, bwoy!" my father shouted, and pushed my screaming brother away from the door. His body made a loud thud against the wall.

I lost count of the lashes. It could have been five minutes. It could have been fifteen. The pain blurred whatever time it took to make my father feel tall again. Darkness grew in and out of the world as I knelt under the blows, and I begged for death to take me. *Just take me.* When he finally finished, my throat was clotted with blood, my face swollen from wailing, my back too bruised to touch. When it was over I crawled to my bedroom like an animal, small as the cockroach he longed to snuff out.

Afterward I stepped into the shower but I couldn't touch my back, which stung tender under the cold water. There was a pitched ringing in my ear. I twisted my torso in the mirror and saw long raised welts and red bruises crisscrossing, marking bloodlines down my back. I was too sore to get dressed, so I called my mother into my room and told her I needed her help to hook my bra. I didn't need her help at all. But I wanted her to see it. What he did. What she did. I wanted her to face it. Our eyes met in the mirror briefly and she looked away. She glanced at my back, then paused. I waited for her to say something, anything. Her frown told me she knew I only called her in to see it.

"You're so funny," she said. I cannot understand, even now, why she said it. Perhaps she wasn't ready to face any of it. Maybe she thought it was warranted, that I was ungrateful, her hurt valid. Or that if she looked away, she could somehow unmake this moment, take it back. I don't know. The moment is unanswered and never-ending. Somewhere in the span of our lifetime together, love and hurt had been hatched from the same egg, sisters in crime. She hooked my bra, and I grimaced. She stood for a breath, never meeting my eyes in the mirror, and said nothing more. She handed me a shirt. Then she walked out and closed the door, leaving me.

Seeing myself in the mirror then, I knew I was nothing. Deserved nothing. I was smaller than a speck of filth in the eye of God, aching to be washed away in its hurricane, to let go of the rotted driftwood I was grasping, and finally drown. I sat with myself and drank this loneliness instead, digging my fingernails into my wrist, and turning away from my brother's soft knocks at the door.

17

Through the Fire

I LOOKED AWAY FROM MRS. NEWNHAM'S FACE, out past her desk full of Catholic relics, all those memento mori that had become so familiar to me in the last few months. The morning after his worst violence, my father had bounded out of bed featherweight and freed, alight with his best mood in months. I awoke to find him cooing to the strums of his guitar, the red belt still hanging next to Haile Selassie on the bedroom wall above his head. Each note he sang made a sharp hook that shredded what was left of my spirit, and I knew then what I had lost. My mother, humiliated by the confines of our poverty, had finally sacrificed me to his wrath. My brother, still too small to save me, had been slammed against the wall. My sisters, fingers plugging their ears, had learned how to sew their own mouths shut. I had no one left to protect me in this world. That look on my father's face, torqued with determination as he swung the belt, played on a loop in my mind, the memory crushing me more than the blows. It still crumbles me to nothing, even now. He had tried to beat the Babylon out of me. Snuff out the woman I was becoming, the one he envisioned splashing him with dirty rainwater on some future street. "Spare the rod and spoil the child," my father told me when it was over. But there was nothing of me left to spoil, nothing to spare. I looked in the mirror and saw only ugly. The matted roots of my dreadlocks and my broken front tooth were ugly. The trees were ugly, the roads were ugly, the sky and glimpse of sea were ugly. But the sun still rose to the bells of the birds, and the banality of the whole scene seemed blanched of mercy. I pushed my breakfast around and spoke no more than needed to be said. I dressed for school and rode along with my siblings to this wretched building, ushering empty good mornings and a covered smile to my classmates as if nothing at all had happened, until months later when Mrs. Newnham called me into her office.

Outside, the sunlight struck the orange trees in a way that called me away from Mrs. Newnham's concerned face. I was a live wire of rage and melancholy. Over the crumbling numbness of the weeks that followed my beating, I withdrew into a permanent hermit crab shell. When I wasn't withdrawn I lashed out, snapping my one claw at everyone in my orbit. I was afraid I would be nothing else but a wound in this world. A thorn in the side of a man who said he was my father. Most days I lunged headfirst into danger if I could find it, searching for my own death knell, rummaging for a sign to absent myself from all worlds. I sat in the principal's office now because I had refused to get dressed for PE, wanting to do away with my body entirely, choosing not to wear any kind of sneakers at all. As punishment, Mrs. Lawrence asked me to write an essay on why PE was important, and instead I wrote an essay about why sports were pointless, which garnered me my first-ever suspension.

"Safiya?" Mrs. Newnham called out to me, waving in the window's middle distance, snapping me out of my reverie. In her hands she held a copy of last year's yearbook.

"Yes, Miss?" I said, turning back to her probing eyes now. She wore a gray and furrowed look.

"I asked you why you vandalized your own picture?" she said, opening the yearbook page to my face, where someone had scratched over my photo in black ink. I looked at my younger self in the picture, and my stomach dropped.

I HAVE NO BOOBS! I LOOK LIKE A BOY! said a thought bubble emerging out of my matted head. My mouth, which was clamped firmly shut in a diffident smile in the photo, had now been redrawn by the doodler as a chomp of massive teeth, one of which was jagged and broken.

"Why did you do this, Safiya?" Mrs. Newnham asked me again. I looked at my ruined face and back at Mrs. Newnham, trying to determine if she was serious.

"Um? I didn't do this, Miss," I spoke slowly and tried to control my tone. I'd never seen this doodle before, and now began to wonder if this was how everyone saw me.

"You didn't do this?"

I shook my head.

"Then who did?" she asked.

"I don't know, Miss," I said, turning my eyes away from the picture, which she still held up to my face. Of course this was how everyone saw me. How stupid to think otherwise.

She licked her smoke-dark lips and closed the yearbook, not quite satisfied. Then she knitted her fingers together and looked at me.

"I've been worried about you," she said. "You were such a bright and lovely young girl when you started. What happened?" she asked me.

I didn't answer.

"Is everything okay?" she asked.

I felt a burning rising in my throat.

It had been so long since anyone asked anything of me so gently. I picked at my pleats and waited for that heavy hoof to unpin me. What could I have said to her then? That everything in the world had morphed for me? That my mother had deserted me in my most desolate moment? That my father's love was now so distant it seemed mythological? That they all expected me to go on living when it seemed there was nothing left of me to love? I looked away from Mrs. Newnham, whose eyes burrowed into me.

Now the tears started spilling over as I looked back at Mrs. Newnham, who nodded slowly, encouragingly.

Finally, the words shook and warbled out of me.

"I hate myself, Miss," I said.

I didn't recognize my voice.

Mrs. Newnham reached out her freckled hands, but I didn't reach back. She withdrew them and searched her drawers for tissue, which she passed across the desk to me.

"You like to write, don't you?" she asked. I nodded and wiped away the tears that were already respilling themselves again.

"You write so beautifully," she said softly. "Have you tried writing it down?" she said to me now. "How you're feeling?"

"No, Miss," I said. I wrote stories of imagined worlds and poems about the sunlight that glinted off the orange trees, but had never tried to pin down the ghost that wrenched this deep ache inside me.

Mrs. Newnham reached for a notebook and a pen and gently slid them over the desk to me.

"Well, why don't you try writing something now? Just write about how you're feeling."

I took the pen and thought for a while.

Then I wrote: *I hate my dreadlocks.*

I looked at the words I thought to myself so many waking hours but had never dared to say out loud. Then I scratched another black mark on the page. And another.

I hate my broken front tooth.
I hate my buck teeth.
I hate the cut above my eyebrow.
I hate my skinny ankles.
I hate my butt.
I hate being a girl.
I hate my body.
I hate being poor.
I hate my life.
I hate my—
I hate my—
I hate my—

I wrote feverishly for almost ten minutes without looking up at her, tracing the knife-edge of my disgust, my confusion, my self-loathing. When I finally put the pen down and looked away from her, I was surprised to find the tears had staunched themselves in the writing. Mrs. Newnham picked up the notebook and read what I'd written, her thinning eyebrows shooting up occasionally. Suddenly I was naked, my heart blasting warning shots in my chest. Folding closed the notebook, she sighed and looked at me, running her fingers through her short black curls.

"Have you thought about what you want to do when you graduate, Safiya?"

I'd thought about it a good deal now that I was in my final year at school. I was fifteen, much younger than most eleventh graders in Jamaica, who graduated at sixteen or seventeen. I had spent the last three years studying for my Caribbean Examinations Council exams (CXCs), the series of final subject tests that all upper-level students in the Caribbean took in preparation for admission to university. But as the school year raced to a close and graduation approached, it seemed I was the only one in my house who gave it much thought at all.

We had never discussed what came after high school in my household. The first and only directive for me and my sisters was to make sure we graduated without becoming pregnant like our grandmother. But my father hadn't bothered to imagine what came next. Going to a university had always been something hazy on the blurred horizon, intangible for us Sinclairs. Neither of my parents had gone to college, and no one in my family knew how to apply to colleges or how we would ever afford them. I was the first—forever standing at the end of the road or at the beginning of one. I had to imagine what was next for myself. All my classmates were planning to go study sociology at FIU in Miami, a combination of words that meant virtually nothing to me, but that sounded like as good a plan as any.

"Go to college in Miami, Miss," I told her. I said it so confidently it didn't even sound like an invention. Buoyed only by the faintest fumes of hope, and no worldly knowledge, I was too embarrassed to admit to Mrs. Newnham that my parents had neither the means nor the proficiency for what to do with me next.

My answer seemed to please her, so she didn't press me for details. "Good," she said, then she rapped her knuckles on the wood of her desk.

"And what would you like to do once you get there?" she asked me.

I looked out the window and reached for the future. There, my hopes hardened into something beautiful again, a kaleidoscope of possible selves beckoning and disappearing at the same time, one girl moving through a splintered world that branched into herself and herself and herself.

"I want to grab the bull by its horns and stitch my name to its tongue," I told her.

"Well, okay!" Mrs. Newnham laughed. "Alright then, Safiya. That's a fine plan." She glanced at her watch and signaled that our session was over. I got up to leave.

"Thanks, Miss," I said, mirroring her smile, the light still reflecting off her glasses.

It had felt good to write it down at Mrs. Newnham's desk—all that frantic, stifled feeling, to leave it withering and pulsing there on the page. It felt good to say what I wanted out loud. At home I started writing down what I felt, turning my mind from the dizzying wheel of stars outside our fifth rented house in the country and looking inward. I returned to that girl at the bottom of the tomb, lost in her catacombs of sand, listening to the ghost sounds of the far waves. At night I waited until the whole house was asleep, then I would lie in bed and write by candlelight for hours. Sometimes I heard stories of the death of other women on the radio and I wrote them down, the gruesome details, mourning the dismembered and despoiled, the lost and forgotten. I imagined their voices speaking to me, as I did with Eurydice, through the lines of a poem. On weekends my mother and I caught each other crossing the river of sleeping and waking; she waking in the blue hour of dawn to begin her housework, finding me in the kitchen pouring a glass of water before closing my door to go to sleep.

A deep silence had grown between us after she pushed me back into the flailing belt of my father. I imagined her growing mossy with cowardice every time she ignored the evidence of his terror. She tried to come back to me not long after it happened, with grilled cheeses and coffee at my door, with foot rubs massaging my chakras. "What's wrong, Saf?" she asked me, eyes trembling. "Nothing," I said, and turned away from her. For the first time in my life we stood on either side of the gate. She was hurt and I knew it, but I wanted her to hurt. "I don't know who you are anymore," she said to me one morning in the kitchen. I shrugged and left her to wonder. "I don't know either, Mom," I wanted to say, but left her words hanging there instead, a mirror large and looming. Months passed this way. Then, without warning or explanation, the beatings that had hurled down on us for the past three years suddenly stopped. I knew it was my mother's doing. She had felt me drowning, slipping out of her hands for good, and could not bear it. She reached for that incendiary power once more, made herself a shield around her children, and put a permanent stop to this chapter of our lives. She wanted no more of the "backra massa business," she told me years later, disavowing the ugly bond between corporal punishment and colonial violence. "We didn't know any better," she would say, years of unspoken guilt tearing at her throat.

As if it never existed, the red belt was retired and disappeared, and my father returned to sharpening the verbal tools in his arsenal instead. Lij was thirteen and I was fifteen, and both of us had grown as tall as my father, though you wouldn't know it from the way we slumped over and listened to his infinite scroll of our wrongs and malformations. We were lazy. My siblings needed to close their mouths when they slept. We had too many cavities. My Adam's apple was too big.

Whatever he said clanged immutably in the echo chamber of my head, because I was fifteen and the mirror was god. One weekend at the beach, two teen boys ran past me and circled back to inspect me closer. From my seat in the sand, I perked up my shoulders and extended my legs, looking away nonchalantly as if I didn't see them. "She kinda cute though," one boy said, as if window shopping. "Nice body," he said, stroking his hairless chin. His friend dragged him back in the sand and shook his head. "Nah. Nah, my yute. Rasta girls are gross," he said, pulling his friend away and laughing. Away they disappeared, like mirages on the horizon. I slumped back into myself. Not long after, I began brushing and subtly detangling the roots of my hair, so it was only dreadlocked from the middle of my scalp down to the ends, while any new growth was smooth and not locked. Every morning before school I brushed down those precious few inches of unmatted hair at the front of my head and kept the strands soft and oiled and shiny. I obsessed over the cut over my eyebrow and started using a black marker to fill in the scarred skin where hair no longer grew. I began unbuttoning my school shirt one button down and wore my tie at my bosom, instead of at my neck like a boy. When I looked in the mirror, I might find something beautiful, as long as I didn't open my mouth.

One afternoon Mom came to my room and told me she had a surprise for me. She was working a new job at a luxe hotel called Round Hill, where she tutored the children of the rich and famous in private S.P.I.C. sessions during the high season. Now as she stood in the doorway, her hair drawn up in a bun, wearing her best calf-length denim work skirt, I waited without expectations for her surprise. It had been nearly a year since she pushed me into the belt, and we still had not come back to each other, even though she had tried.

"I'm gonna pay for you to fix your tooth," she told me. "Now that you're almost sixteen, I think it's time."

I clasped my hand over my mouth in disbelief. She had saved all her Round Hill earnings from the Christmas season, and in conjunction with Grandma's dentist and dental insurance, she was going to pay for me to have my tooth capped. I ran to the door and gave her a hug, thanking her over and over. The gate between us flung wide open again. We held hands and locked pinkies as we made the plans. That weekend Grandma traveled four hours from Spanish Town to come get me, and we rode four hours back to Spanish Town on a cramped minibus. The next day she took me to her dentist, who numbed and prodded and drilled and mended. When she was finished, she held the mirror up to me and said, "Smile."

I smiled the whole bus ride back to Montego Bay, running my tongue over my new front tooth, laughing and joking with Grandma, paying no mind to the sweaty passengers packed around us, or the choke of the exhaust as the bus prattled along the perilous road. I let the country breeze sweep over my face as Grandma and I sucked on oranges, ate roasted peanuts, and popped big laughs. When I got back home, I ran through the gate and up the stairs and burst through the door with a smile. My mother and father were watching television on the couch. Mom jumped up to greet me.

"Hey now! Let me see! Let me see!" she said, coming closer to look at my new face stretching wide in a manic smile. "Wow. You look so beautiful," Mom said, brushing her hands over my head, hugging me. "Now you can graduate in style," she said, and did a shimmy.

"Thank you so much, Mom." I hugged her again and again, then launched into a raucous retelling of everything the dentist did, how I was afraid of her needle, as my mother listened with delight, with Grandma chiming in.

My father, who hadn't moved from the couch since I came in, finally said, "Let I man see it, then."

I turned to him and smiled wide, with one hand on my hip. He must have thought this was a mark of vanity, for after a glance, he turned his attention back to the television and smirked. "Yuh got something in yuh teeth. Don't forget to brush them."

I closed my mouth shut and shrunk off to find a mirror.

I arrived at school that Monday morning like the Cheshire cat, smiling so wide I could feel the heavens mirroring in my face. I couldn't wait to see my schoolmates' reactions. I skipped into the classroom, smiling good morning to everyone, with no hand over my mouth for the first time since I began at St. James College five years before. Some girls smattered out a polite hello, or good morning, then went back to their conversations. I slid into my desk under the bright fluorescent light of our eleventh-grade classroom and tried to join in their conversation, more talkative than usual. I smiled every chance I got. Their conversations of last night's beach bash continued uninterrupted. If anyone had noticed the difference, nobody said so. By the time the lunch bell rang, no one took notice of me. All the joy and confidence I'd been clinging to vanished again with a profound ache, a hammer clanging a puny nail.

At lunchtime everyone had left the usual picnic spot on the lawn except for Heather and me. We sat awkwardly for a while under the mango tree in silence. She loomed so large over my world and its boundaries, over my anxieties and my parents' failures, but I realized we had never had a single conversation alone. Now we both pulled at the crabgrass under our pleated skirts, as the breeze picked up the feathery hairs at our temples. In a few months we would be graduating and the world that divided us would grow only wider in its chasm. I looked at her face. Pleasant, placid. Perhaps a bit haughty. But not satanic, nor cruel. As the wind whispered over our silence, I wanted to disrupt that peace. I wanted to wound.

"Hey, Heather," I said. "If you were going to slit your wrists, how would you do it?"

I watched her face. Her expression didn't change. I'd heard that her cousin had tried to slit her wrists after her father left her mom and moved to Canada.

Without even hesitating or turning toward me, Heather said, "You know, most people think you cut across your wrists, like this." She held out her pale hands to demonstrate, sliding her thumb across her wrist. "But to be most effective, you have to slice the blade down your veins vertically, like this." She ran her fingernails down the green veins of her wrist, leaving red lines where the thumbnail slid.

All the air left me as she spoke. Her pupils had gone wide as the moon, and she looked out ahead of us, to someplace unseen.

"You just have to remember," she said, with the faintest hint of a smirk. "Down the highway, not across the street." She ran her fingernail down the length of her wrist again to show me. *Down the highway, not across the street.*

It was as if I'd fallen from a high tree. I was feeling rotten about my life, my uncertain future, how my tooth had gone unnoticed, and hurting her seemed like a way to vent my own pain. I was doing just as I had learned from my father. But she'd seen right through my ruse and would never give me the satisfaction of seeing her wounded. All that misplaced bravado and silly strength I felt evaporated as she turned the hurt back on me. She might as well have given me the blade. Maybe she could see me after all. Maybe she had always known. That I was not the weapon. I was only the wound.

As my graduation crept closer and no concrete plans were made, the fog of my disappointments shrouded everything. One evening, under the bruise of dusk, I asked my mother about going to college in America, and her mouth quivered. "How would we afford it?" she asked me, eyes wide. I was fifteen and had no answer. I had no internet or computer. No college counselor or mentor to guide me. Mrs. Newnham never revisited the question of my college education after that day in her office, and I would spend the years of limbo that followed wishing I hadn't been too embarrassed to ask her for help. My mother could only press her hands into mine and say, "Something will work out, I know it." She had lived on a cowrie shell dream for so long she didn't know how to plan more than a week into the future. Her chakras and mantras were a good salve when I was younger, but they could not get me to college. I wasn't going to close my eyes and wake up in Miami, no matter how much my mother willed it so. My father, on the other hand, seemed content to keep me under his watch.

Nothing frightened me more than the uncertainty of what happened next. Fixing my tooth had not changed the trajectory of my future, nor sutured my cutoff world. I was caught in our household's monsoon of chaos, and all I craved was my own bleak sense of order. At night I began dragging a pair of scissors down my arm, pulling one ache to the surface instead of another, bartering numbness. But the scissors had been used to cut ganja and were now too dull to draw blood. So it was not blood but fire that came for me in the end.

Sometime after midnight, as the end of the school year approached, I lit the candle next to my bed and lay thinking about what I had just heard on the radio—somewhere in the country a young girl my age had been molested by her pastor, so she killed herself by drinking Gramoxone, a weed killer that turned her insides to mush. I wrote this down in my journal, imagining the darkness of the underworld if I succumbed to it.

I put away the dulled scissors, set aside thoughts of Gramoxone, then blew out the candle and went to bed. I dreamt of a moth diving black into the sun, of the sun calling out my name, an unearthly voice.

I awoke to flames licking up the fringe of the curtain, burning at my sheet. The heat was suffocating. From beyond the wall of flames I could see my mother, her face warped with panic, screaming my name, beckoning to me. My sisters' voices were shrill as their shadows called for me too. My body hesitated. I could not move; I had been yearning so long for some kind of light, and now I did not want to escape. My mother ran back for a wet towel as the flames crackled the nightstand next to me, and a painting I had made began to burn at the edges. My brother was shrieking now, filling buckets of water with my father. My mother, draped in the wet towel, approached the fire and grabbed me, pulling me away to the cold air outside. My parents ran back inside to put the flames out with buckets of water, and dawn rinsed the night clean. My siblings and I coughed the darkness out of our lungs and clung to each other.

It was Ife who prickled awake in the night and went to tell my sleeping parents that I was on fire. I shook like a breadfruit leaf in the blue mist, unable to face my family. The thought of them coming to harm racked me. I sobbed. We all wept, smoke rising, at how close we had come, how close we all were. The heat had seared the hairs of my skin.

When the fire was finally out, my father skulked back outside and hurled his shadow over me.

"Yuh stupid, girl?"

"No, Daddy," I said.

"So why yuh never blow out the rass candle?"

"I did, Daddy." I swore I did.

"You take I man fi fool?"

"I'm sorry. I thought I blew it out. I'm sorry."

"Yuh nearly kill all ah we, Rasta. Damn stupid."

I only wanted to kill myself, I wanted to tell him then. That it was an eerie coincidence. A specter of my desire fluttering in the curtain. But I offered no defense. There was no defense I could give that would remove this lingering darkness, which sat like a heavy saddle of tuberculosis in my lung. Four months later, by the time the ash and black in my corner of the room had been painted over, I graduated high school with no future ahead of me; no college, no job, no prospects, nothing but the dead air of the combustible days, the dull scissors, the Gramoxone, the struck match.

18

Silver

THAT FIRST YEAR AFTER HIGH SCHOOL moved in slow motion. The days trudged like a sea of tar, sucking me under. My parents had no plan, no road paved beyond this moment for me. How far I had fallen, how heavy. I spent almost every day of my sixteenth year inside the house, staring at my ruined days, wondering how it had all happened. Hadn't I done all that was asked of me? Learned every spelling bee word, won speech and math competitions, studied and passed all my final CXC exams. I had been "excellent." Now I wore it around my house like old clothing: the weight of my failures, my loneliness, my unbelonging. And life galloped on without me as if I had never existed. My brother was fourteen, my sisters twelve and seven. I began worrying what future might await them. I wished more than anything that they didn't have to see me like this. Each day my family got dressed for school and work and left me there in bed, shrinking away to nothing. Every evening they returned, having lived a day out there in the world, finding me just where they had left me hours before—slowly becoming the furniture, part of the repainted wall and the red floor. And when they asked me what I had done, I could either spin them a fable or say nothing, longing for the thorny trees and the giant birdcatcher spiders in the yard to take me. I had nothing but my thoughts and myths and poems, and what good was that to anyone?

I needed purpose, I needed order. Some sense that my life might be my own to mold. If I couldn't make it to college, I decided that my education would be in my own hands. During that first year after high school, an American family-friend donated a secondhand desktop computer to my family. It was the first computer we ever owned, and it came with a Microsoft Word CD and a digital encyclopedia called Encarta. We finally had a landline installed, and an internet connection. After everyone went to bed, I spent many late hours with Encarta opened on the desktop, clicking from one entry to another, devouring, devouring. I memorized Poe and Dylan Thomas and bled my own dark yearnings into verse. I had an easel, I had paint. I tried painting myself into the frame. I would read every entry under Philosophy, taking notes on Plato, Socrates, and Aristotle, trying to pronounce Kierkegaard and Nietzsche and Sartre, pacing back and forth while I thought about existentialism and nihilism and how my father always said "Rasta don't deal in ism and schism." I would type in "Astronomy" and read every possible entry, trying to identify constellations in the night sky with my naked eye. Then I moved on to Botany. Then the life and teachings of Confucius. Soon I began yearning for the nighttime, when the whole house was asleep and I could feel some sense of purpose again. I imagined my gone grandmother Isabel watching me as I scribbled in my notebook in these small hours. She had died by the sea three decades before, but I carried her here with me like a shell that I kept pressed to my ear while in the country.

I spent most of my waking hours leaping from each era of literature, consuming century after century and clicking on the name of every poet. Sometimes the entries included a brief recording of an actor reading an excerpt of the poems, and this is how I stumbled upon the entry on Sylvia Plath. I clicked the recording of a poem called "Daddy." The voice was that of a Black woman reciting the first lines of "Daddy": *You do not do, you do not do / Any more black shoe / In which I have lived like a foot / For thirty years, poor and white*, she said. I was transfixed. Somehow, I understood. I played the curious clip over and over, then found the full poem on the internet. I memorized it, studied it. I carried the lines around with me for weeks, recognizing so intimately the speaker's own troubled relationship with her father, feeling strangely seen by how much it mirrored my relationship with mine. Some days I imagined I slept in my own black shoe, airless and windowless, closing in. I had not known that a poem could slice so closely to the personal. I sought out other Plath poems, and fell into their strange, lush, and heavy bleeding diction. Once I read that she had taken her own life, I thought it was a sign—that she understood me somehow, her breath whispering across the veil. I saw myself as the hothouse orchid, myself as a huge camelia, myself as a phoenix rising from the ashes to eat men like air. *Beware, beware.* Now poetry nursed itself on my veins.

I spent many manic and insomniac months building poetry as a home for my most private parts, work that must've looked to an observer like nothing at all. When Rashmi, one of my old high school friends, returned home for spring break and called me up to ask what I had been up to, I couldn't say "I've been reading the encyclopedia," so I just diverted the question back to her. She had been two grades below me at St. James College and left in the ninth grade to go to private school in Miami. She asked me to come sleep over and I welcomed the change of pace. Her family had a large mansion as their main house, while Rashmi had her own guesthouse where we hung out and sometimes snuck out to chill with the rich daredevils of Montego Bay. I crossed into another world to see her; a place where two Black maids who wore pink uniforms and called her "Miss Rashmi" appeared every mealtime to ask her what she wanted to eat. We stretched out in her living room and waited to be served as she told me about boarding school in Miami, about her tennis lessons, and all about the cute boys there and what their cum tasted like. "Classes are so boring, though," she said. "Look at all these books I have to read for my exams." She pointed to a stack of books that made my eyes water. I stood up to sift through them, their covers and pages still brand-new, and my heart skipped when I saw *The Collected Poems of Sylvia Plath*.

"Oh my god, you get to read Plath?" I asked. "I *love* her."

Rashmi snorted. "Oh god. I can't take another minute of her," she said. "Our teacher makes us listen to all these recordings of her reading her poems, and she has *the* weirdest accent. In one poem she pronounces the word 'Daddy' like 'Doddy' a million times. 'Doddy' this, and 'Doddy' that, 'Doddy, Doddy, Doddy.' She sounds fucking demented."

I said nothing and watched Rashmi as she laughed and kept saying "Doddy" over and over again in a strained accent. For so long I'd envied her life, but it was only pity I felt for her then, seeing the truth of it: how empty her life now seemed, how artless. Watching her mock so flippantly a poem that meant the world to me had me briefly daydreaming of my palm-slap printed across her face.

Of course, she didn't know what she had, because she had always had it. I would have given her all my possessions then, meager as they were, just to hear Plath reading one of her poems. But I went home with my bile instead. That night Rashmi called again and I didn't take the call. Nor the next day. I realized that I wanted no visions of my old friends' lives in Foreign. I had watched them all move away to America, to colleges and family jobs, to shiny new lives. It became harder for me to feign interest each time I heard from them, to hide my envy, to cull my disappoint-ment. Their joy may as well have been a knife, slowly shunted into a waiting ventricle, my life draining away before me month after month.

My family had moved again, to our fifth house in five years, this time to a country town called Bickersteth, which was tiny, even by Jamaican stan-dards, with modest houses flanking the sides of a mile-long road, winding stutteringly up a steep hill. The town was unmoved in time, still with the dusty languor of three or four decades, going along at its own slow clip. We arrived in spectacle as the only new villagers in almost a century. The villagers gaped, some with mouths open and others closed tight, their fists and hearts clenched as my father unpacked cases of guitars, my mother's dreadlocks cascading down her back as she lifted furniture like Samson, while my siblings and I ran around the yard with our dog, Rusty. Because my father worked nights, many days he and I were the only people at home. He often slept in the daytime, and I stayed out of his way. But when he was awake I held my breath, tiptoeing around him while he listened to the news on the radio and quarreled out loud with the angry callers.

He was never good at managing his disappointments or tempering frustration without firebombing the nearest person in the house. Now I was the only person in the house, and his tongue was ready. One after-noon he woke and gathered his dark gaze on me. He stood in the door-way of my bedroom and watched me as I wrote in my notebook. I looked away from his stare as my heart thumped in my ear.

"Why the I never do anything?" he asked me. "Every day I man wake up you still sitting there in the bed, doing nothing at all."

I longed to tell him that something miraculous was happening while the household slept. That I had been writing, and it felt like oxygen. That nothing at all on this earth filled me with more purpose than a poem. Surely he would understand, since he was moved by some higher power to write his reggae songs?

But I had no chance to respond, because he was already raining down a blitz of complaints. He stood over me, snatching my light away, word by word. His career had been a failure and now I was his failure too. He wanted me to be a scientist or a businesswoman, and I had ruined my life by not taking high school physics and economics classes like he told me to. I never cooked or cleaned the house. I was nasty and unbecoming. I sat stone-faced and listened. When he finished, I managed to squeak out that I'd been writing poems. My father laughed a black laugh that did not touch his eyes. All at once, the beautiful city I had been building was reduced to leaves and chaff, blown down easily in his hard wind. He shook his head to the ceiling as if to say he couldn't believe this was his daughter.

"You're really worthless, Rasta," he said. Then he turned and left, my hand clasping tight at my own neck.

That night I walked to the stony hill behind our house, dodging the litter of glass bottles and half-buried rusted cans that had lain there for decades. Beyond the house, no lights were visible except for the one flickering flame in my half of the bedroom I shared with my youngest sister. Uncertainty had returned, a hungry abyss opening beneath me. Maybe what my father said was true. Maybe I was worthless. I stood at the top of the slope and looked out at my inheritance, our rented house, old and filled with mice. There, my father and his cruel tongue slept. Outside, the darkness spread for miles, pregnant with what was unseen in the Jamaican countryside. The trees surrounding me loomed tall and quiet, and I thought of the one big knife in the kitchen, the one my mother used to chop her almonds, its rickety handle, the steel stained almond-red. The rungs of the ladder I'd descended were long gone, and all I needed was a push. I thought again of Heather's directive: *Down the highway, not across the street*. I was sixteen. A year had passed since I graduated high school, and here I still was, caught in my father's hurricane, drowning.

There was no world for me except the one I had been building in my mind. No way ahead. I knew I could not live here with my father and survive. Among the hill's wreckage I saw a long shard of glass, exposed and shining. I picked it up and shuddered as I touched the sharp end to my wrist. The crickets screeched in my ear and my eyes blurred with tears, as my cry became a beastly moan. I thought of my dreaming siblings and my mother, trying to preserve something of them before I dug the cold point into my veins. I shook as I clutched the shard, mouth stringy and gasping for air. I wept, wishing my gone grandmother Isabel could hear me now. There, on that desolate tin-can hill strewn with rocks, from somewhere in the desperate depths of my body I cried out to the air, "Please help me."

The low clouds drifted, exposing a full moon, and a catch of light glinted silver off the glass shard. *Silver flows through my veins*, I thought. Words hardened around that pearlescent beacon. My face was wet and cold, exposed in the spotlight. *Silver is the moon I swallowed.*

I dropped the shard to the ground and shivered back to my dim-lit room, reaching for my notebook. *The words I bleed are silver.* I wrote in a fugue state, engulfed by white smoke and a billowing georgette dress and my hair strands spiraling silver. Electricity gathered between the words. *My belly swells and it'll be a while, but I know more silver is welling inside.*

I nursed the poem like hibiscus silk. There were no words or blows that could pull me away now, for the veiled world I had first glimpsed when I was ten now opened the slick throat of itself, and pulled me, fully formed, from out of it. In the chaos of our rented house, under a borrowed moon, I discovered that a poem was order. It was certainty. And, for the first time, it seemed possible for me to write my way out. There was no looking back. I wrote possessed, each night drawing closer to the girl who walked barefoot into the sea, leading her to the surface. And the light out there was the one we had made, a universe speckled with all that silver.

Eurydice, in the end, would save herself. A week later, I asked my mother to mail an envelope of three poems, including "Silver," to the editor of the *Jamaica Observer* Literary Arts supplement, which appeared every Sunday with new fiction and poetry by Jamaica's best writers, and for which I had not garnered the courage to submit to until now. For a long time, I thought no more of the shard, of the knife.

A few weeks later, the phone rang, and my father yelled from his bedroom for me to come pick it up. I walked ten paces across the boundary into his bedroom, where the sun glinted through the curtains. My father gave me a suspicious look. The one he always wore whenever someone he didn't know called me at home, a look that made me nervous. He passed me the telephone and left. I took a breath, watching the cord spiral as I raised the receiver to my ear. On the line was an older man with a deep and playful voice.

"Hello, Safiya," he said. "I am the editor of the *Observer* Literary Arts, and I was blown away by your poems. I'd like to publish them." He spoke with a lilting Trinidadian accent, and there was joy in his voice. Or perhaps the joy was all mine. Maybe he'd heard me squeal, for I was already leaping five minutes into the future, screaming about what he had just said.

"I think you have an incredible poetic talent. We need to meet immediately," he said. My voice shook with deference as we made arrangements to speak again, and then the voice was gone.

I clicked the phone back into the receiver and noticed my hands were shaking. Or perhaps it was the ground that shook as I ran out of the bedroom into the light, giddy as the heavens with the news.

III

LIONHEART

O daughter of Babylon, doomed to be destroyed,
blessed shall he be who repays you
with what you have done to us!
—Psalms 137:8

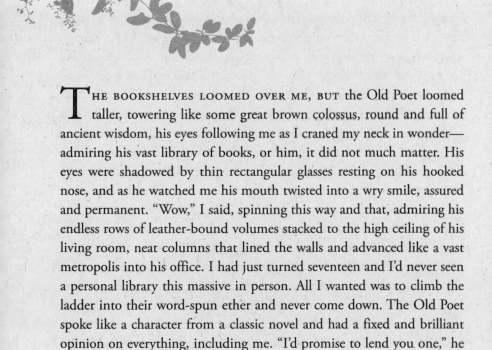

19

Galatea

Тнe bookshelves loomed over me, but the Old Poet loomed taller, towering like some great brown colossus, round and full of ancient wisdom, his eyes following me as I craned my neck in wonder—admiring his vast library of books, or him, it did not much matter. His eyes were shadowed by thin rectangular glasses resting on his hooked nose, and as he watched me his mouth twisted into a wry smile, assured and permanent. "Wow," I said, spinning this way and that, admiring his endless rows of leather-bound volumes stacked to the high ceiling of his living room, neat columns that lined the walls and advanced like a vast metropolis into his office. I had just turned seventeen and I'd never seen a personal library this massive in person. All I wanted was to climb the ladder into their word-spun ether and never come down. The Old Poet spoke like a character from a classic novel and had a fixed and brilliant opinion on everything, including me. "I'd promise to lend you one," he said, his eyes twinkling from behind his glasses, "but I don't know how you take care of books yet." His Trinidadian accent rising and falling like a wave, he continued, "When I lend out a book, I assume an inevitable loss. That the book in many ways belongs to the reader now." I frowned, taking it to heart that he thought I could ever ruin a book. I reassured him that I treated all books with the utmost care and would treasure any of his that I might be so lucky to read.

"But you write notes in your books, don't you?" he asked.

"No . . ." Apart from my high-school textbooks, I always shared books with my siblings, and never had a book that was just for me, one that I could make a permanent mark in to share my thoughts with my future self.

"Well, you should always write in the margins as you read," he said. "Make that a regular practice."

"Yes, sir," I said.

I arrived at his gate that afternoon feeling that I had stepped into another life, waiting for the man himself to appear, to prove this was not a dream. On the wall by his gate there was an elegant wrought-iron sign affixed in italics that said *Sequestra*, Latin for "to set aside, to separate," I later learned. From the outside, his house looked like a foreign sanctuary, a serene villa with arches topped by scalloped Mediterranean red roof tiles and a neatly manicured lawn, his yard frocked with foaming bougainvillea, pink hibiscus, and the verdant crush of fruit trees, all shivering alive with the buzz of insects. The Old Poet was tall and had a slightly round belly, visible underneath his polo shirt. His smile curled to his eyes as he approached me at the gate, and said, "Come on in," like we were old friends. Inside, it was just as I imagined a well-off Caribbean man's house might be: the lingering musk of oiled mahogany and rum, walls adorned with bright paintings and side tables bearing untouched vases and wooden statues from places he had traveled. Throughout the house were framed pictures of his two daughters, twice as old as me. In the living room was a set of rattan furniture carefully arranged around his coffee table, where there were more books, including a biography he had written of a famous sculptor. The Old Poet had a helper, a middle-aged woman who greeted me in the foyer adjacent to the kitchen. She helped him "keep house," the Old Poet said, while he did more pressing things; like run the Literary Arts magazine in the *Jamaica Observer*, conduct poetry and fiction workshops, and write books of poems and short stories. *More pressing things*, I remembered later, were separate from the domestic.

He motioned for me to sit at one end of the big rattan couch and he sat at the other, turning to face me. The ceiling fan whirred overhead. I had the distinct sense I was being judged and measured; worthy or unworthy. My eyes darted away from him; I was afraid to say the wrong thing, a feeling that would never leave me when I was with him. His eyes lingered over my dreadlocks, which were tied in a ponytail with a long gothic-black ribbon.

"Well, you're a strange one, aren't you?" he said.

I didn't know how to respond.

"All the best poets are," he said, winking to reassure me. When he spoke, his lips twisted into a quizzical smile. His droll expression seemed to me some aspect of a national character; if Jamaicans wore an immutable furrow, Trinis seemed to bear an immutable smirk.

"Thank you," I said, straightening my posture to seem more assured in my strangeness.

"I was blown away by the poems you sent me," he said. "From the first line I could feel the prickle of something completely different. I read so many writers every day for my job and I knew at once."

"Thank you," I said again, looking away with enough measured humility that he wouldn't notice the meteor shower that streaked inside me.

"I could see Plath's influence in the work right away," he said. "In that first hair-raising poem."

"My father didn't like it very much," I told him. My voice was quieter than I expected as I held my palm inside my palm, both of which were sweating.

"Well, I can't blame him." The Old Poet chuckled. The first poem of mine he published had been called "Daddy," written after Sylvia Plath's own famous poem that had extended a light to me in the unfurling darkness.

The day my poem "Daddy" was published in the Literary Arts supplement of the Sunday *Observer* was one big excitement in the Sinclair household. I ran around buzzing and announcing to everyone that my name would be in print: a marker of greatness. My parents were ecstatic. My father, who read the Sunday *Observer* every weekend, was the most excited of all of us when, lifting the paper, he saw that the poem's title was "Daddy." I didn't bother to warn him that it was not a tribute to him. I didn't tell him that this was a persona poem, an act of imagination, or explain that what he would find was a tribute to a young girl from the news who drank Gramoxone to kill herself because her father had molested her. I didn't caution him that the language was visceral and the details gut-wrenchingly vivid. Instead, I watched him as he opened the paper to the page and savored the long droop of his face as it fell into a sad, cross-stitched quiet. He closed the paper and went away into his room alone, folding into himself for the first time that I could remember. He said nothing to me about the poem that day and would say nothing more to me about my poetry for a long time. I was surprised to find some glee in it—seeing that my words could affect him after all. I knew then that I could finally build myself a world that was beyond his reach. That on the page I was not the princess, I was the dragon. I wanted him to see the cruel world nakedly, the way I wanted all men to see the cruel world, their deeds burned to ash on my tongue.

I said none of this to the Old Poet. Not yet. Instead, I shared that after "Daddy," my father no longer seemed interested in anything I wrote.

"Listen," he said, shaking his head. His flash of hair so gray it was white. "If I wrote anything with the specter of my parents looking over my shoulder, I would be too crippled with fear to write anything at all."

It was all quite Freudian, the Old Poet explained. Poets had to sever the umbilicus to write their true self. I made a note to discuss all of this with my brother, who'd been reading *Oedipus Rex* in his eleventh-grade Lit class to prepare for his upcoming CXC exams. Though I had aced my CXCs more than a year before, the financial path to university had only seemed more impassable, just as the path to poetry was beginning to open. Lij and I had been arguing about nihilism and the idea that our fates might be irrevocably fixed. My brother was allured by fatalism, but I was adamant that I was authoring the narrative of my own life.

"What other writers have you read?" the Old Poet asked me. "Who do you like?"

Another test. My stomach lurched, not wanting to get it wrong under his curling wry smile. "Well. I really love Edgar Allan Poe and I like Dylan Thomas," I said.

He laughed. "So, you have a flair for dark melodrama," he said. "That much is evident from your poems. The sheer audacity of them." *Sheer audacity*, I echoed to myself, stamping this moment in place indelibly, a text to revisit later, combing over his every word.

"I also like Shakespeare," I added for good measure.

"You read *The Tempest*?"

"No," I said. I'd only read *A Midsummer Night's Dream* and *The Merchant of Venice* for school, but their monologues and dizzying wordplay had left me drunk.

"*The Tempest* is his finest work," the Old Poet said. "How it moves like the sea. And in every line, you hear the lapping waves of a poet who is nearing the end of his life."

As he spoke, all was still, and I knew I was hearing something for the first time that would always matter a great deal to me. An anchor for a girl who was adrift. We spent many moments this way, face-to-face in private mentorship, when I could do nothing but listen, awed by the way the Old Poet could so clearly and deeply see the world. The way he saw me.

We fell into a fertile cosmos of our own making, talking poetry into the afternoon. Our tea had gone cold, untouched, and I had no memory of his helper even bringing the cups to us.

Before I rose to leave, the Old Poet went into his office and returned with a small hardcover book in his hands.

"We'll start here," he said, handing me the book with a clang of finality. Its worn cover was a frayed blue linen, and along the spine in gold lettering it read *Poems of Gerard Manley Hopkins.* I squeaked and thanked him. I had passed the test.

"You will come here every week for a private session," he told me. "And you will join my weekly poetry workshop meetings."

I thanked him again.

"At *no* cost," he added emphatically.

Until then, it hadn't occurred to me that this was something for which I might have to pay. I was only seventeen and just beginning to learn the cost of things. I thanked him again and walked out to the taxi waiting at the gate.

The next day, there was an email from the Old Poet waiting for me. *I fear you will eventually exhaust me completely,* he wrote.

My skin prickled at the subtext of his message, and instinctively I looked over my shoulder to see if my father was there. This was the first time anyone had ever communicated with me like this, with a private river of meaning coursing beneath the words. I was flattered and intrigued. A little nervous. I read those words until they were a flash of neon, a searing

photo negative I sat with for a long time until I mustered all the right
words to reply.

There was more than one way to make her. A blank block of marble chiseled away insistently with iron, or an empty wire frame, molded into the
figure of the sculptor's imagination, his warm hands smoothing her limbs
with clay. Either way, the perfect statue emerged, a blanched reflection of
the maker himself. My mother had agreed right away that this would be
a good thing for me to do, to be instructed in poetry by a distinguished
man. At my behest, she convinced my father to let me go and live with
my grandmother in a cramped and yardless housing scheme in Spanish
Town, where I would stay for a few months. Twice a week my grandmother hired a taxi to drive me an hour and a half to the Old Poet's house
in Kingston. We spent many sunlit days in Sequestra, me and the Old
Poet. In this seclusion, I learned how to read meter and mark scansion,
studied forms and rhythm, divining myself into the poet who was divining me. I edited my poetry on the computer at his desk, going over my
poems line by line. He deleted and rearranged my work at his will, trying
to show me the secrets of assembling a real poem. "A real poem," he told
me, according to Nabokov, "registers with the reader not in his head or
heart or even his gut, but in his spine."

When I was not with him I spent the rest of my week alone in Grandma's rented house, reading the books the Old Poet loaned me—Auden,
Walcott, and Yeats—and studying the page-worn books I borrowed
from the library at the high school where my grandmother taught—
Shakespeare and Spenser—hoarding in my mind every line that flashed
with a dazzling color or startling sound. When I returned the Hopkins
collection to the Old Poet, he immediately flipped through the pages to
see what marginalia I had left. Sheepishly I had scribbled some light notes
and underlined my favorite stanzas in pencil. I had been too nervous to
actually write in his book with ink.

"What is this?" he asked, flipping through the book.

My cheeks burned. "My notes, like you told me to do," I said.

The Old Poet went to his desk and got an eraser, then with all his weight on the page, started rubbing away all my penciled notes and underlines from his book.

"See how easily I erased this?" He showed me the clean pages, annoyed. "*Always* leave a permanent mark."

"Yes, sir."

My freedom was an intoxicating gift after years of being cooped up at home and the misery of St. James College. I burned my evenings at Grandma's house by recounting everything the Old Poet said during our meetings. I devoted daily practice to reading through the dictionary, gathering the meaning and root of each unknown word, gems clinking in my heavy sack. I treasured that collection, plucking up words as often as I could, adorning each poem with as many jewels as possible, assembling one sparkling garland after another. It was my first small escape, to spend so much time away from my father, and it was as if the roof of the world had blown open. Though I missed my siblings and my mother, I felt alive again with my hours and days mine alone to fill. Soon it was the Old Poet's voice that began replacing my father's, his thoughts reshaping the tenor of my days. I began to write from the spine, existing in the tremor of my most cardinal self. I slinked away upstairs after dinner to avoid Uncle Clive, passing long hours in my bedroom reading or writing new poems by candlelight. "You will spoil your eyesight," Grandma chided, pushing her thick glasses up on her face as evidence. But whole poems came to me at night, and I scribbled at a fury, chasing images and sounds and a deep wellspring of words. Sometimes when Uncle Clive shambled home late and turned up the television too loud, I could hear my grandmother amble downstairs to shush him. "Clive, Safiya is *writing!*" she would whisper, as if she were in church.

"I hate to think of you there in Spanish Town," the Old Poet told me once, after I described daily life with my grandmother.

"Why?" I asked him.

"It's just . . . not a place for someone like you," he said. "I can't imagine any art being made in such a place. Poetry requires a sacred space." My grandma had no internet and no computer, so whenever I was in

Spanish Town he called it "the Dark Ages," since all our communication was severed. Perhaps he imagined littered shantytowns and warring gangs like the nightly news portrayed, but to me, it wasn't that bad. It was Grandma's space, therefore it was a part of me. It had her warm mugs of Milo and her baked chicken and the familiar smell of camphor in every room. We watched *Jeopardy!* together and felt buoyed when we got the answers right. I never left the house enough to know that I was living in an artless place. All I needed was a room and a pen and some light to read at night.

The Old Poet made me memorize a poem every week. "The best way to really understand a poem is by embodying it," he said. I made a sacral vessel of myself, immaculate and vestal, as I recited poems for him alone. First, we started off easy, with short poems, Yeats and Hopkins, couplets and rhymes that grew easy in the mind and ribboned out of me as I held his gaze.

After my first recitation, he was impressed. For the first time since I met him, his lingering smile was one of genuine pride. I told him that my siblings and I had been memorizing and reciting poems with my mother since we were children. "Well, you should have said so from the beginning!" he said. After that he seemed to take my recitations as a challenge, assigning longer and more complex poems every week; three- and four-page poems of Walcott, Auden, and Stevens. One week, he asked me to recite Wallace Stevens' "The Idea of Order at Key West," a poem that swept me to the coastline as I stood before him and spoke:

> She was the single artificer of the world
> In which she sang. And when she sang, the sea,
> Whatever self it had, became the self
> That was her song, for she was the maker.

With each line, I felt the gentle rhythm of the water, calling me back to the seaside where I was born, where my mother had first taught me to read the waves like a poem. As the familiar music poured from me, the Old Poet nearly wept at my performance, misting over. When I was finished, he asked me to perform the miracle again at the workshop.

The workshop poets were all women two and three times my age, all of whom had come to poetry later in life and had sons older than my father. They were tender and unseen and marvelous women who had nursed their poems as a hobby until they finally answered the insurgent call in retirement. They were travel agents and journalists and librarians who spoke with the crisp English of rich Kingstonians and who joined in on frowning on my commute from Spanish Town. I was startled and intimidated by the lived maturity of their poems, as much as they seemed dizzied and tolerant of my own mythic imagination. But they were all natural aunties to my tremulous lamb, nurturing and cooing after my poems, even befriending me. There was nothing to do but to oblige the Old Poet, so I faced their eager smiles with "The Idea of Order at Key West" held flimsily in my head. Their faces beamed, sunflowers and satellites. I began. *"She sang beyond the genius of the sea. / The water never formed to mind or voice . . ."* When I was done, they all howled and applauded, then made the Old Poet promise that they wouldn't have to start reciting poems for him as well.

Where my father pressured clay onto an empty frame to build the perfect daughter in his own image, the Old Poet chiseled away at me, determined to perfect the poet within. Back at his desk we pored over my pages, parlaying over edits. There seemed to be no other world beyond this world. I marveled at his hands, which flew like wild swans when he spoke, as he challenged me about what a line meant, what I was really trying to say. "Dominate the poem without reducing it," he would tell me, his palms circling their large wingspan overhead.

So, I wrote him a poem from my heart. I brought it to workshop thinking no one else would know who I was addressing, but all the auntie-poets smiled slyly at me during our break and said, "So . . . you wrote a poem about the Old Poet," like it was some girlish rite of passage, which made me even surlier because the Old Poet had ignored it completely. My blush turned slowly into a bruise. The next time we were alone, I braved him about the poem.

"You had to write it, of course," he said. "But I won't discuss it."

"Why not?"

His mouth drew into a line.

"My worst fear is being written about," he said.

One afternoon he decided to drive me into Kingston to meet the taxi driver at a closer pickup spot, so I wouldn't have to "perish all that way to Spanish Town." His car was dated and ordinary, a very clean white Toyota Corolla. We continued our philosophical sparring of the day as he drove. After baking in the city heat, we stopped at a mall for refreshments. The Old Poet climbed out, and I sat with the quiet strangeness of myself, here, in an esteemed poet's car, grabbing juice. This must be the chapter before she falls, I thought. If my parents taught me anything, it was to keep watch for the next disaster at hand. Happiness was only a trick of the light. When the Old Poet returned to the car, he lingered by the driver-side window with our drinks in his hands. As I waited for him to get in, he leaned his head down by the half-wound window and cast a peculiar look at me.

"Now I know I can never marry you," he said.

My eyes went wide as a sky with rain.

"You didn't reach over and open my door for me."

I lurched my body over to his door and tried to pull the handle open.

"It's too late," he said, brushing my hand away. "The moment already passed. You can't change my mind now."

All night I replayed the moment in my bed at Spanish Town, punishing myself in the dim shadow of the kerosene lamp for not reaching out. Not because I wanted to marry him, not even because I was surprised by the suggestion of it, but because I didn't want him to see me as flawed. My scarlet mark turning to flint in my cheek.

We never spoke of it again, and I was glad. I'd hoped he would forget it entirely, so I could reach for his door another time. Later I confessed to him that I felt myself being pulled irrevocably toward some tragic fate. That I was doomed for a love so violently passionate that it would draw blood. That I longed to be taken apart entirely. How else would anyone know I was alive?

The Old Poet sighed. "Life is not like a novel, kid," he said.

But how else to explain this bright accumulation of days to a seventeen-year-old who exchanged words with one of the Caribbean's greatest minds? Did she not stand near the window of some momentous scene in her white georgette dress, waiting to enter the frame?

The ceiling fan wicked overhead, making ghosts of the curtains.

"Will you come and read to me?" the Old Poet asked, removing his glasses. "When I'm in the hospital?"

I searched his iron gaze and found he was sincere.

"I will leave some of my books to you in my will if you come," he said.

"Are you sick?" I asked, trying to seem calm.

"Not now," he said, "but it's inevitable."

He held my gaze as he looked into his future. I saw in his unguarded eyes an old man open for the first and only time.

Outside, the wind soughed through the trees that surrounded the yard.

"I will come and read to you. Of course I will come."

He nodded. Then the moment passed, almost imperceptibly, and he turned his gaze from me.

"You'll outgrow Plath eventually, you know," he said, his mouth now twisting back into a smile.

"Absolutely not." I shook my head.

"Trust me," he said. "Give it time. You'll find more substance in Emily Dickinson when you're older. She's the far greater poet."

I made a show of pouting and turned away from him.

"I think you will outgrow me, too, eventually," he said. I turned back to look at him. His face was ashen and quiet, resigned.

"Impossible," I said. I couldn't imagine it.

"You will see," he said, with finality.

But I could not see. For there was nothing then beyond the half-light of the afternoon filtering in through his window, each day held like a velvet petal in my mouth.

20

Dance of Salome

THE FREEDOM I HAD FOUND WITH the Old Poet was like a wildfire catching. I spent my days obsessing over ways to leave my father's house, his sharp gaze darkening the horizon. A whole year had burned away since I graduated high school, and though I regularly published my poems in the Sunday *Observer*, it became clear that my parents would never have a plan for me. I was petrified by the possibility that I might never leave this place. That my life would never change. I had seen my own mother try and fail to escape, even as her strength had pulled her as far as the gate. The Old Poet tried to steer me closer to him, encouraging me to apply to the University of the West Indies, the only major university in the Caribbean. But my parents simply could not afford the UWI tuition and weren't able to cosign the colossal bank loan needed for enrollment. With palpable sadness, my mother confessed the severity of the situation: that even if I got one of UWI's scholarships, which only covered tuition, they would not be able to afford my food or housing. Now the prospect of my solitude combusted with my ambition, and I was afraid. Since the day my father had traded in the red belt for the precise and indelible cruelty of his words, I lay awake most nights just longing for a moment of tenderness. There was the sad yet tacit truth of it: I dreaded the thought of finding myself back on that desolate hill, with a shard of glass held to my veins.

"If I have to stay here in Jamaica, I don't believe I will survive it," I confessed to the Old Poet one afternoon as we discussed my future. We never spoke much about my father during our meetings, but it was all there in my poems.

His eyes went dark as he listened. After a long pause, he said, "I think you're right."

As a new year began, I'd seen a new opportunity to escape, so I ran. With my back bending under the weight of my books, I sprinted to a model scouting event. A friend of my mother's had told her an agency was scouting for models not far from where my SAT prep classes were and insisted that she send me. "Her complexion too pretty not to send her," she told my mother, then pointed out how skinny I was: "Look how she mawga. She a born mogeller." My mother had looked to me, her face asking the silent question, and I had nodded. One way or another, I would make it out.

Three months earlier, I had asked her to enroll my brother and me in SAT classes so we could start preparing for American college applications. She asked me how she would afford to send us if we got in. "We will get scholarships," I told her. We both knew getting a full-ride scholarship was my only chance of leaving home. We'd discussed our financial situation and knew there was a narrowing road ahead. But they saved up what they could and paid the fees for me and Lij to go to SAT classes twice a week. And that afternoon, when my mother asked me if I wanted to go to the Saint International model scouting event, I had everything to gain.

Mom hired a taxi to speed me down to the hotel. The event was nearing its end by the time I climbed the stairs in search of the conference room, huffing under the weight of my books. I looked for any sign of beautiful people, any sign of hope. My sandals clopped hard against my heels as I raced down the hallway, counting off the lost minutes in my head. Judging by the time on my watch, I was too late. But I wished for some tenuous Jamaican punctuality. For most of my adolescence I had given up all interest in beauty or my appearance, after years of weathering the taunts boys lobbed at me and my sisters. I had even begun to believe it: that my body, under the banner of my dreadlocks, swathed in the cloth of my maker, was undesirable. Then I fixed my tooth and so many women, friends and acquaintances, began suggesting I go into modeling or enter beauty pageants. And now the door was in sight.

By the time I got to the conference room, the casting was over as I feared, and in front of the partially closed double doors stood a grimacing security guard.

"The event is over. The doors are closing," the security guard said, her fingers in the loops of her belt, next to a baton.

"Please, Miss, just let me try nuh?" I asked her, shifting on my feet, wiping the day's sweat and dust from my face.

The guard maneuvered her body to block my way.

"Okay," I sighed, as I turned to go. I started heading toward the waiting taxi with the weight of my homework still on my back.

"Wait!" I heard a man's sharpened voice ring out. "Security, stop that girl."

I was already halfway down the hallway, lost in the underworld of my own thoughts.

"Miss! Ey, Miss!" the guard now shouted to me. "Rasta girl, come back!" she called out.

I turned back to look.

At the entrance a slim, bright-eyed man beckoned for me to come back. He introduced himself as Deiwght Peters, beaming wide, radiating a reassuring warmth. He told me about the Saint International modeling agency, which he founded to celebrate Black beauty in the modeling industry worldwide. While he spoke, he circled me with a feline liquidity, sizing me up like a museum artifact. He moved unnervingly close and studied my face. I stood still and let him see me.

"You have a very unique look," Deiwght said to me, his eyes gliding over my dreadlocks, which were tied back with my favorite black ribbon and had now grown halfway down my back.

"We have to get you," Deiwght said as he looked at me, nodding yes to his hovering assistant. He looked at me and saw something that I had not yet seen for myself.

"Hold your head up for me," Deiwght said, positioning me against the makeshift white background along the conference room wall, gesturing quickly for his assistant, who was already bouncing toward us with the Polaroid camera. Deiwght positioned the lens on my face and I looked straight into the light.

I officially signed as a Saint model to the silent disapproval of my father, who pulled on his precept and looked to the ceiling as if calling on Jah. I don't know what magic my mother worked behind the scenes, but my father, with a brooding resignation, eventually agreed that I could try it. When I left for Kingston, I knew he was displeased, but he had carved out no other plan for me beyond escaping teenage pregnancy in high school—so I could either seize whatever opportunity arose or I could work in the hotels, an idea he rejected so vehemently that I was sure he must have known, and known intimately, what young, working Jamaican women did to survive in hotels, at the source of Babylon.

I went back to Grandma's house in Spanish Town to begin weeks of model prep all leading up to the Fashion Face of the Caribbean event in Kingston. Deiwght taught me to glide with one heeled foot in front of the other without ever looking down, to walk as if I owned the room. He taught me how to walk tall in all the things that made me singular. To appear both interesting and disinterested. To find the light wherever I went.

I became a many-limbed girl, a laughing cyclone moving in and out of the most beautiful clothes I had ever seen. Pants and sequined halters and ruffled dresses and stilettos. I reached for the fantasy of who I could be, draped in swan-lengths of tulle. The first time I wore makeup, the makeup artist stepped away to show me my face in the mirror and drizzled, "See? You barely need a thing, honey." I gazed out and my glistening face gazed back, somehow suddenly twice myself.

My body was a gift, but I didn't quite believe it, not until the Fashion Face of the Caribbean event. I looked out into the stage lights, bright as the moment of transfiguration, and sailed down that first runway as the crowd roared, cheering on the Rasta mogeller who smiled wide as the moon, lustrous and full under photoflashes that would anoint me in tomorrow's paper. I started to believe it then. Believed in my body, the thrum of its radiance, accepting its gift when Deiwght grabbed my beaming mother and shook her, saying, "*Your* daughter? She is one of the classics!"

That summer, when Rashmi, my friend from high school, called, I answered. Modeling, I discovered, was its own shimmering currency, and I relished clinking each new coin on this dipping scale. This time she didn't have to ask what I had been up to or pretend to be interested. "I hear you're a model now," she said with some jealousy, and described how her mother saved all my modeling photos from the newspaper to show her when she returned home from Miami.

I went over to see her then because I wanted to be seen. Now, as we chatted about my modeling, she brought out the clippings her mother had saved, the photo of me on the runway, incandescent. *Fashion Face of the Caribbean Top Ten*, it said. I towered in the column of the photo, a Technicolor girl too tall to see her feet, my smiling face painted for the gods, a bright wheel of stars in my eyes.

We spent the rest of the week hanging out. As MTV blared on in the background one day, I mentioned to Rashmi that I was also publishing poems in the newspaper.

"Oh god, you know I'm not smart enough for any of that!" She laughed. "I barely read."

Summer melted kisko-sweet and neon in my hands. My sisters and I stayed up many nights under a chittering moon, belting out our favorite Beatles songs as I painted their nails and recounted all my new adventures in modeling. Shari, who was now nine, had grown into a prize-winning dancer, and was eager to show me a new piece she had choreographed herself, along with the costumes she'd designed. At thirteen, Ife was already charting her own escape, revealing her plans to take a whopping thirteen CXC subjects in her final year, even though most students took no more than seven. Lij, who was fifteen, was our household's glory, now a famous debate champion; he had carried his high school to victory schooling baldhead boys every week on prime-time television. We were a coven of overachievers, outdreaming the confines of our small world.

When summer was over and my siblings were all back in school, I went back to Spanish Town, continuing my poetry sessions with the Old Poet half the week and showing up at castings all over Kingston the other half. Nighttime was still for poetry, and I spent the late hours at Grandma's house nibbling away at the dictionary while writing by lamplight. I carried my poetry notebook wherever I went. While waiting around at rehearsals I crouched over my pages, scribbling.

Meanwhile, the Old Poet scoffed at this ridiculous double life, telling me that modeling was a "terribly silly business," and I would soon get bored of this frivolous phase.

My father, on the other hand, had grown more militant while I was away in Spanish Town and said nothing at all of what I did in Kingston. He had started attending weekly Rastafari meetings that he called "reasonings," where a small circle of about a dozen Rasta bredren from around Montego Bay would meet at Tafara Products to have philosophical discussions about their livity. This was as close as the Rastafari came to a kind of church: men sitting around a drum circle, pulling on their precepts and chanting out the name of Haile Selassie I, decrying the state of systemic downpression for Black people in general, and the Rastaman in particular. Women, of course, were not invited. All the Rasta bredren in my father's circle viewed the world through the approval of the other Rasta breden. Whatever one Rastaman might think of his daughter also became my father's view, which became the other man's view of his daughter, and so on. They cultivated a fragile ecosystem of beliefs, each trying to outdo the other for who was most militant, whose daughter was most humble, their livity a tangle of roots without water. My father observed me with a reptilian quiet. Whatever he thought of modeling or poetry passed through the filter of my mother and arrived to me in Spanish Town cauterized or arrived not at all.

Yet, I wanted to believe that my body was a gift. At Grandma's house, for the first time since I had pulled on those jeans shorts in Cuba, I stepped again into that body, brandishing legs and midriff whenever I went out to Saint meetings, skipping through the sun in short-shorts and belly-skin shirts. I was learning how I wanted to be seen. My grandma raised no objection other than asking on a few occasions, "Saf, is that what you're wearing?" To which I would reply, "Yes, Grandma!" and hop into the chartered taxi. Some days I rifled through her barrel of vintage clothes from many waistlines before me, some falling apart and everything smelling of camphor balls, beautiful and ancient yards of gabardine and chiffon and cotton poplin. Her best clothes I kept and altered with scissors and basic needle and thread, transforming long librarian skirts into pleated teases as short as Britney's, turning old jeans into denim thigh-high boots, spinning chiffon scarves together into barely there shirts with floating sleeves, silk into angel wings.

One weekend my father rented a car and drove to town for a meeting with music producers in Kingston. On his way into Kingston, he stopped by Grandma's house to pick me up for a model casting not far from where he was headed. The casting call instructed us to dress for a music video that was "fun and young and sexy," so I spent the night creating an outfit from Grandma's old clothes. He honked impatient blasts from the horn and I walked out, trying to pretend I was bulletproof. My father's eyes bulged wide as I swooped into the car. "Oh, Rasta," he said, but not to me. He covered his hand over his mouth, his eyes darkening. We were told to come prepared to dance. I was wearing a very short pin-striped pleated skirt that I had cut from one of Grandma's old skirts, adorned with safety pins along the waist and hem like a punk. My fingernails were painted black, and I wore a pink spaghetti-strapped tank top that showed my black bra straps underneath.

He couldn't look at me. The words he did not utter simmered off him.

"Deiwght said I should dress for the brief, Daddy," I started explaining to him, my voice clear and not shaking. Being away had emboldened me. "It's a casting for a music video and they want the models to come dressed like they're on MTV." It was a dancehall video, but I thought that was better left unsaid.

My father and I arrived in Kingston under his arid silence, languishing in the dusty heat. After navigating the unfamiliar city roads for the better part of an hour, we pulled up late to the address of the casting. There was a large iron gate that opened onto a gravel driveway leading to a far house in the distance. I could see scores of brightly attired young people waiting on the veranda. Instead of turning in, my father stopped the car outside the gate, still not speaking to me. I waited. The path up to the house was long and rocky and would be perishing to walk in this heat. I turned to look at my father for the first time in two hours. He pointed out my window. "It's up there," he said. His hand stretched stiffly across my face as if this same hand had not made me.

"I can't walk all that way, Daddy," I said. "Can't you please pull in?"

My father took a long look at the people gathered in the distance. The people who he thought would gaze into the face of a Rastaman as I left the car dressed as I was.

He shook his head. "No."

I felt a deep jab inside my chest. I picked up my handbag and opened the car door, but before I climbed out, he turned to look at me.

"I'm ashamed of you," my father said.

I clutched the handle of my bag but couldn't look at him.

"Okay," I said. I wouldn't let him see me flinch.

I was prepared to dance. I got out of the car and started walking up the rocky driveway, my gaze straight ahead. I was surprised at how little I felt it at that moment, the old shame and longing for his approval. All those months I'd spent out from under his thumb had taught me something crucial. Nothing would deter me from where I was going, as long I could escape him. Ahead of me was a path I would make for myself, and I was ready for the dance. The building and its eyes in the distance emerged as I moved farther away from him, dust splattering my heels as I walked alone, one swift foot in front of the other.

By the time I arrived on American soil, Lower Manhattan was rubble and smoke in the aftermath of 9/11. The world had shifted on its axis and the American dream had lost so much of its sheen. I'd already weathered the shame of standing in line with hundreds at the US Embassy in Kingston to plead my case for a visa to a white man through bulletproof glass, all hope in my throat, waiting to touch the hem of Uncle Sam, rehearsing my story and watching to see who would be turned away, praying it wouldn't be me. I'd already weathered the guilt of my mother, who didn't hide her disappointment at the airport when she said, "I can't believe you're only seventeen and going to America before me." And when I finally touched Foreign, as Deiwght corraled us through the blue notes of the underground saxophone players and the zombic crush of the subway tunnels, a Black man told me, "God bless your hair, sister," while later in Barnes & Noble a white cashier laughed me out of line because she needed to wade through my accent. But I had made it out. I had made it out! I ran through the freezing streets of Brooklyn and rode in a yellow cab and walked into a store where I could buy five thongs for five dollars, so I bought ten. When I finally touched down in Miami four days later, clutching my portfolio in the sterile Wilhelmina Models office, surrounded by South Beach's finest glass windows and glass tables with all my glass hopes, sitting face-to-face with the famous one-named German model sighing sweetly over my photos, and her gaze halted at my dread-locks, I shouldn't have been surprised at what came next.

"Can you cut the dreads?" she asked me, her soft accent blunting the impact of the words. Draped in a crisp all-white outfit, she lifted her red frames to her hair as she looked at me.

If only it were that easy. Back in Kingston, the hairstylists would leave my dreadlocks untouched, tied up in a ponytail with my good black rib-bon, deciding the problem was unsolvable.

"Sorry," I stuttered, sinking into my chair. "My father won't allow me."

Before we met her, Deiwght told me she was "a living legend." Now in her sixties, she was quite striking, tall and lithe with cropped blond hair, but had let the Florida sun have its way with her skin.

She dropped her glasses back onto her nose and looked over at Dei-wght.

"It's her religion," he explained. "Her father is Rastafarian. Very strict."

"Oh," she said, leaning back in her chair. "That's a shame." She looked from my face to my portfolio photos again and smiled too politely. "The dreads just aren't versatile enough."

The road between my father and me was woven in my hair. Long spools of dreadlocks tethering me to him, across time, across space. Ev-erywhere I went I wore his mark, a sign to the bredren in his Rastafari circle that he still had his house under control. Foolishly, I had believed that my dreadlocks would make me one of a kind, since I'd never seen a model with locks. But this was a profession in which to be emptied of oneself, and I was still too much of him.

Later that night I recounted the disappointment of my agency visits on a long-distance call with my mother. The consensus was that I needed to cut my dreadlocks and lose weight in my cheeks, even though I was five foot nine and only weighed 108 pounds. The first thing I asked my mother when she got on the phone was if I could cut my locks, pressing my luck.

"Oh, Saf," she sighed. "I think you already know the answer to that one."

"Mom, I have no hope of doing this if I don't."

After a long pause she said, "I will see." Which meant she would go and talk to my father, as if she were setting a meeting with the pope. Despite all the rebellion I now tended, I knew cutting my dreadlocks was a point of no return: I would never be allowed back under his roof if I did it. It hadn't even crossed my mind to cut them without his approval. At seventeen, that was still one step too far to cross alone. Whatever discussion passed between my parents, I never knew, I only received the denial through my mother's rose vine as she returned to the handset, sweetened and softened for me to receive it.

I asked her if I could visit my auntie Audrey, who was now only a short drive away in Fort Lauderdale. It had been almost thirteen years since I had last seen her and my cousin Jason at White House, and if I didn't see them with my one-month visa now, I might never get another chance. "Maybe I can extend my plane ticket and go see them?"

"NO!" The blast of my father's voice boomed suddenly in my ear.

The phone slipped from my palm. He'd been eavesdropping on my call with Mom. Even here, across the ocean, I could not be myself. His reach followed me like a tentacle, roped tight around my waist to drag me back. My wish to stay longer shriveled lifeless in my hands.

"I man knew you were trying to run away."

"No I wasn't!"

"Don't lie to me, girl," he said. "Yuh think I man don't see the I getting caught up in the wiles of Babylon?"

My ears burned as he spoke. I had no intention of running away. It hadn't even occurred to me until now that some might stay here illegally. My father's vexed certainty gave more of himself away than it did me.

"Don't you dare try to stay in America," he yelled. My mother's voice had disappeared from the line completely.

"You get back on that plane and you come home, you hear me, girl?"

It didn't matter that I was always going to come back home, because he didn't believe it. My hands shook. I longed to sever the line, longed to sever all of what made me immobile, all of what came from his world and restrained me. Even as I found myself assuring him, promising him, I realized the sad truth of it. If I stayed in Jamaica, I would never escape him.

21
Leaving Sequestra

Y BODY WAS MY FATHER'S AGAIN. He forbid me from cutting my dreadlocks as the modeling agencies wanted, so those faraway foreign hopes snapped shut like a shell. This, it seemed, was my first failed escape. I was not yet eighteen. The hair on my head belonged to him and to Jah, and therefore my body belonged to the Rasta bredren in his circle. I had no choice but to return home. The Old Poet, who had been advising me to give up modeling and concentrate on my poetry, was pleased. Now my mind belonged to him again. Once again, I found myself in his study one Saturday afternoon.

It was June, in the restless maw of summer, and everything nursed the need of everything else. The fruit ripened recklessly, perfuming the air with orange trees, overripe jackfruit sweating like men, and the soft, purpling blush of the star apple, beckoned. On the blazing streets and in the privacy of kitchens came the suck of fresh water through jelly, sugarcane juice licked clean from sticky hands. In every Jamaican house, green lizards and soldier ants darted in and out of open windows, pressing their pale tails and feelers through holes and crevices, warm nights gathered owl-moths in the hungry web of the Anansi. Everywhere we dreamt with the heat boiling our blood unruly, a bushfire of impolite bodies.

Around the Old Poet's garden, an unseen net of honeybees and dragonflies thrummed from every unruly vine, and I sang that week's recitation like a wind turning through the slutty trees. *Had we but world enough and time, / This coyness, lady, were no crime.* I'd been tasked to recite Marvell's "To His Coy Mistress" for the Old Poet, and held for days the roguish words like water in my head, *My echoing song; then worms shall try / That long-preserved virginity, / And your quaint honour turn to dust, / And into ashes all my lust,* until I stood sweetly before him and bid the words gush out. He listened in the creeping heat with a sated quiet, occasionally closing his eyes and mouthing along with me, *My vegetable love should grow / Vaster than empires and more slow.* His favorite line, he told me later. When I was done emptying the words into his mouth, he asked me to do it again, so I did.

"Do you understand it?" he asked, peering over his glasses into my face. Outside the whir of the bees and the red-legged thrush pushed in.

"Yes," I said. "I guess men from the olden days were no different than now. They all want the same thing."

"You're right about that," he said.

We combed through the poem again, retreading the words relentlessly line by line until I grew tired of Marvell's pleading, until I felt his mistress's coyness becoming mine.

After my recitation lesson we worked on polishing my poem "Silver." The Old Poet slid the pointer across the screen, adding caesuras and deleting lines, questioning and rearranging my stanzas. Time slipped into a humid fog as we clicked back and forth, passing the mouse between us. The day's heat pressed in all afternoon, beading our bodies to sweat inelegantly, making us aware of our warmest parts. "This may be your best poem," he told me, as we read over the finished result.

I thought of myself back on the littered hillside of Bickersteth, the broken glass clutched at my wrist, the helpless words breaking over me.

"I have something to tell you," I told him.

"Does it end with you being wildly fucked by a lake under moonlight?"

My mouth swung open, and I caught myself. He smirked.

"No." I was seventeen, and had never even kissed anyone, much less anything else.

"Then I don't want to hear it," he said, and disappeared into the kitchen. My mind rang from the shock of the words. That visceral picture flashed hot behind my eyes, and I forgot what I was going to tell him anyway.

As I turned back to "Silver," his words kept ringing. My body sticky with the murmuring unrest threatening to break in. *But at my back I always hear / Time's wingèd chariot hurrying near.* I surged on, face lit by the glow of the screen. Suddenly a shock of cold pressed at my back. I jumped in my chair. Behind me, the Old Poet held an icy glass of water against my exposed shoulder. Instinctively, I did not move.

When I was eleven, I had learned something crucial about danger. Back at the old yard in Farm Heights where we'd eaten the green cherries, I once climbed the June plum tree alone, clutching the crux of branches, and roosted under their shade. I rested that way until a large bee zagged down and landed on my face. Before I panicked, I reasoned with myself. I was too high up to fall without injury, and any sudden movements would cause the bee to sting me. Above, I spotted another bee crawling along the tree's green, unmoving trunk and saw that it did the tree no harm. So, I decided to make a trunk of myself. No fussing, no moving, simply becoming imperceptible. The bee crawled over my face, across my lips, its furry legs tickling my nose. I stayed that way for several minutes, entwined with tree and bee, not moving, until the bee had tracked pollen all across my face and flew away, leaving me unstung.

As the Old Poet pressed the cold glass to my shoulder, I stayed still as I was in that June plum tree. The vagrant hiss of the garden growing louder now as he slid the glass across the middle of my back.

"That's so cold!" I said finally, too loudly, hoping he would get the hint. Here in the Old Poet's house, where I sat for countless weeks before, the heat had now shifted into something unbecoming. I retraced my steps, my looks, my words, trying to scan for the turn of climate in his office.

He peeled the glass from my back and placed it on the desk next to my hand. When it made a soft thud against the wood of his desk, I realized his helper was not at home.

"I brought you some water," he said, sliding his hands across my mine.

"Oh, thank you," I said, feigning surprise. I could see he already drank from the glass. There was a white glob of food residue on the rim, which disgusted me. I looked away and did not drink.

The Old Poet sighed. "I can see you don't want to drink after me, eh?" he said, looming above as I sat in his chair, at his desk, alone in his house. "I'm not carrying plague, you know."

"I know," I said. I picked up the glass and took the smallest sip of water to appease him. The noisome heat and my discomfort deafening. My recitation still lapping my head like a river. *Had we but world enough—*

The Old Poet spun my chair around to face him, grabbed my face with his hands, and smashed his lips into mine. I recoiled, but there was nowhere to go from his large grip, so I let my body go limp, dead as the brass knob of his front door. His face was cold and prickly from a morning shave, his folds of skin rubbery and foreign, swallowing my face. Behind the heave of his body, the office door. The hallway. Then the living room. Through the front doors. Then the gate. I followed the way back but could not move. My arms were straw, useless at my sides like my old Raggedy Ann doll, unspooled button-eyes and all her good stuffing torn out. It was not how I imagined my first kiss would feel, cold and dead with my eyes counting every overgrown hair on his nose, his alien face smothering me. I fixed my eye on the slow crack emerging from the wall behind him and waited for it to end. He pressed at my lips and the garden's hiss was deafening. I knew the exit was behind him but I could no longer see it, so I watched the crack in the corner of the wall where something nasty had surfaced, black archangel or giant horsefly, and did not move.

When it was over I said nothing. He peeled his face away from mine and I gulped for air. As he rose from me his smile was gorged so full that I wondered if this was what all the kisses in my life would be like. My body had already been emptied of itself, my girlhood vanishing through the door without me. When the taxi pulled up and I walked out the gate, I heard nothing but that unholy hiss—not Marvell's poem or the broke beat of my own ragged heart—only the cold stamp of the Old Poet's glass against my back, marking me.

It was years before I revisited that ugly afternoon, and when I did, I could only do it on the page. It was longer still before I ever said a word to anyone. I stuffed the afternoon inside my seams and carried it around in silence, fretting over getting the Old Poet in trouble. His grand reputation on my silver hook. I agonized over the idea of our poetry sessions ending, and the dark unfutured days that would again lay ahead for me.

I worried that no one would believe that I had done nothing to invite it, least of all my father. No one would believe that it had not started out this way, that it had been pure, once. Hadn't it been pure, once? I convinced myself I needed his lessons more than my crooked shame would haunt me, and found myself on the threshold of his door again. There I walked the tightrope of my body and tried not to do anything at all that might possibly be tantalizing. Even though, last time all I had done was sit in his chair. But, something had shifted for me. I reasoned with myself and made excuses, pushed the odd feeling away, and kept on as if nothing *that bad* had happened, until some picture or memory or poem would stir that afternoon to the surface of my mind like mud in a clear pond, even months or years later.

As for the Old Poet, his world kept spinning on its golden axis. He never mentioned that afternoon and left me alone to myself. A few months after my eighteenth birthday, he published "Silver," and I felt anointed. The Old Poet chose my work for global anthologies, praising me as "an extraordinary eighteen-year-old from Mobay who reads the dictionary for pleasure." He called me "the baby" of the workshop but published more of my poems than anyone else's in the group, once even publishing the poems of my two younger sisters under the banner "Three Sisters, Three Muses." He arranged for my first reading as a co-headliner alongside him and two other esteemed Caribbean poets, men more than three times my age, reading to a packed crowd of over a hundred in a Kingston auditorium. My silver spread wide on every tongue. Another writer published an Op-Ed in the paper titled "In Praise of Safiya Sinclair," to my mother's screams of delight and even a "Praise Jah" from my father. "Silver" won the second prize at the *Jamaica Observer* Annual Literary Awards, making me the youngest person to ever win in those awards. I knew that the Old Poet had a hand in choosing the prizes, and briefly wondered why I was only second.

My mother took the four-hour drive from Mobay to attend the *Observer* award ceremony. She seemed so delighted to be free with me here in Kingston with the hors d'oeuvres and wine being passed around, which she sipped all night as she slipped into easy conversation and fast company, laughing with the other writers and auntie-poets and editors as if it were the most natural thing in the world to her. She had twisted my dreadlocks that afternoon for the event, and I tied my hair up in a large black ribbon, which matched the black sleeveless beaded dress that barely reached my thighs.

When the Old Poet wove his way through the crowd to greet us, he already smelled of rum. He was sweating under a black blazer and I realized this was the first time I'd seen him dressed up and playing host. I felt a secret thrill that I was as tall as him in my heels. When I reached in to hug him hello, he slipped his hand up my dress, grabbed my thigh, and whispered in my ear, "Finally, you're done with the prudish bullshit." He winked at my mom, who did not hear him, exchanged loud pleasantries with her, and was gone.

I looked at my mother, but her face registered none of the shock that must have clouded mine. I pulled her aside.

"Did you see that?" I asked her.

"No, what happened?"

I told her what the Old Poet did. What he said.

Her face twisted into disgust as I told her, and she shook her head, turning to find him in the crowd. She ran her hand down my arm. Then her eyes glossed over with a dark wine-calm, a wordless faraway look, and she shook her head. She waved her hand between us, as if shooing away the thought like a gingy-fly.

"Don't pay him any mind, sweetheart," she said to me over the loud chatter of the room. "He was just acting crazy because he was drunk."

I frowned at her. "That doesn't make it okay."

"No. But that's how all men act when they're drunk. Just try to avoid him for the rest of the night," she said. She was passing down something about the world to me just then—the world as she found it and survived it, ever since her mother died. She'd been trying to escape for a long time. Not just the man who had grabbed her on the bicycle as a child, or the street louses she had to fight off on her way home from school, but eventually the advances of her own grandfather from whose drunken fondling she ran away. This she would only tell me about years later. The world that sent her running and hiding from unwanted hands and mouths and tongues was the same one I now moved through—and she expected nothing but the worst from men.

I shrugged and nodded a faint "Okay, Mom," then pressed that ugly afternoon further down into silence before glancing over at the Old Poet and rejoining the crowd.

By the time I was eighteen, "Silver" was the radiant star divining my days. My poems had been inducted into the Jamaica Archives, and I was asked to deliver a guest lecture to the department of Literatures in English at the University of the West Indies on becoming a writer. If I had never imagined myself as a writer before, this invitation etched it indelibly. Imagining college students and professors waiting for something wise and beautiful to come from me, still unmatriculated, filled me with dread. I spent the days agonizing over my lecture and emailed the Old Poet to tell him I was terrible with beginnings. *I know how to end things*, I wrote. *I just never know where to start.* He wrote me back within the hour and said, *Here's your first line*: *"When I first heard that I was asked to speak here today, I had a moment of unreality."*

That's where I began, as I stood in front of the most attended Friday class the department ever had, the classroom flanked by students and gray-haired poetry profs and bright-eyed members of the public. My mother was in the front row, clucking and puffed feather-proud alongside the auntie-poets from workshop. Next to her was my new friend, Ann-Margaret, another young poet about ten years older than me that the Old Poet had recently added to our workshop. "Now you have someone your age to be foolish with," he said. My father, who had driven us to Kingston, was not there. He had meetings with more Kingston musicians, he'd said.

What an odd thing it was, an audience so attentive to every word that I tended, watching my thoughts come alive in their faces. "Why do I write?" I asked the crowd, catching my mother's eyes but unable to look at all in the Old Poet's direction. "For me, the question seems synonymous with *Why do you breathe?* The answer is simple . . . I write because I have to. It is as natural and as uncontrollable as my heartbeat. Sometimes it *is* my heartbeat, my very essence and survival."

I looked down from the lectern now into the pleased-as-puss smirk of the Old Poet, his lips curling with something like pride. "As *someone* once said to me, a poem is a thing . . . a cathedral of sound and imagery, and writing a poem is often like having the wind of some great power rush through you. I always find myself empowered, a mortal on the other side, with verses of immortality." When the audience applauded, I felt taller than I'd ever been on any photoshoot, locking my gaze then with my mother, whose dark eyes glistened, overcome.

An English prof then opened up the lecture for audience questions, and a strange Rastaman in the audience was the first to take the mic.

He stared me down with one palm out, as if he was begging. "Gimme some of the silver, deh," he said.

My mother gasped.

The university crowd chattered in dismay, a ripple of anger and confusion churning over the gathering.

"Pardon me?" I asked him, shaken, but trying to give the man some space to clarify. Perhaps this was his way of asking me to read my poem.

"Gimme some of the silver, deh!" he asked me again, his graveling voice almost like a plaintive song, now with both of his hands outstretched.

After this second plea, Gwyneth, my favorite of the auntie-poets, took the mic from the man's hands, as two big UWI students escorted the Rastaman out.

"Gimme some of yuh silver, deh!" I heard him still shouting as he was being ushered down the hallway.

The Old Poet, who had taken my silver without asking, rose and apologized to my mother for the inappropriate question, cracked a joke to reset the rhythm, then the Q&A went on without further incident. Even after he was gone, I heard the Rastaman asking me for silver, and I wondered if his desire would have ever been sated with just a poem. Days later, I still heard his melodic plea, long after the gravel of his voice was gone.

That night after my lecture, and before we made the long drive back to Montego Bay, the Old Poet invited me and my parents over. He had a gift for me, he said. My parents arrived at Sequestra bearing a bag of fresh fruits, which was always their way of repaying someone who had done an invaluable service for our family. In the face and height of the Old Poet, my father was almost deferent, his voice softening as he spoke, his personality becoming almost unbearably affable, as it always did whenever he met a successful Caribbean elder. We walked into the Old Poet's living room, where my mother marveled at his books, her face mirroring my own reaction the day I had first entered, right down to the "Wow!" The Old Poet led us to the rattan couch, where my parents sat quietly, listening as the Old Poet and I talked over the day's lecture.

My parents looked so small there under the Old Poet's high ceilings, and so foreign, in this house where I spent almost two years becoming more of myself. Beyond them was the office, and I was grateful that it remained out of sight.

"I'm gifting you a book from my library," the Old Poet told me, as the ceiling fan whirred overhead. His original test passed, at last. "Pick any one you want."

"That's so irie, sir," my father said. "Give thanks."

I vaulted out of the couch and scanned his bookshelves, Penguin Classics and old leather-bound volumes and matching sets from the Library of Congress. As I pored over the choices, my parents and the Old Poet traded nice words about me, a rope of pearls I was secretly coveting.

My mother and father watched as I made my choice, pulling the book off the shelf. "This one," I said. I'd been eyeing it for quite some time. *The Canterbury Tales* by Geoffrey Chaucer.

"You don't make it easy on yourself, do you?" The Old Poet smirked. My parents laughed. "No, she doesn't," my mother said, as a point of fact.

The Old Poet walked us out to the driveway where we exchanged goodbyes. Before I slipped through the iron gate of Sequestra for the last time, he hugged me and gave me a quick peck on the cheek. My mother and I got in the car and he waved at us. "Drive safely."

Once we were in the car, my father slammed his door and peeled away in silence. As we turned out of the quiet of the Old Poet's neighborhood, my father sped up and swung the steering wheel wildly, his hands flying off the wheel, sending the car fishtailing down the dimly lit street. My mother looked over at him from the front seat, but he didn't look back. I could not read the thunder that darkened his face. There was no music. Only the wind pummeling through the open windows as he careened down the street. Mom looked up to the ceiling and closed her eyes as the current lashed through her hair. By the time my father screeched onto the main road, my mother and I were clinging to our door handles and seat belts. I scanned the moments behind us for meaning. I was completely stunned by this implosion of his mood. He'd just been smiling in the Old Poet's driveway and now he looked possessed. We sped down the freeway, darting in and out of the lane of cars, my father occasionally lifting his hands from the steering wheel and holding them out, as if ready to take flight. I was terrified. The careening motion flung my body from side to side in the back, straining painfully against my seat belt. I looked up to my mother again, wishing she would say something in the face of this madness. But she said nothing as her hair whipped her face, and so I spoke, finally.

"Daddy!" I screamed, the harsh freeway wind battling my voice. "Can you please slow down!"

Calmly, so calmly, as if he were readying himself to pray, my father closed his eyes and swung the steering wheel again, swerving the car. Then he looked straight at me in the rearview mirror.

"Did the Old Poet just kiss you on your mouth?" he asked me, his voice calmer than the dark furrow of his face, collapsing into his scar.

My eyes splayed wide.

"No! He didn't, Daddy," I pleaded, shocked at the question, my heart thundering as I spoke, thinking of that day in the office, pushing it further away.

"Then what did I just see, girl?" he asked me, his foot pressing hard on the gas, his hand slapping the wheel. My mother's body juddered into the side of her seat.

I knew it then by the way he asked. We were over the edge now. If a truck tore toward us on this highway, he would let it flatten us. If some deep ravine appeared wayward out of the night, he would sail us out into its depths.

"He kissed my cheek, Daddy! My cheek." My voice wavered, and not because of the one-hundred-mile-per-hour winds battering my face, but because I realized that I should have expected this. That my father had offered the Old Poet deference and fawning smiles and saved his anger only for us, just as he sang like a prince to the tourists every night, then brought back his worst self to our family. My mother, gone as limp as I had been that scorched afternoon in Sequestra, let her body be shaken from side to side as the car roared forward.

I looked at him and did not know this man. It was not just my obedience he wanted, but something much more lethal. How far would he go now to scald me clean? My panic melted away to resignation that this terror would never end. Not even if I pleaded. He pressed his foot into the gas again, and my innards ached, queasy, my shoulder smarting from being thrown.

"I man don't want you going over to his house again," my father said. He slammed his fist against the steering wheel and swung. "You hear me?"

Yes, I said. Yes. Hoping in vain that this would make him stop. But in the neon scream of traffic, as the braying wind tore tears from my eyes, there was nothing else left in me. I let my body soar as my mother did hers, closing my eyes and floating elsewhere, letting the wind and the night and his anger take us—home or wherever else he planned for us to go.

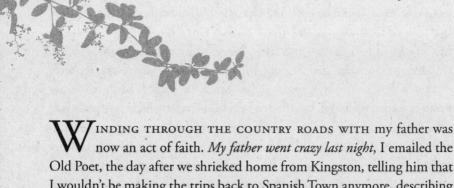

22
Coven

WINDING THROUGH THE COUNTRY ROADS WITH my father was
now an act of faith. *My father went crazy last night*, I emailed the
Old Poet, the day after we shrieked home from Kingston, telling him that
I wouldn't be making the trips back to Spanish Town anymore, describing
my father's reaction to what he thought he saw between us. *He was more
upset than I've ever seen him*, I wrote. The Old Poet's response came back
in that unruffled blue font, cavalier and unconcerned. *Your dad is of a very
different generation than me*, he wrote. *He will always need something to
rage against.* The way the Old Poet dismissed the whole event startled me.
His response made my father seem so pitiful. Not the god of anything. By
and by my father began appearing to me the way the world must've seen
him: an emperor denuded.

He had always been ruler of the house and there we were at his mercy.
But now that we lived up in the hills and he had his own car, he was
ruler of the road, and we were subject to his whims and his rage. Any
disturbance or disobedience now had him threatening to throw our lives
over into the ravine, while he drove leaden-footed down the murderous
unrailed gully at Long Hill, or blared, red-eyed with his hands flying off
the wheel in the middle of downtown Mobay. This unnerving darkening
of his spirit coincided, in my mind, with the arrival of a Rastaman who
styled himself Jahdami, whom my father met at one of his weekly reasonings at Tafara Products, and with whom his paranoia seemed most dangerously combustible. In the months following their meeting, my father's

temper became only more nefarious, slowly dragging my family down a path of devastation we are still reeling from, even now.

Perhaps my father had felt his influence dwindling after my brief modeling career and two years spent under the Old Poet's instruction, for what hold he still had over my sisters and me he clutched at ravenously, fastening the rope tighter around when we could leave the house. Which it turned out was never. Before my father had a car, he would only allow us to ride alone in the taxis he had chartered, with taximen he had vetted. But now he took sole control of our movements, shuttling us from home to school and SAT classes and back. None of us, including my mother, could drive. So when his car pulled out of the grassy driveway, we were exactly where he knew we would be. Stuck in amber. Meanwhile my brother zipped up and down the road on his bicycle, which my father had taught Lij to ride, but not the rest of us. It was unbecoming for a Rasta-woman to part her skirt and mount a bicycle. On weekends my brother took the country bus or public taxi into Mobay to hang with his school-friends or his first girlfriend. "Just be safe, Fyah," my father told him, dapping my brother's fists to celebrate his new brown-skinned girlfriend. "Protect yourself, Tafari," he said, "and don't get her pregnant." My sisters and I could only fold our skirts and look on at his rich teenage life.

Soon I buried all hope of ever leaving the dusty snow globe of Bick-ersteth. Once you turned off the main country road and entered the vil-lage, time and neglect settled like long-ago dust over everything, where the villagers inherited the odd country phonetics of the last two genera-tions, which over a century had gradually warped the name of their own town to "Bakerstep." And so we woke up each morning in a home that did not quite exist, dreamt up in a viscous tongue. When my chance to leave as a model slipped through my hands, I could tell my sisters wore my disappointment as their own. I was eighteen, Ife was fourteen, and Shari only nine. We three spent our time together wishing we were free from the confines of Rastafari, free to be ourselves. Without being taunted on the street, without being cowed at home. It had been a year since the Old Poet had pressed his face into mine, and six months since my father had barreled us down the highway. As the weeks galloped past, my father grew more extreme in his beliefs, spurred not only by his weekly reasonings with Jahdami and the other Rasta bredren in his circle, but by a labyrinth of disinformation he found on the internet, where he had become ensconced in conspiracy theories about lizard people and the Illuminati, all the proof he had been desperately seeking; that Babylon had a global master plan to destroy the Rastaman. And his daughters. Sometimes I would hear him recounting his conspiracies to my mother, who listened on—in feigned interest or quiet alarm, I could never tell. She had no email address and little desire to use the internet, it seemed, keeping her hands occupied with hours of housework instead. She was usually so tired at the end of each day that she fell asleep on the couch before the clock struck seven. When my sisters and I were alone, Ife, who was a star student of science and logic, would handily dismantle each of my father's irrational declarations, calling it "Jah Jah brainwashing," while Shari and I cackled along. Together we formed a coven that my father could not infiltrate, conjuring the women we wanted to be in the world.

My father closed his fist tighter and tighter around us until he was the overseer of all our days. Babylon would not pollute the purity of his daughters any longer. At Bickersteth we nursed on solitude without solace, like all girls forbidden from the world. We became reluctant shut-ins, my sisters and I, our daisied hours spent reading and embroidering, sighing languidly from behind our curtains as we watched the slow drama of the country road pass by. Marl-dusted workmen guffawing, the shiny car parked next door blasting Celine Dion's entire song catalog every evening, and schoolgirls our age, dancing up and down the street glowing a sun-shower of sins we ached to be under. We gathered our understanding of the world from books, the internet, and cable television, and formed an unbroken circle around what we all liked and what we didn't—our songs, our poems, our oneself dependent on each other.

Soon there was the only slow crawl of history directing our days. We wove bougainvillea and pink ixoras in our dreadlocks and called ourselves dryads. Ife taught herself Elvish, and sang out to the heavens so beautifully, the world stopped in its tracks to listen. Shari saved a baby chick from the farm supply store, named her Chicky, and trained her to eat the mice multiplying quietly under our floorboards. I cradled my sisters' heads in my hands and showed them how to tweeze their eyebrows, how to paint geometric shapes on our nails. I drew charcoal portraits of my family, presenting them as gifts each time someone had a birthday. Almost a year passed this way. My sisters went into the world for school, but I was pinned in place, aching for the loss of the freedom I had only glimpsed, slowly forgetting how to fly. Our mother, when she was not with us, began privately tutoring the children of a local businessman several days a week. Day after day we waited, for nothing, for everything to happen.

I had almost surrendered to the river of nothingness when the letter arrived. Returning from running errands one static afternoon, Mom handed me the heavy envelope with interest. It had been nearly a year since I communicated with the outside world, and any contact now seemed its own kind of magic. I tore open the package and gasped as I read. Addressed to me at White Sands Beach Post Office was a letter from the 2003 Global Young Leaders Conference, inviting me to represent Jamaica at a meeting of politically minded young people in Washington, DC, and New York City that summer, which was only in a few months. I was chosen based on academic excellence via my SAT score, which I'd received the year before. Mom screamed as I read the letter out loud to her, rapid-fire and disbelieving. "It's a ten-day trip," I squealed. "It says I get to go to the UN! And the Department of State!" We didn't quite know what the Department of State was, but it sounded rather important. "Oh, my girl," Mom said, holding my hands and spinning me. "You are amazing."

Buried in the letter was the fine print regarding the cost, and our joy was short-lived. I had been awarded a partial scholarship, but the remaining cost of the GYLC trip was more than four months' rent for my parents. "I have to go, Mom," I pleaded. The dangled promise of leaving was almost too much to bear. "I have to." Her eyes lowered and she looked away from me, even as she promised, "I will do my best."

By May the deadline to send in my conference registration arrived, and I stayed in bed and wept. My mother came home and nudged her head at my door. "You're going," she told me, and smiled. She conjured it, somehow. Grandma had given some, a concert promoter who wanted to see a young Jamaican girl at the UN had given some. And then she mustered up some courage and asked the local businessman whose children she had been tutoring, to help her. After listening to her trembling petition, he said nothing at all. "He just gave me the whole amount in cash," Mom said. "I burst into tears when he handed it to me."

"It's going to happen for you, love," she said, squeezing her copper warmth into my hands. "No matter what."

Hand in hand we both approached the reinforced plexiglass window at the US Embassy and handed the white man the 2003 Global Young Leaders Conference invitation. My mother's voice quivered when she explained that she would like to accompany me on the trip. The last time she had applied for a visa she was eighteen, and she had been denied, flung through the revolving exit of shame. Now at the terrifying window again, she performed the speech we practiced, detailing why she needed to travel with me. "My daughter and I have a symbiotic relationship," she explained, brandishing her favorite word like a new dress, and the agent laughed.

He stamped our applications and handed us a blue slip.

Before we turned toward the door, my mother reached into her bag and pulled out a copy of *Rocking You*. Her hands shook as she slid it under the agent's window. "As a thank-you," she said, bowing her head. "This is my husband Djani's album." Surely, my father must have put her up to such a humiliating gesture. Her submission infuriated me.

The agent slid the CD back to her with a smile and said, "We're not allowed to accept gifts."

She ran to catch up with me, and I couldn't be angry as we passed arm in arm through the shiny glass doors.

Less than a month later, we were in Foreign, twirling side by side until my mom and I separated for the duration of the conference. I jingled along the patriotic trail of American history the conference had laid out for me. I inspected the crack in the Liberty Bell, ascended the Empire State Building, and sailed around the Statue of Liberty at sunset with my fellow young leaders. America told a beautiful fable of itself. I shook hands with a white man who cried about his quest for peace in Myanmar. I slept in a college dorm with a white roommate who said she only needed to shower every other day. During the day we practiced speeches on the floor of the UN, while I begged my peers not to spoil *The Order of the Phoenix* for me until I could buy the book. At night I jotted down

my poems and cried. I wished to meet a boy my age who understood the
nature of my loneliness. And my poetry. My emails to the Old Poet grew
sparse, and the time spent away from him only brought me clarity, and
well-worn shame.

After so much time spent shut inside at Bickersteth, I had nearly
forgotten it—that there was a whole world out there just waiting for me
to make something of it. Looking back, it is hard to believe how easily I
slipped into my hope again, as I walked wild-eyed through the streets of
Foreign once more, thankful for this second temporary escape, breathing
free and not thinking of my father waiting across the sea.

I spent the last day of the conference at the National Mall exploring
all those grand and dazzling museums. I crossed from building to building and dashed from room to room, trying to remember every detail,
pressed deep in beeswax, to describe to my siblings later. Spaceships and
planets, prehistoric skeletons, I cataloged in my mind everything Lij or
Ife or Shari would have loved to see. Strolling the long corridors of the
Smithsonian in amazement and in guilt, I longed for them. I turned the
corner of a quiet exhibit and collided with my mom, who had been staying with a family friend and with whom I could only communicate by the
landline at the conference hotel. We squealed and jumped in each other's
arms to the alarm, then delight, of onlookers. She had been shadowing
my itinerary in DC all week, but we had missed each other at each loca-
tion. And as we stood here together, dwarfed under the marble columns
and mammoth bones, we marveled at the surreality of being here together
at all. This was Mom's first trip to America, and she experienced all of it
like a candy she let dissolve slowly on her tongue, savoring the most minute details she would recount to me years later.

"Do you know there is something called space ice cream?" she asked.

We turned hand in hand about the towering halls of the dinosaur exhibit, stopping to observe and admire every beautiful and ancient thing.

"Yes," I said, having also been to the National Air and Space Museum
earlier in the day. "Did you try it?"

Mom nodded and opened her purse, showing me the many silver
packets of space ice cream she had bought for my siblings. Then she
sealed her eyes shut. "I didn't think any of it was true, you know," she
said. "Men in outer space. Rockets. Walking on the moon."

"Mom, what—?" I unlinked my arm from her.

"Sorry to say. I didn't think it was real until I saw the rockets for my-self." Her voice was tender and humble, bargaining, the tone she leaned on whenever I was too impatient with her.

We slowed our pace now as I listened to her describing all she had learned at the National Air and Space Museum, her words almost ringing off the walls with excitement. I looked around to make sure none of my GYLC peers were nearby. I tried not to get frustrated, as I often did, with the startling naïveté of my forty-year-old mother. I wanted her to walk through the world with the same certainty as I did, but that was not who she was, and there was no shame in her to show it.

"I didn't know what to think!" she told me, her gaze widening as we stood in the shadow of the tyrannosaurus. "For a long time I believed him, that it was all Babylon's propaganda."

"Mom, please stop." My temper simmered as she spoke. I wanted to clasp my hand over her mouth and smother all these senseless words. We promised ourselves when we got off the plane that we wouldn't talk about my father. He had a way of overshadowing everything that was inescapable.

Despite myself, I could feel my anger rising as I listened to her now, fueled by my own shame. This day, long coming, had finally arrived: The roles between us had reversed. Years ago, mother and child had blurred, crossing each other under some ancient arch where she emerged as the one in need of teaching in my impatient hands. I pulled away from her again and pouted.

"How was I to know?" she asked me, as if asking for clemency. "How could I have known? That he was wrong."

She needed someone to bear witness to what she had discovered, not about the world, but about herself. And him. So I listened. She squeezed my arm again to calm me, then linked her elbow back inside of mine. We continued walking along the radiant hallways, dwarfed under the vast ceiling and wide-as-a-river rooms, while she unreeled a frantic retelling of the world she was exhuming. I rested my head on her shoulder as she talked. It finally struck me then. This was her first time stepping out-side the bubble of Rastafari on her own since she went up into the hills with my father at nineteen. It was its own kind of wonder to behold, her moment of emergence. Her eyes were luminous as she talked, awareness unfolding like a petal after water. She could see it now, the world beyond my father.

"Thank you," she whispered to me. She laughed, and I laughed along with her. And soon we were a pair of giggling witches, our shoes barely touching the polished tiles as we kited away. There was freedom in knowing something for yourself. Just as I had come to learn by leaving the underworld on my own. There was nothing else like it. The sweet realization of a whole wide-eyed world, glowing and boundless, just waiting to be discovered, lighting the path to all of what was possible.

Our screams pealed through the rafters of the Miami airport. Letting go of our luggage, Mom and I crashed into the hungry embrace of Auntie Audrey, who was also screaming. It had been over a decade since we had seen her, and Mom was not going to touch Foreign for the first time without also touching her sister. We lifted our bags into Auntie's Mercedes and laughed with our whole throats all the way to her house. "Roger just got me this car," she told us. I didn't even have to cross the gates into her lakeside community to know she was living the American dream. She had a husband and a green card. She had her own car and knew how to drive it. She had a manicured lawn by a man-made lake; she had a dishwasher and a washing machine that she never touched, because she had a cleaning woman who came daily to operate them. Her house was a mansion of polished tile and crystal and gilded décor that seemed lifted right out of a magazine.

Nestled outside in her backyard we laughed, our voices hoarse while watching the sun dissolve into russet over the lake. As we talked into the night, it seemed no time had passed at all, and we slipped comfortably into each other's arms again, under the warm wool of family. My cousin Jason now had an American accent, an American swagger, and all the athletic charms afforded him by a football scholarship to a private school. Auntie, too, had her sugary twang, though with her sister she fell boundless into an unbuttoned patois, both of them raucously reminiscing about their seaside village White House, about their parents and the duck-egg past they had both fled.

"She sound sweet though, eeh?" Auntie said to Mom, gesturing to me. "Boy, you barely have a Jamaican accent. You sound more American than me."

"It's true," her husband, Roger, agreed. "I can only tell with certain words when you stress your *T*s."

Mom nodded along proudly and told them I went to school with Americans, that's why I talked so proper. I accepted the piercing scrutiny of a family reunion and slid under their microscope.

Auntie Audrey's face was beautiful, warm and done up, eyes lined dark and her lips shimmering with a pink lipstick.

"Your mom told me you were modeling. When you gonna enter Miss World?" she asked me. Her hair, long and straightened, was blowing in the wind as she spoke.

I told her I didn't model anymore, that I was only a writer now, and poetry was my passion. That even in my passport my occupation said "Writer."

"Poetry?" Auntie Audrey laughed, giving Mom a questioning look.

"Mhmm. She's been published in the newspaper and everything," Mom said. "She even lectured at UWI on poetry."

Roger chuckled. "But I've never heard of anyone doing *poetry* as a job," he said, the house light glinting off his blue eyes. "I guess it takes all types."

I looked at Mom and pulled my mouth taut into a pout.

Auntie threw her hair over her shoulder. "You know, I think that's rude of you to say, Roger." She smiled at him dangerously as she spoke. "Yes, the world takes all types to go round. But there's nothing wrong with her doing her poetry if that's what makes her happy."

"No, babe. You're totally right," Roger said to Auntie. He patted me on the shoulder and winked in reassurance. "I believe in you. I do."

As I listened to them talking, I was shocked. I'd never heard my mother challenge my father like this in my whole life, neither to defend me nor give her opinion, much less for him to agree so amiably and come to see her view of things.

"I disagree with my husband on a lot of things." Auntie turned to me and Mom, laughing. "But I let him know it. That's why we cannot talk politics in this house!"

Roger threw his hands up in mock-surrender. "I agree with my wife," he said, and laughed. Then he parted the sliding doors and slipped back inside to the kitchen, where he ordered us all food for dinner.

The next morning I woke up to a corvid chattering, Mom and Auntie Audrey cackling over coffee at the kitchen counter. My mom was loud and unstoppable, her voice trilling operatic through the house, and Auntie's voice rose to meet her, their clamoring joy two birds flittering around the ceiling. I felt my impatience rising, but I wasn't sure why. I had never seen my mother this way. Hair loose, face loosened and animated with jokes and quick blasts of patois, her voice blaring out news of home, teasing about old friends they didn't like, and telling me my thighs looked rosy when I was sitting down. Here, in America, something had ignited in her that rattled me. She and Auntie Audrey had their own coven, one I could never be a part of. A dark jealousy twisted in me. Why hadn't she been this way at home with us—outspoken and headstrong? It stunned me to think that perhaps this was my mother all along, this volcanic woman having the best morning of her life, reunited with her one true sister in this world. A sister who gave her something I never could, who reminded her of joys that I could not, for there was always something of my father in me.

"Mom, can you stop being so loud and brawling!" I yelled, clattering her reverie to a halt. Behind Auntie's shocked expression, a snatched reflection of my face. My brows knitted, face pulled dark and grimacing. All that was missing was the scar.

Mom frowned at me and wrenched her body away, and I felt my breath leave me.

She spoke without turning back to look me in the face. "You're acting just like him." Her voice was low and deathly. "And you're making me not want to be around you."

My chest flooded. The barbed repulsion in her voice struck me down, and I immediately wished I could take it back.

A slow burning horror rose up in my throat.

"I'm sorry," I said, ashamed.

She didn't answer. Her back was still turned as I moved toward her. A cleaving ache overtook me now, my hurt and guilt drowning everything else. My face twisted into a cry.

"Mom, please. I'm sorry."

My tears were stinging at my throat.

"Mom, I'm sorry. I'm so sorry," I pleaded. I promised myself, I promised her, that I would never be like that again. When I reached my arm into hers, she reached back into me. But as she held me I was terrified of myself. All those years of mistreatment in our house had warped me, and anger had become my first mode of expression. Anger and cruelty. My mother's drowned silence wasn't a natural aspect of her character but evidence of my father's force. And now here I was, his hideous student: I had learned too well how to hold her under water. I resolved to excise his monster from me.

"Well. I think we need to go shopping," Auntie said, the silence shattering back into laughter.

At the mall, I slipped black nail polish and smoky eyeshadow into our shopping cart. Already the morning's catastrophe was swept clear away. I wanted so much to be like my mother, so patient and forgiving, to be a person other people clung to. To laugh with my whole mouth open and not have a care, as she had that morning. When we walked past the jewelry store, I decided I would do it.

"I want to pierce my ears," I said. Mom and Auntie Audrey were shifting their way through trays of sparkling earrings and bangles in the jewelry store.

"Let's do it!" Auntie said without hesitation. I looked to Mom and she nodded. Both of them had pierced their ears when they were very young. Neither of them had ever had to think twice about such a thing.

"Are you sure?" I asked my mother.

"It's your body," she said. "You're becoming a woman now, and you have a right to decide about your person." Auntie nodded along. I'd never heard my mother talk this way. Whether it was being away from home, or being with Auntie Audrey, even for such a short time, something pivotal had shifted in her, and I was grateful for it. She spoke to me now from a deep well of wisdom, like a woman shaken out of a coma.

I sat in the chair and nodded yes to the two blue dots the woman had marked in the centers of my earlobes. Mom and Auntie Audrey stayed back and watched, holding their thumbs up and smiling at me. The iron

clamp felt cold upon my ear, my face shining in the mirror on the wall
in front of me. When the first rod snapped through, the mall's chatter
muted to a pinprick. I welcomed the pressure, the release, the quick sting.
I was four months away from my nineteenth birthday, and I had taken
another step through the gates of Babylon, the sweet pain a holy reminder
of the life ahead of me. My mother and I knew my father would be livid,
but we shook his impending wrath from our heads like carefree women.
Our freedom was short-lived and we both knew it, but just this once we
wanted to pretend it was truly ours. When the woman raised the clamp
and asked me if I was ready for the next ear, I was already nodding, yes,
please, yes.

    While in the dusky verdigris of the countryside, my father had spent
this time on the phone with his new friend Jahdami, stewing. Each day in
our absence he went deeper into the darkness, amassing rockstones forged
there in a righteous fire, his slingshot armed and waiting, his aim steady.

23
Jezebel

WHEN I STEPPED BACK INTO THE rocky netherworld of Bicker-steth, my father glanced at my new earrings and grimly shook his head with disgust. "You're lost," he said. For days he cursed the loss of my purity. My body was supposed to be Jah's temple until it was my husband's, and now I had defiled it. "Vanity is a reckless sin," he told me, his words clenched to a whisper. Right back into my cage I went, locked in with my sisters once more, the three of us ruing the pink shriek of youth we were missing, our bodies a prison house. This time my father slid the lock tight and buried the key. He could not be a righteous man with a wayward daughter whose sisters studied her every move. But if I was under his eye, I was under Jah's eye, and I might still be hammered aright.

He began burning frankincense and myrrh every day, lighting a putrid incense that he swung from an ornate silver lamp like an orthodox priest, choking us. He took an impish pleasure in walking through the house with thick clouds of black smoke curling around him, overpowering every room. Ife was sensitive to smoke and would fall into coughing fits whenever he burned it. I would pinch my nose and sneeze, which my father took as a personal affront, making sure to linger, swirling the incense around me more. "Stop acting stush like yuh grandmother," he chided. But if either of us closed our bedroom door to hide from the smell, he would bang and force the door back open, billowing in the dark smoke. Perhaps it was a solution prescribed by one of the Rasta bredren from his meetings, a cure to purify what was unholy in his daughters.

Beneath it all, I believe he burned his incense because he wanted to terrorize us. Perhaps this terror was the last control he had left, giving him some shabby semblance of power in a world that reminded him every day that he was powerless.

Every week he returned from his Rastafari meetings, the more militant he seemed. His anger hardening evermore to brimstone. It was there, in these meetings, that I suspected he had fallen under the thrall of the Rastaman named Jahdami, a man whose face was coiled like a black adder, eternally waiting to strike. Jahdami was about fifty years old, a decade older than my father, and had recently returned home to settle with his wife and children after living in Foreign for many years. At first glance Jahdami was a typical Rastaman, drawing what he needed from the larger tenets of Rastafari and molding the rules to fit his own household's livity, with himself as godhead and ruler of all things. But to my eyes, he was an outlier in the way he also drew from extremist ideology and harmful archaic practices to suit his purposes, constructing his own violent interpretation of an austere version of Islam most commonly known as Wahhabism, which then started to grow popular with my father and some of the other Rasta bredren. Jahdami moved through the world not with peace, as Howell originally envisioned, and as many Rasta bredren island-wide did, but with violence. He believed in polyamory for Rastas, with multiple wives and girlfriends on the side. He believed he was righteous in punching his son with a closed fist or beating him with the flat side of a machete, and he believed in disciplining women and daughters alike with a striking hand or foot. He cheered on terrorist attacks and supported female genital mutilation. He was the man my father now spent most of his days off with, the one whose voice seethed through their long conversations on the phone.

My father would return from their meetings with a forked tongue, starved for someone helpless to cower under him. Out there, with his reggae career stalled, Babylon's foot was on his neck. In here, he demanded obedience and divine attention, our purity a gauge of the power he still wielded. He had been going to those Rasta meetings for more than a decade, but in the two years since he had met Jahdami, he became viciously narrow-minded, tyrannical in the extreme. The more radical his outlook became, the more reckless he got. One night he got on the hotel stage and ranted about the evils of Queen Eliza-bat, cursing her for at least ten minutes to the hotel's guests. Some of the guests filed a complaint with management and he was let go. After that, my father grew only more convinced that Babylon had deliberately derailed his career. From then on, every time he opened his mouth, it was not a song that came out, but fire.

The scorch-marks of his anger were everywhere I looked, my family withered and blistered. The night after I got back from my trip to the United States, Ife pulled me aside and told me that my father had threatened to break a chair over her back while my mother and I were gone. She had been crying from period pains, which triggered his anger. Her gentle spirit reminded him too much of his own mother, and he always flared up in a rage at the first hint of her tears, telling her this was a sign of weakness. She was only fourteen. He watched her like a hawk, convinced she would also get pregnant in high school. I did my best to comfort her that night, as her tears spilled over, and promised myself I would never forgive him. But I did not confront him. Rather, my silence knotted up inside me. Long before I left for the trip, I had felt it tangled there, after Shari had burst into our bedroom and heaved into me, crying. She had been rehearsing a dance to be performed for Queen Elizabeth's visit in 2002. When my father found out, he erupted in a blast of curses, forbidding her from going. "No yute of mine will evah bow to that vampire Eliza-bat!" he roared. "Fire bun Babylon!" Shari had whimpered in my arms, gasping as she recounted it. Only ten years old, she was already the keenest student of his cruelty—the way he treated the rest of us had hardened her too early, and I could see her mind had swiftly turned away from him. Each day that I looked over at my growing sisters I was frightened, seeing their lives and mine slowly becoming a closed loop.

My nineteenth birthday passed at home, locked under my father's glare, the mere fact of my body's maturity offending him. It had been two months since I returned from the trip to the United States, and that time had only sharpened my sense of what I had lost. If I closed my eyes I could almost feel that freedom again—the wind at my back as I moved through the world as myself, never once worrying about the ladder being kicked out from under me without warning. I held on to that glimpse of liberation for as long as I could, trying to avoid my father by nesting in my room, but some days he would seek me out, heavy with nothing but venom.

One afternoon he came back from a Rastafari meeting in a black agitation. He squinted at me as I walked into the kitchen, muttering something under his breath. It seemed that everything I did now was a scourge in the eyes of Jah, a daughter whose ruin also ruined him. I tiptoed around the couch where he watched television and tried not to look at him. Whatever had happened at his meeting, he couldn't let go of it, hours later. He passed through the girls' room, as he sometimes did to get to Lij's bathroom, inspecting that our beds were made and our place was tidy. I ignored him as best I could, pressing my face into my book. When he passed back, I saw that he had a Sunday *Observer* rolled in his hands, which he dropped at the foot of my bed.

"You know what Jahdami said to I and I this day?" he asked.

I closed my book and swallowed a sigh before I looked at him. "No, Daddy."

"That the I write like Shakespeare."

"Oh." I was surprised to hear it. Flattered, even. "Thank—"

"Him tell I man that you only write for white people," he spat. His face taut, knotted. "You use their words. Not I and I words."

I could barely catch my breath. He moved closer to the bed and glowered.

"You don't write for us," he said.

His words tore me open, a knife ripping longways through my soft tomorrow. It shouldn't have surprised me, that he knew precisely how to wound me. But it did. Tears rose hot and bitter in my throat. I held my knees and pinched at the soft underside of my skin.

"That's not true, Daddy," I said. I hated my quivering voice, my body trembling as he fumed over me. "Many Black people like my poems."

"Jahdami is right. Some Kingston people might embrace you and love you, but your poetry will never do anything for Black people. It's worthless. You will never get anywhere with this poetry." He flicked the newspaper toward me and stormed out.

When the door clicked closed and his footsteps had gone, I turned my face into my pillow and sobbed. He had hacked at the one thing in this world that gave me purpose. That had kept me alive these past few years, my driftwood in the midst of his storm. It wasn't his baseless accusation that tore at me, but the way he had so callously dismissed all my efforts. All night I wept with the crushing realization: After more than nineteen years, my father still could not see me. To him, nothing I wrote would ever matter. Poetry was the voice I had forged because for so long I had been voiceless; I had written every word because I wanted him to hear me. Now I knew he never would. My chest heaved, puncturing. There, in the wound he had made, all the hushed grievances of the countryside plunged through me, and the cruel hurt of his words lingered long into my days, into my weeks, until it hardened like basalt, a black tumor I carried around with me, clenched like a fist.

My father stopped calling me Budgie. Every day he brewed uglier, and every day he strayed further from the man who had placed his hands on my mother's stomach at White House and named me. Nobody was safe from his fire, not even my brother. My father terrorized Lij about his teenage acne, telling him he bore pestilence because his livity wasn't right. One night after my father's car turned down the hill and left, my brother finally buckled under years of torment and wept. My sisters and I were so stunned by his crying that we formed a circle around him and bawled, open-mouthed and primal, doused in sweat and tears as the years of pain passed through us, each one absorbing the other's hurt. I bared my teeth and clutched my siblings, barbed in anger because I felt helpless.

One evening, only two weeks later, I found my mother crouched alone in her room with her head in her hands, looking like she had seen a ghost. I pressed for more, but she wouldn't say. So I sat with her and waited. It had been four months since we returned from Foreign, and the boisterous hours of our trip were now just a faded echo in our heads. When we returned, I had watched her slip right back into the stupor of our unyielding life in less than a week, burying the woman who had glimmered alive in the presence of her sister. Her alarming regression had crushed me, and I began to feel that I might never escape this life myself.

"You have no idea what it's like," my mother whispered to me now, through her tears. I kneeled in front of her and listened. Her breath was strained, her eyes wide with a terrified look I had never seen. "How much I absorb, you don't even know. Just so you don't have to—" A burning knot rose in my chest as she spoke. My father had been cursing her for ruining his life, she said. He blamed her for having four children, blamed her for this burden that sunk his dream of stardom. I clasped her palms as she spoke, throttled by my powerlessness. Throughout my adolescence, I had always sensed there were struggles and calamities my mother had shielded me from, but this was the first time she had ever opened up to me about them. It devastated me now, to hear her describe it.

"Mom, why don't you ever say something?" I asked, my voice breaking around the words. "Why don't you just leave him?"

Her eyes peeled even wider at my question and she put her hands over her ears and shook her head like a toddler, frightened at the thought of it. So many years I had wished for the woman who had almost left him to return. The twisted pallor of my mother's face told me that woman was long gone. I was nineteen and sheltered, still too young to understand what my mother herself had lived through since she was nineteen. Even as I comforted her, I was oblivious to the signs of what she had been experiencing my entire life. How one could live under the influence of a partner so long that any other possibility seemed terrifying. How one could be isolated from your family, controlled, and made powerless. How one could be too shell-shocked to ever leave. How so few women ever made it out.

But in this moment, caught under the hammer of my own abuse, I didn't have those words; all I had longed for was my mother to protect me, for someone to speak up for me, like Auntie Audrey had done with her husband. As I embraced my mother and consoled her, I recalled what I had already learned under the dinosaur bones. There was no one in this house to stand up to my father's terror. My sisters, my brother, my mother; they had all confessed his misdeeds to me because they wanted, as I always did, somebody to defend them. And now there was no one ahead of me except for me.

In the weeks after my mother confided in me, I made of myself an adder's nest, distilling my family's hurt into my own furious venom, so the next time my father came back angry from a meeting with the Rasta bredren, I was prepared. My sisters and I were watching television, making a garland of our future selves, daydreaming of the first thing we would do when we were free. Lij had gone to debate practice and was not at home. I sat at the computer, adjacent to the television, turned away from the couch where my sisters were seated. My mother hovered in and out of the living room, getting up to check her pot in the kitchen every now and then, prepping for my father to head back out to work. That ghostly look I had seen in her eyes that night never left me. Weeks later, her face had already grown older, more sunburned and carved with frown lines, stone-gray and fixed in hypnosis, bound to her duties by some invisible rope. At that moment, my father stalked into the middle of the living room, his dark smoke stifling the air. My sisters and I averted our eyes, cautious as he stood among us, breaking our sacred circle. He looked around at me, Shari, and Ife and shook his burning head.

"I and I must be cursed," he said to none of us in particular. He liked his audience silent. He liked his women pliant.

"Jah know, star," he said to Mom, who had returned to rest on the arm of the couch next to Shari. "I man was just at Ras I-gi's house and his eight-year-old daughter cooked Ital breakfast for all ah the Rasta bredren them. And she served all of us. Eight years old. Such a beautiful spirit. Quiet and I-mble as ever."

Mom did not respond, beyond maybe a slight nod of her head. But he didn't need us to respond. My sisters drooped in their seats as he spoke, bent by an unseen force. I kept my back to him and didn't move.

"Watching her made the I so ashamed of my daughters. I man don't think one of you ever boil a pot of water for me. One ah yuh ever even pick up a broom?"

Mom got up from her perch on the couch and disappeared into the kitchen; I turned to watch her go and caught a brief glance of tired resignation in her face. I wished Auntie Audrey were here with me under this hot light, somewhere at my back to defend me. She was afraid of no man and spoke her mind clear as cut-glass to anyone.

"And you—" My father turned his fangs on me. I kept my back turned and didn't look, but I could feel his leer fixed on my every movement. "I man hate how you just corrupt your sister them. More and more each day."

My face burned as he spoke, but I didn't react. He always needed something to ram against. I kept my gaze fixed on the computer screen.

He skulked closer to me.

"You're worthless," he said with reptilian calm. "You will never get a husband because you don't know how to cook or clean. Yuh think I man don't see you, how yuh gallivant round here in shorts and earring, gyrating your body? You are nothing but a Jezebel."

Blood rushed to my ears, and the roof of the house pulsed with the heartbeat throbbing at my throat, trying to pound its way out. I took my hand off the mouse.

"Yeah," he said, his voice a cold knife, knowing he finally hit the right vein. "You are nothing but a Jezebel."

I sat unmoving in my chair and closed my eyes. Here I was, in that familiar fire. For an entire decade I had lived under his ugly words, cowered under his cruel hands, swallowing his venom in silence. But as soon as he spat that word at me, I knew exactly who I was. Without opening my eyes, I spoke, finally.

"You can't talk about me like that," I said. My voice came out too clear, like birdsong. I turned to face him. "I'm not going to accept it anymore."

His eyes bulged wide. I could see nothing now except his face, his mouth a black fissure, opening.

"I'm not afraid of you," I lied. "No one else will say anything, but I will." I couldn't see my mother, but felt the hot gasp of the household drawn tight, my sisters sitting straight up in their spines, watching me.

"You better stop talking, girl," my father warned, his voice hard. He didn't look at me when he said it.

Nobody spoke. He was arched on his feet, his gaze deadly and poised to pounce. Wild goats kicked in my chest.

"No. I won't stop talking." I did not flinch. I would be a lionheart, just as he had always instructed. "Please stop speaking about me like I'm not there," I said. "Don't tread on my name."

At that, my father's eyes narrowed into blades and he rushed toward me. His hair slashed about his shoulders as he shook his head. His mouth spittling as he spoke. He towered above me, his scowl so close I could feel the warmth of his breath, and he raised his heavy hand in the air. My heartbeat sounded in my ear as he loomed, but I looked up from my chair and kept his gaze.

Watching him there, I finally felt it. A kind of heady current. A small smirk unzipped across my face.

Sudden thunder crashed upon me, my father a gnash of teeth and dreads bearing down. "Yuh rude and disrespectful gyal!" he howled in my ear. "Ah don't know where yuh mother get yuh from, but you are not my daughter."

"I wish I wasn't."

All the years of silence in the face of his terror had boiled over in me; my mother's words, my sisters' words, my brother's pain, all our fear and hurt and choked animus now poured from me like lava. The dark stone of shame and fear that he had lodged in me all these years felt like it was crumbling away, releasing me from something I once thought endless. I gasped at the weight of it, leaving.

My breath stilled, heart slowing black as a river.

My father hulked over me with his fist clenched. I felt the heat of his hands approaching my face. I did not blink.

His fist became a finger, jabbed at my forehead like a loaded weapon. "You must have man to take you in, gyal, that's why you talking to the I so crazy."

I held his gaze. If I had gotten up from my chair then, he would have seen it: I was tall as him now, a little taller. I had pulled iron through fire. Iron from iron. And it wasn't him who smelted her, it was me. Outside, the night air hissed as I watched him. His shadow blotted out the glow of the ceiling light as he loomed over me, but there was light enough out there, and I knew it: Only I would shape the woman I was becoming. I didn't know what it would cost, nor how long it would take, but I was willing to sacrifice everything to do it.

"I hope you have somewhere to live," my father snarled. "Cause you can't live here. When I man come back, you better not be under my roof."

24

Harbinger of Babylon

I PACED THE DIM VERANDA AND LOOKED out into darkness from the house's high perch on the hill. My father had screeched out for work and would be back in the morning, his threat to be gone before he returned ringing its death knell in my head. My siblings had gone to bed terrified at the thought of me being thrown out. As I searched the darkness I thought about my sisters, wondering if this was the future that also awaited them. There were no streetlights out there. Nothing but a clear sky speckled with more stars than I had ever seen. Under their myriad glinting eyes I wondered where I was supposed to go. Once daylight broke, my father would tear back up that hill, wanting nothing to do with me, and what then? He was wrong. There was no man out there waiting to take me in. My only friend, Ann-Margaret, from my old poetry group, lived more than a hundred miles away in Kingston. My grandmother, who had no car and no cell phone, was asleep and unreachable in a labyrinthine housing scheme in Spanish Town, four hours away. Everyone else I had ever shared a laugh or a furtive word with had already flown off to brighter suns. The sea was now so faint on the horizon that I could no longer feel the pull of its waves.

Around me loomed the dark ridge of the mountains, serried and vigilant. Out here was the bread and backbone of our country. The thick countryside where our first slave rebellion was born. Voices of runaways still echoed from these impenetrable hills, where a vast network of caves had formed from limestone overrun with bush, and where Maroon warriors waylaid English soldiers who couldn't navigate the terrain. The English would yell commands, only to hear their own warped voices hollering back at them, until they were driven away in madness, unable to face themselves. Now this chattering night wore me mad, a cold shiver rushing down the bone. A girl, unable to face herself.

I traced the black outline of the tangled forest below. The eyes of something unseen looked back. Something sinister. The ghost of a slow mist coiled in the valley, and something shook across the street. There, emerging from the long grasses, was a woman in white. The woman appeared like a birdcatcher spider ambling out of its massive web. Her face was my face, but numb and smudged away. Her head was bowed, her dreadlocks wrapped in a white scarf atop her head, walking silently under the gaze of a Rastaman. This was the future that awaited me at my father's hands. The pale specter that first appeared to me all those years ago at Kwanzaa, as I fled the deflated room of Rastawomen. I shivered as I watched my gray self glide down the hill, placid in her white georgette dress. All the rage had been smothered out of her. Gathering her long skirt with the day's shadows, all her dreams set to fire long ago. She cooked and cleaned and demurred to her man, bringing girlchild after girlchild into this world who cooked and cleaned and demurred to her man. Next there was a baby in her belly, and a baby on her arm, while her Rastaman squirmed in bed with another woman. To be the humbled wife of a Rastaman. Ordinary and unselfed. My voice and vices not my own. This was the future my father was building for me. I squeezed the cold rail of the veranda as ghost moths danced around my face. I needed to cut that woman's throat. Needed to chop her down, right out of me. I had to leave her to leave this place. I had to run.

"Wherever you're going, I'm going too."

My mother's voice rang through the space between us like a bell. She stood in the doorframe in her black nightgown, her dreadlocks streaming down her back. Her face calm and groggy. "It's me and you. Alright?"

I nodded.

"It's chilly. Come back inside," my mother said, her voice sleep-weary but warm.

I took one last look into the night, where the woman's gray silhouette faded slowly into the dark, then I stepped inside.

My mother took my hand. Her face was stern, her brows knitted into a dark line. "Listen to me. As long as I'm living, no child of mine will ever be on the street," she said. All the fright I'd found in her that night she wept on the floor had fled. There was no world in which we would ever be separated, she told me now. "Never ever." She pulled me into her embrace, and I stayed a while in her arms then, feeling a safety I hadn't felt in years. I nestled against her and cried, awash in gratitude that she had saved me, again. I had not understood until that night, when she pulled me in from the terrible specter of the dark, that when it came to her children, my mother had always been strong. It was she who had arranged for me to study poetry. She who had insisted, against my father's objection, that I be allowed to model. It was she who had gotten me to the UN. She had always been there, guiding the most crucial moments of my life like an invisible hand. Just as she had raced across the sea to save me from drowning, when faced with the renewed prospect of losing me, she said never again.

When my father turned into the driveway the next morning, still raging at my outburst, my mother stood unflinching and told him what she had already told me: "Wherever she going, I'm going too. No way on this earth you go do to my child what your mother did to you." She was as staunch as I'd ever seen her then, her face set with a quiet fury. And that was that. My father could not imagine a life of labor without my mother's hands. So he decided it was not me but the house that was cursed, and we moved again.

But the haunting stayed with me, and followed. After that night, I knew nothing in my life could ever remain the same. I was now resolved in what I eventually had to do. To save myself from a future I was now fixed on unraveling, I had to rend myself free of her. I had to leave.

The sea was only a short drive away and the wind always wrung with salt. Here, at our sixth house, in a neighborhood called Ironshore, my mother and I settled into our bones again. I was nineteen years old, and for the first time I had my own room, and I stayed away in there day and night, reading and writing. My father and I courted a polite kind of truce, dancing around our grievances and never speaking of that night again. But all the ugly things he had said weighed on my mind as heavy as the dreadlocks atop my head. The specter of the woman in white had disturbed something already tenuous between us. My dreadlocks tethered me to her, because they tethered me to him. And every day I longed to be the sharp knife, severing.

Soon my mornings in Ironshore began with me sputtering awake from the same recurring dream. I dreamt I was chewing on newspaper, mouthfuls of bitter ink and gray mush, all night unable to speak. I'd gasp awake, moaning, with my jaw tired, trying to say something. After weeks of dreaming about chewing on newspaper, I asked my family what they thought it meant. My parents kept a dream book that told them what lotto numbers to buy, but no one had a satisfying theory for my mouth, clamped shut and straining around bitter newspaper pulp. No one, except my father. "Maybe you need to wash out your mouth with soap," he said.

I started avoiding going to sleep to avoid the dreaming and stayed up reading the novels I begged family friends who visited from the United States to bring me instead: Dostoyevsky, Kafka, Hesse. I got lost in their dark cathedrals while the shrieking crickets soothed me still. I wrote poems about imagined loves, imagined worlds. Despite what my father had said about me, I became the handmaid of the family, spending my hours and days cleaning up after my three siblings and my parents, who all had someplace to be, who all clattered dish after dish in front of me to clean. I stood at the kitchen window washing that teetering mountain of pans, lost in my own catacombs. This is how the terror appeared to me again: as I lifted my tired head from the kitchen sink, I saw myself at the gate outside, standing under the mango tree, my white georgette flapping in the sea breeze. The silent woman who was my future doom. She stared black from beyond the gate, her eyes gaping wide and unpeopled. I wanted to claw my way out of her, to leave this place. But every night I stood by the kitchen window washing dishes, and every night she was there, gazing back at me from the throat of night. The longer the days stretched between me and college, the longer I lived under my father's roof with no hope of leaving, the longer she stared out at me. As the weeks stretched on, her visage crept closer, slipping like smoke inside the front gate, standing moonstruck in the middle of the yard, until she was almost in the frame of the kitchen windowsill.

Until finally we were face-to-face. As through a mirror broken, she wore my face, only older and marred with scars of distress, neglected and weary, never speaking. She had nothing to say. She only stared at me with eyes wide, sometimes with sticky-handed shadow-children pulling at her hem. And then one night I reached out, and suddenly our hands were touching. Bloodline to bloodline, through the frayed veil of my future and her.

Dawn broke and I woke unable to move. Unable to speak. Underwater and pulsing with fever, my throat burned and my limbs ached. I swam sweaty and faint-headed in my sheets, and cried out. Burning up in my bed, I was torn to weeping, which only flooded me with more pain. My mother sat at the end of my bed and massaged my feet, plied me with coconut water, soup, fresh juice, mint tea. Nothing worked. After three days I was still beached, squalling, twisting in that specter's nightmare. One night I gasped awake in the black, nearly strangled in my sheets, and for the first time wished I did not, after all this time, have my own room.

Dragging at the sheet of my bed, barely visible in the dark, was a tiny figure, mewling across the floor. A baby. It cried for me like a cat, and the sound struck me. Slowly it trawled its glowing silhouette across my floor, pulling at my bed with tarred hands. I could not move. All the walls unpeeled with that unearthly crying. Behind me, I could feel her there in the corner. Staring in warning, the woman in white. And now this creature, which called for me, called for her.

I woke breathless and weeping, still aching under fever, and threw up fluid clear as ocean water.

My mom stayed home with me through the fever, nudging her head through the door often to ask me how I was doing. My voice cracked as I told her, "Still sick." She brought a tray of tea and crackers to my room and sat beside me with fretting eyes, pressing my chakras with her hands. Some days she retold the folktale of how our lives began, anchoring me in the world with her. Sweat drenched my bed, and I could keep nothing down. Gone gray and skinnier than I had ever been, I was battling the fourth day of fever, though it felt like ten. "I can't take it anymore," I told my mother.

Each day I watched my life stretch out before me in unceasing nothingness and wondered what it was all for if all that awaited me was becoming a Rastaman's wife? Becoming as dutiful and self-effacing as my own mother had become, she who buried her wants so deep in that unknown place that she forgot what they once were. Who was I becoming now, nineteen years old, and already four years out of high school?

"I want to die," I told my mom on the fifth day, sobbing into her chest.

Crumpling into me, my mother shook and I shook with her. "No," she said, rocking me back and forth. "No no no no."

"If you're dying, I'm dying too," she said. "You're not going anywhere without me."

She pressed her warm hand to my forehead, and her sixth finger gently scraped my skin.

"Anywhere you're going, I'm going," she said again, cradling me in her warmth. "So please tell me. What can I do?"

My mother called a friend to come help her do it the morning after my fever broke. She chose a day she knew my father would be gone. My siblings were all gone to school and her friend, Sister Idara, arrived with a smile, ready. First, they poured hot cupfuls of water over my scalp to soften the hair, then they massaged my roots with both of their hands. I leaned my head over the laundry sink as they lathered my dreadlocks and scrubbed. I closed my eyes and tried to imagine what would happen next. The two women lifted me by my arms from the sink and wrapped my damp hair in a towel. We three walked together arm in arm to my bedroom. There was no sound but the mourning dove cooing through the house. My bedroom curtain lifted in the breeze as I knelt beneath them. I nestled nervous between my mother's knees, and waited.

"I went through this with my eldest daughter too," Sister Idara said to my mother. "After all the anger, we got through it. Distance helps, of course."

Sister Idara was Jahdami's American wife. She lived abroad with her two children for most of the year while he was down here, making trouble for the rest of us. She was a plump and jovial Rastawoman who kept her dreadlocks and body shrouded in matching African fabrics. She shined wise and warm with natural kindness, and no matter how hard I pushed my mind, I could not imagine her coiling in bed with a cobra like Jahdami. My mother had asked her to be here because she was a perfect shield. My father could not unleash his anger on Sister Idara since she was his good bredren's wife, and since Idara was scheduled to fly back to the States in a day, he could only spit fire over the phone. "Have you told him we're doing it?" I asked my mom. "No," she said. "But I don't need his permission."

Mom told me to hold down my head and I held down my head. She asked me if I was ready, and I said yes. Beside me, the sea breeze made womanly shapes in the lace of my curtain, and no one among us spoke. I don't know who held the scissors, or who made the first cut. All I heard were the hinges of the shears locking and unlocking, the blades cutting. And then, long black reeds of hair came loose in their quick hands. My dreadlocks fell around me like ruined limbs. I closed my eyes then, because I could not look at what I was losing. I had railed for so long and had not expected it to matter when the moment came. But now I found that it mattered a great deal. My throat burned with peculiar remorse as all my dreadlocks fell away. For what was Medusa without her snakes?

There was hair. So much hair. Dead hair, hair of my gone self, wisps of spiderweb hair, old uniform lint hair, pillow sponge and tangerine strings hair. A whole life pulled itself up by my hair, the hair that locked the year I broke my tooth, hair that locked the day we caught cane ashes in the yard. Hair of our lean years, hair of the fat, pollen of marigolds hair, my mother's aloe vera hair, my sisters weaving wild ixoras in my hair, the pull of the tides at our sea village hair, grits of sand hair, hair of salt tears, hair thick with the blood of my own cut wrists. Hair of my binding, hair of my unbeautiful wanting, hair of his bitter words, hair of the cruel world, hair roping me to my father's belt, hair wrestling the taunts of baldheads in the street, hair of my lone self, hair wrapped atop the ghost woman in white's hair, red thread of hair, centuries of hair, galloping future of incorrigible hair, all cut away from me.

When they were finished, my neck and head were so light they swung unsteady. The tethers had been cut from me, and I was new again, unburdened. Someone different, I told myself. A girl who could choose what happened next.

My mother held before me a mirror, and a strange young woman blinked back. I felt exposed. This was the first time, since birth, that my hair had been cut.

"How do you feel?" Sister Idara asked. I touched my hair, now a soft and short Afro as black as lamb's wool. When my face shone back at me I didn't recognize myself.

"I don't know," I told her. I was trying to take it all in, this unfamiliar weightlessness, turning my head this way and that in the mirror, trying to find a light or an angle that suited me. Agitated that there was none. "Better. Much better."

My mother gathered all my shorn dreadlocks from the floor, now long and dried dead things, twigs and string and a decade of dirt and lint. She swept them into a black Lada bag.

"You want to keep them?"

"Yes," I said. My answer surprised me. The bag was lighter than I thought it would be when I lifted it from her.

I rose to hug them both and felt I might float away. Unanchored and dizzy, I thought I was free, until I thought for the first time of my father. His anger. What he might do to me.

"Don't worry about that," my mother told me. "I will take all his ire."

I thanked them and pushed my fingers through my curls, collapsing into the warmth of their bodies. Like a blessing, their hands pressed earthlike and light over me. We stayed that way for a moment, breathing each other's power. And like a fringe of thread tickling against me, there at my shoulder was the whisper of a third hand, another woman, birthing me again into this world.

By the time he had bucked and lashed and burned down the altar of my mother, all my father had left for me was his hurt. Hurt that I had chosen to shed this sacred marker of Rastafari, the mark I had worn since I was eight years old. Hurt that I had begun to sever myself from him. Hurt that I was no longer recognizable as his kin. Now whenever we went into the world together, nobody believed I had come from him, people mistaking me on several occasions for his young lover. My father was grievously wounded, and I was a daily reminder of the injury. My mother seemed unbothered by it all, stepping into a kind of shift of power, her energy bursting bright and growing with the days. I could hear her laughing in the light of the kitchen with her friend Auntie Crista, who was not a Rastawoman, but one of my father's ex-girlfriends from his days as the teen heartthrob of Future Wind. She lived close to us in Ironshore and began coming over more often once we moved to this new neighborhood. She and my mother were in the midst of some long-ago reverie as I approached. Both my mother and Auntie Crista had been born with hair so straight no pencil would hold, slipping through their strands like silk. Even though my mother had dreadlocks, all my life I watched the root of her hair grow so quickly and so straight that her dreadlocks never stayed locked at the crown of her head. Meanwhile my cropped Afro had grown rapidly wild. I had no idea what to do with it, and Mom offered no instruction, so different was my hair texture from her own.

"Her hair so thick!" Auntie Crista said, looking over my head.

Mom agreed. "And she tenderheaded like wha! When I tell you she used to scream as a girl just to see the comb."

I avoided the comb even now as there wasn't a single one in our house, choosing to let my hair do whatever it was doing instead. Both my sisters had greeted me with glee when they first saw me without my dreadlocks, and liked to push their hands into my hair, their own eyes glazed with hope.

"Djani mussah been upset though, eeh?" Auntie Crista asked Mom, and my mother shook her head and made a stoneface that said you don't even know the half of it, then pressed her finger tightly to her lip.

"I'll tell you off the air," she said to Auntie Crista.

The worst of my father's anger scorched behind closed doors, muffled badwords and thrown objects and chanting out for Jah. My mother never shared the details with me, but my siblings and I overheard him hurling his rage. Afterward he didn't speak to me for weeks, averting his glances. He was slow in coming to terms with his disobedient daughter, and must have wondered, as I did, where I was taking myself—and our family—next.

One afternoon he finally approached me like a zoo patron approaching an animal pen. Circling me on the veranda, he observed my shorn hair, which was now so thick my fingers pained to detangle it. All my life I'd been told not to touch my hair, so I had grown used to ignoring it. Now my hair consumed my days, the washing and conditioning, the frustration at waking up with knots, the impatience at wanting it to grow back to the length my locks had been. My father looked over my head in its thick and untamed state, and he was pleased.

"Your hair looks just like mine when I and I was a boy," he said, smiling wide as the midday sun.

As he fawned and complimented my hair, the frayed woman emerged from the wall behind him. Speechless in her white dress.

"This hair is your strength," he said. "Leave it as it is, and it will grow." Her eyes wide and unblinking. Saying nothing. Only waiting for me.

The hair salon exhaled chemical smells, peroxides, and burnt hair. Eight months after I cut my dreadlocks, I was on the verge of my twentieth birthday. I stepped into that mirrored world for the first time and felt timid, as all the women's eyes turned to look at me. I studied the pride of women, eyes glazed under hot comb and scissors and flat iron, with pink rollers in their hair. I waded shy into their reaches, soothed by the hum of blow dryers and tongue after tongue of gossip. They laughed loose and free, jangling with gold earrings and false fingernails. All heathens, all unclean women. I waited alone among them with teeth chattering, uncomfortable and uncertain. Auntie Crista had driven me to the salon and said she would be back in two hours. My mother had given me the money I needed to do it. "If that's what you want to do, then I support you," she said.

When the hairdresser looked over my head, she called it "virgin hair." She pushed her fingers through my tangled curls and frowned. "Is dread you dreading?" she asked when I sat in her chair. I didn't need to answer, for she already stood over me with her comb and started slathering the white cream on my scalp. Cool to the touch at first, then a strange tingling sensation that gave way to a burn, my skin giving way to flesh underneath. "It's burning?" the hairdresser came back to ask me after ten minutes had passed and I said yes. "Tenderheaded, eeh?" Under the fluorescent light, head burning, avoiding myself in the mirror, I felt more exposed than I had ever been, so naked in my wanting. I was frightened by my uncertainty at what kind of woman I should now become. Before I went to the salon, I snatched the Lada bag full of my shorn dreadlocks and threw it into the trash. I had kept it under my bed for months. I winced as the hairdresser chatted with her friend and washed out the relaxer.

When she was finished, my hair was soft and fell at my shoulders. I swung my head side to side and smiled. All the women in the salon now crowded in, drooling over me, running through the familiar litanies. "You should be a mogeller," and "You should enter Miss World," and "Girl, your skin color cyaan buy inna Chinese shop!" I felt anointed by them, my own gaze following the pavement shadow of a girl with long hair, running my fingers through it, loving the reflection of myself.

"Wow. You look Chinese!" Auntie Crista said to me when she came to pick me up, running her fingers through my hair. "It feels so much better now, right?"

I shook my head to and fro, feeling even lighter-headed now. When the breeze grazed my scalp I felt oddly unprotected. My parents had always told us that our natural hair would save our skulls from injury, and I could not help but wonder if I had lost some of my power. My heart fluttered with a brief remorse then.

"Yes, better," I told her, pushing the feeling away.

"Now let's find you a Prince Harry!" she said, and we schemed on the drive home.

Back home I looked in the mirror, ran my hands through my relaxed strands, and stroked the parts of my scalp I had never felt. When I moved my head I was surprised each time I felt a soft tickle at my cheek. "Wow," my sisters and mother said, combing their fingers through my hair too. "It's so pretty." My brother smiled when he saw me and also complimented my new look. Now my shadow was no longer my shadow; she was a new girl who liked the look of herself, chasing her silhouette head-first into a tree. And, this is how my father found me the night he came through the gate to his home's ruin, his daughter gawking transfixed in the mirror, trying on a lipstick Auntie Crista had slipped into my hand.

I walked out of the bathroom with my straightened hair and he froze.

"Hi, Dad," I said. His eyes looked through me with disbelief.

In the fraught scar of his face I saw a reflection of myself: processed hair, lipstick, gold earrings. His lips pursed.

I think my father realized it just then. That nothing Rastafari moved through me anymore. I had fought and snuffed that woman out of the world completely. The one he wanted me to be. I had cut her throat. I watched her hands at her severed neck, still trying to speak, soundlessly. Her pale silhouette fading into the wall, taking that forsaken future with her.

I waved to him again and he looked right through me.

I felt a jolt of fear run through me then. If my father could have burned me alive, I am sure he would have. His dark eyes excised me from him the way I had already excised him. I waited for him to say the black words, to unleash the inferno of his thoughts, abjuring. I waited for his lips to invoke Jah, to strike me into ash.

But it was not fire he had for me, but cold. Cold river water that had been seeping up from the earth between us since the day I first bled in his bathroom. And today it rose dangerous and rushed between us, frigid and silent, its dark current now a wide expanse, sweeping me away.

My father shoved past me as if I were not there, even as I spoke his name.

I was now one of them: a baldhead. Eater of dead animal flesh, eater of men. A sinful and joyriding Jezebel, one among the horde of unclean women, skinning out at carnival, gyrating to dancehall music in the street, parading with the lewdest and crudest jingbeng, sated under cold plantation rum. A whore among the white-wigged Kingston lawyers and the gang-bought police clad in Her Majesty's colonial khaki, shaking hands with the governor-general and the prime minister. A bloodsucker lost in the gated homes of bloodsuckers, practicing the haughty unbroken English of bloodsuckers who summered elsewhere. I was the mother of the wolves at the megaphone, suckling the CIA-bought politrickster pretending he couldn't spell "bread" to win the country vote. The mistress of the johncrow hotelier who snatched up two hundred miles of clear coastline, building barbwire fences around the beaches and hotels that kept my family out. I was the heathen woman opening the wet seam of herself to herself, looking out upon my damned kingdom.

My father slammed the door against me, for I was not there. It would be one long year before he uttered another word to me, for I was nothing but a wanton ghost to him. One of the lost. The harbinger of Babylon.

IV
MERMAID

born in babylon
both nonwhite and woman
what did i see to be except myself?
—LUCILLE CLIFTON

25

Daughter of Lilith

M Y FATHER'S SILENCE SPREAD LIKE A fog over everything. Weeks
passed and he spent not a single word on me. Purse-lipped months
came and went and he looked through me like an apparition. I was the
ghost of Ironshore, skulking through my discarded days pale as a jumbie
bird. My hair, my insistent plague, possessed his waking mind and day
after day, I felt smaller. Living with his closemouthed punishment brooding heavy and unhatched between us was a sullen undertaking for me,
until it wasn't. Until the silence itself became a kind of freedom. Once
my family left for school or work, I nestled into my solitude. I wandered
the yard in needful snatches, writing poems like gulps of September rain.
I tore through my stacks of books, tailoring my own weekly curriculum,
wondering after the first woman who said "No." Lilith was her name. The
First Woman, made from the same clay as Adam, who had refused to be
subservient to him. Her defiance led to her banishment from Paradise,
her name erased from all biblical accounts. Night monster, they called
her. Demoness of Babylon.

I, too, was the first exile.

Now every day that I woke, I said no. I stepped headfirst into my role
of ghoul, haunting every room. I ate and slept as a woman carved down
to nothing but her starkest needs, hanging my one omen on the gate like
a pale flag: all who enter beware. I began painting myself a mask that
courted my father's discomfort. When I was invited to read "Silver" for
the prime minister at the National Youth Awards ceremony in 2004, the

first thing I did was buy myself a pantsuit. Then red lipstick, then nail polish. When my father, impressed by the large honorarium accompanying
the invitation, asked me if I would contribute some to the "family pot," I
told him no, reminding him that he said my poetry would never get me
anywhere, sipping then on the wine of his embarrassment. I painted my
nails black, painted my eyes black. I longed to startle anyone who came
near, waving foolhardy semaphores of whatever black thing I was feeling.
Daughter of Lilith, I called myself. Winged and taloned, I swatted away
my father's disapproval with the strength of the woman I could someday
be. She who would write herself back into the frame.

This defiant need is what dragged me to the print shop. I placed an
order for a white T-shirt to be custom printed, and the word I chose to
display across my chest was now causing a stir around the shop's iron
press. The young woman who handled my printing gazed confused over
the text, her eyes trying to decipher the word. More workers gathered
while she prepared the sheet of paper and arranged my T-shirt under the
large iron.

The manager, an older woman, hovered, glancing sideways from me
to the text and back.

"You know what this word mean?" she asked the young woman.
She shook her head. Then the manager cupped her hand and whispered
something into the printer's ear.

She cast a frightened look at me. "Oh Jesus!" she said.

Her hands shook as she peeled my finished shirt from beneath the
press, holding the shirt away from her as if it might ignite into flames. "Is
this okay, Miss?" she asked me.

I studied my white T-shirt where the word **ATHEIST** was now printed
in a bold sans serif black font.

"Yeah, that's great," I said, pretending not to notice the crowd of eight
or so staff, some whispering about "devil worshiping," while one man in
the store-back made the sign of the cross. My nails were painted black,
my eyes lined with the darkest kohl. I held each of their gazes and flicked
my hair, now pin-straight and swooped into a half shadow across my face.

The manager hesitantly rang up the sale, and just before she handed
over my T-shirt she asked, "Are you a Visigoth?"

"No." I laughed and thanked her. A cowering baldhead was always a cowering baldhead. The trembling shop parted as I walked through the crowd, which was still whispering heresy and pointing at my back.

When my mother saw the T-shirt, she could only laugh at this unusual and provoking daughter she had birthed, and though my father threw up his eyes to Jah, he knew it could be worse. I could be a Christian.

I'd printed the shirt because I wanted to offend. Not just the sensibilities of my devoutly Christian nation, but the Old Poet specifically. He had recently written a Sunday column about being a die-hard agnostic, and I wanted to jab at him. To leave him with one final word. It had been almost a year since we had spoken. After a few pointed email exchanges where he accused me of ingratitude and lacking humility, we stopped communicating. Like my father, he punished me with his silence. Then I got an email from an unknown editor at the *Observer* telling me I had won an award. At the award ceremony, the Old Poet and I stayed on opposite sides of the room, and I avoided his stare with my red-lipped scowl. With distance, I had gained a clearer understanding of our time together, and that ugly afternoon, which still left me stumbling and mawkish. Now, it had brimmed over in me as rage. Over time, I found the farther I had gone away from the Old Poet, the farther away I wanted to stay. I made no attempt at pleasantries or conversation that evening. Once I accepted the envelope with my prize money, I took one last look at the Old Poet's face—had it always been so unsmiling?—and turned away from him for good.

Though I was the first one to pull the thread, I wasn't prepared for Ife being the first of us to leave, but it was no surprise to any of us when she did. Ife spent her every waking hour plotting her escape, already erecting a future beyond my father, who didn't spare her his vitriol, inventing a future beyond us. On weeknights she ate dinner in her room, choosing to pore over her homework alone, while the rest of us played board games or watched TV. Patient and kind, she always gave her last word and her last laugh to me and Lij and Shari, as we three bullhorned our way through most conversations. I was twenty, Lij was eighteen, Ife was sixteen, and Shari was eleven. Ife spoke less than we did, but her voice was a gift. She answered the call when life's quiet moments struck her, singing her soul up to the rafters and making me believe in the divine. It was this porous nature to the sounds of god that made my sister easily wounded, her spirit shattered easy and often by her three siblings' rough nature. "Don't let anyone disrupt your orbit," I told her one night after Lij, under a black mood, taunted her until she cried. "Make yourself impenetrable to all." My father spent years trying to push her to be a professional singer, but Ife, being most like my mother in spirit and in mind, wanted to be a doctor instead.

When her final Caribbean Examinations Council results were announced, she scored the highest marks in all thirteen subjects across the entire Caribbean. She was lauded nationwide in the newspaper and called to Kingston to be trophied and garlanded by the Minister of Education. This led her to be scouted by an American boarding school that granted her a full-ride scholarship to attend twelfth grade, which would have her picking any American college she wanted in a year's time. We squawked round the house in one big excitement when we heard the news. I was too happy for her escape to tell her how deeply her departure would sting.

It was in her leaving that the great unraveling of my family began. A few weeks before she left for Foreign, Ife asked my mom to cut her dreadlocks as well. Since I had done it, she was no longer afraid to answer her own longing, to sever that tie completely. This time, it was Mom and I who formed a circle around her, draped her over the same laundry sink, and poured hot cupfuls of water and thickening soap over her head. When the cleansing was over, it was the two of us who walked Ife to my bedroom, where she knelt as Shari watched intently. Mom and I held a dreadlock in each of our hands, asked if she was ready, and started cutting. When it was over, I passed my sister the mirror and asked her how she felt.

She stroked her short curls and smiled. "Happy to be rid of the parts that felt like baggage," she said, "and to be more myself."

Before she left for America, Ife also went to the salon and relaxed her hair. I made myself a shield for her. My father was violent in his silence, fuming against us in the house. He did not speak to my sister for weeks, not even the night before she got on a plane to go to boarding school for a year, more than a thousand miles away in the American Midwest. But Ife seemed unrattled by his gloomy drama, perhaps because she was already looking ahead of her, away from home, her future stretching luminous away from us. On the eve of her leaving, my siblings and I sang for her, so in Foreign she would not forget that she was loved.

Mom had been wiping away tears all afternoon. We stayed behind the ropes of Departures at the airport and watched as Ife handed her passport and plane ticket to the immigration agent, then turned to wave to us one last time. Just then, her warm smile flooded me with the deepest ache, my body trembling to wave back, struggling to hold my own parting smile as she slipped through the lit hallway, and then my dear sister was gone.

The three of us who were left behind huddled together like ragged survivors on a desert island, watching the sea for any signs of hope. Though Lij and I had both been accepted to the American colleges we applied to the year before, none of them had offered either of us a full scholarship. For now, those dreams were grounded. One of the schools, Bennington College, had offered both of us partial scholarships, the difference of which was still too steep for our parents to afford. After a night of fretting over our future, my brother told me he was giving his scholarship to me. I tried to dissuade him, but he'd already decided. "I know how much you've wanted this, Saf. You deserve this," he said. The heat and sweat stuck us to our chairs, to our fate. Shirtless and determined at the computer, my brother pressed send on the email, relinquishing his place, along with his scholarship at Bennington, to me.

By morning the Admissions Office replied with words that crushed us double. It didn't work that way, they said. One student could not roll their funding into another's, even if they happened to be related. But for reasons lost to me now, I still clung to the blind belief in a different outcome. I asked my mother to pay the small enrollment fee anyway and defer my enrollment for as long as we could, as long as it took. Hoping for some future magic.

Rather than hinging on this unknown hope, my brother made a different choice. Faced with his own forking future after Ife left, my brother, who was an island-wide debate champion, decided to enroll at the University of the West Indies to study law. The founder of our SAT classes tried to discourage him, telling Lij that he was "Dartmouth material." And though I, too, tried to convince him to wait a year and reapply to

American colleges, he had already made up his mind to leave us. To leave me. My mother enlisted a close family friend to cosign the mammoth bank loan for UWI that my parents could not afford alone, and I worried how graduating with debt in Jamaica might shape the rest of my brother's life.

Lij and I spent the humid night bellowing our old songs together, his head resting next to mine, our private language wistful and sticky as summer. He was leaving for UWI in a few days and we had not spoken of it.

"Are you sure?" I'd asked him before he signed the loan, hoping he would change his mind. "How will you pay it back?" Now I asked him again, over the plaintive sounds of Kurt Cobain and the lake of fire. His mind was fixed. My brother had always believed in a kind of mythic fate as his guiding hand. He was happy to let the compass needle swing wildly, and follow. "Why don't you come too?" he asked me. My mind was also fixed, and only my own hand would ever do the guiding. I told him that my best chance as a poet was leaving Jamaica.

"Look, Saf," Lij said to me. "You can stay here and be a house rat. But I cyaan live another moment here with this man."

It was the hardest to accept, his leaving. Ripping through the emotional clutter of that evening, his face was determined. After my brother had loaded his best friend's car, I could hardly tear myself away from him. No matter how bad things had gotten, I'd always thought we would be in this war together. He had grown much taller than our father as he had grown older, which made me feel safe. Made me believe my father might think twice about reverting to physical violence while Lij was in the house. But now he was clambering into a car to drive away. Mom looked to the heavens, saying "Oh Jah," as he went. I watched my one brother disappear down the road, and grasped at Shari like a life raft as she wept. I was the eldest and yet I was a lonesome failure, forever left behind. For months I clung to my brother's far voice, his last warning still echoing in my ear.

Without my mother I would have lost all hope now that my younger brother and sister were gone. That year, we deferred my enrollment at Bennington and would continue to defer for another two years, buoying our hopes until another empty year rolled around. Each time she said,

"Maybe this year will be different," and I believed it. I had to believe it. After Lij left, a blur of weeks and months passed, while Shari and I grafted as two twigs to each other, twining into one blossoming tree. We were all each other had left. I still dedicated myself to poetry as if my survival hinged on it. Outside of the Sinclair household, Ann-Margaret, the other young poet I'd met back in the Old Poet's poetry workshop, was my only friend. Sometimes we would talk on the phone about our passion for poetry and our love of Plath, and I would listen with vicarious hunger as she described her affair with the man she loved.

I never left the house except to go to the movies or to the beach with Shari. She was eleven, and I was twenty, but most days it never occurred to me that I should need any other friend but her. On weekends we clung together like twins, dreaming and drawing and plotting for when Shari could pierce her ears. As time passed my father left me to myself in a resigned kind of peace, which slowly grew into acceptance, even pride, when he saw that my teens had elapsed without a whisper of a boyfriend, much less pregnancy.

It seems incredible to look back on this time now, and even more peculiar to write it down, as I try to make sense of it. For these five years after leaving high school at fifteen, this unnatural hermitage was all I knew—reading the growing stack of books in my room and dreaming of far moons, faraway boys. Because of my father's unpredictable moods and controlling reach, my freedom had never been a given, so whenever it was taken away again it was not a shock. I had almost grown accustomed to it, until nighttime struck. When the house slept, my haunted stasis overtook me, and I sometimes mourned the world I was missing, the neon scream of my teens passing me by in my bedroom. All this time spent in seclusion would have felt unbearable if it weren't for poetry. If it weren't for my poems, I wouldn't have survived it. I was convinced that my isolation was some poetic rite of passage; that *this* was how all the great poets before me had lived. I thought about how Emily Dickinson, secluded under her own unfulfilled hopes and desires, had burned with a singular intensity at her desk, distilling her grief into hundreds of poems. How Plath, heartbroken and closed off from the world in the countryside, wrote in just five months the staggering poems that would make her name. Poems that would eventually find and transform my sixteen-year-old self. So I did not rue the outside world too deeply, because as long as I had a poem in my head and a pen in my hand, I believed all this strife would shake out right in the end. Each word, each poem, would one day revise the trajectory of my life. When I got the call to come to Kingston for the Nobel Laureate's poetry workshop, I finally felt the air of possibility shift around me again. Derek Walcott had landed on the island and was teaching a workshop for Jamaica's finest poets, and I was one of eight who were chosen to be a part of it.

I walked into the workshop at twenty dizzy with nerves, clutching a sheaf of poems that I planned to show Mr. Walcott afterward. The workshop occupants were two or three times my age, except for one other young poet, a dreadlocked youth so shy he uttered not one word the entire meeting. I turned away from him the way I looked away from my former self. Mr. Walcott sat at the head of the table, gray eyes glinting as he loosened gem after gem. We all gulped every word, scribbling notes, trying to osmose everything. I scavenged greedily from where I sat. He asked everyone at the table to name the poets they were reading. I made note of what everyone said, to make sure I would say something entirely different to impress him. "I'm reading Georg Trakl, Rilke, and Paul Celan," I said. "I'm in a deep German phase." Everyone chuckled and so did Walcott, his eyes sparkling as he nodded at me in approval. "Great choices," he said. When the workshop was over, I shadowed Mr. Walcott down the hallway and bleated out my request to show him some of my poems. I'd practiced my speech several times, rehearsing how to ask this giant to look over my poetry, and now it all spilled out in a quivering jumble, which seemed to warm him to me.

"I've been told about you," he said, and my insides plunged. I had not spoken to the Old Poet in almost a year. Now I wondered what he'd said to Walcott about me. How much. "Follow me to the lobby," he said.

I walked behind Mr. Walcott to the hotel lobby, where we sat in two tufted armchairs facing each other. I handed him my printed-out poems and waited with a stone in my throat as he read over them.

He peeked over the sheets of paper at me, then back at the poems. He peered down at me from his reading glasses.

"This is serious," he said.

"Thank you, sir," I managed to say.

"No, it's not a good thing," he said, pointing to one of the poems. "You can't be beating the reader over the head with a hammer like this, every line." My pages shook as he spoke. "You need to give them room to breathe."

"Yes, sir." My hands were trembling, threatening to fly off without me.

"We need to meet again," Walcott said after he finished flipping through my poems. "Come back tomorrow at noon for lunch."

As I got dressed to meet Mr. Walcott the next morning my phone rang. It was Lij. "Hey, love!" I chirped. My brother's voice shook on the other end of the line. He'd been at UWI five months now, and he sounded so different than the last time I'd heard him. At university he'd taken up my mother's habit of smoking spliff after spliff to blur the edges of his hours; his professors had not taken kindly to a Rastafari student in their halls, and his college days were marked by their mistreatment. He was raspy-voiced and low now, none of his usual electricity, all his chatter drained from him. "Saf. I need your help," he said.

"What's wrong?" I asked him, my voice pitching.

"Saf . . . I've been starving over here . . . I was hoping . . . I was hoping you could help me with something to eat." My brother was a proud man. He would never ask anyone for help except me or Mom, and if he was asking me, it had to be dire.

I ached as he spoke. I didn't tell him I was scheduled to meet Walcott in less than an hour. "Of course. Of course I will," I said, my eyes watering. "Tell me where to meet you."

I'd been staying in Kingston for the first time with Ann-Margaret, who had offered to host me when I came for the Walcott workshop. She now drove as fast as she could, zipping through the roads, all while worrying over the clock and my meeting time with Walcott. I couldn't leave my brother in the lurch, tell him as he was starving that I had somewhere else to be. We were one spine, one blood. The car sped through Kingston to the Mona Campus. I hopped out and hugged my brother, who was all bones and dreadlocks, which were now almost touching his backside. "Thanks, sis," he said, his eyes dark with sadness even as he smiled at me.

I handed him the fish sandwich and fries I bought with my savings from the poetry prize, and his voice wavered. "I love you."

"Love you too," I whispered. We pulled ourselves apart and he waved us goodbye. Ann-Margaret peeled again through the streets of Kingston and I kept watch of the clock. Ten minutes late. We zipped through side streets, my stomach lurching as the time ticked by. Fifteen minutes late. When Ann-Margaret finally squealed into the hotel driveway there was no time for parking, so I just flew out the car door and sprinted through the lobby, looking for signs pointing to the restaurant. Twenty-five minutes late. I tore past slow-strolling patrons, gasping out apologies as my limbs became sticky with sweat. Thirty minutes late. My heart thumped as I flew, searching for what reason I could possibly give to Mr. Walcott to excuse this. My brother's emergency felt too private to share. When I arrived at the hotel's outdoor restaurant I saw him standing at the bar, and I clattered up to him and yelped "Hellosir I'msorry sirpleasesir," in one heaving breath. Once he saw me approaching, he turned his back to me and crossed his arms. Almost immediately I began to cry.

"I'm sorry, sir," I said, running around the mute wall of his back to face him. "I'm sorry. I'm so sorry. Please." He turned his back to me again and I started sobbing in the middle of the restaurant. Then Mr. Walcott's eyes caught mine. Perhaps it was my tears, or something else unknowable that softened him.

He turned to me, touched my elbow, and said, "Stop crying. Go and clean yourself up and come back."

When I returned from the bathroom I joined him at the table he'd taken in the shade.

"I'm furious with you," he said as soon as I sat down. His eyes unfeeling, arctic. "This is just not done. This is as if I showed up late to meet Auden. Unimaginable," he said. I apologized and started tearing up again.

"No more tears," he said. "We're here now."

I gathered myself and nodded.

"You look like a waif," he said. "Are you hungry?"

While we ate, we pored over my poems, which he went through like a butcher, slashing, carving. "The lines need space to sing," he said. "These images are good but lose potency when you string four of them together at once."

"Yes, sir," I said, only listening and nodding.

Soon the sunshine burned high and overtook us in the shade. We talked about Coleridge and inventing hyphenated words, we talked about Yeats and Brodsky and Heaney. I ran like a madwoman through the temple of everything I knew, flinging open doors to find the right words, the right names, trying to catch the keys as he threw them at me. Until it seemed we were speaking a kind of jazz. He asked me what poems I had memorized.

"Well, I have about eight of your poems memorized," I said, suddenly nervous again.

"Eight?" He seemed impressed.

"Yes, sir," I said, listing the titles of his poems I had by memory. "But please don't ask me to recite one," I begged. He laughed and agreed. In the end I recited Stevens' "The Idea of Order at Key West" for him. He closed his eyes and listened, rapping his fingers every so often on the table as I spoke.

"Beautiful," he said when I finished. "What year are you in college?"

My cheeks flushed and I looked away. As the afternoon lengthened, I'd been feeling more comfortable with him. I decided then to throw off my embarrassment and take the plunge. I shared with him the truth, explaining that my parents could not afford to send me to college just yet.

"That's a shame. If you get yourself to Boston," Walcott said, "you can audit my class at the university. I will arrange it. Just get yourself there."

A surge of hope, then. Joy striking me in the right light.

"Yes, sir." I nodded. "Thank you."

Afterward he walked me back to the lobby where my parents were coming to meet me. They were taking food and supplies to Lij at UWI before taking me back home.

While I waited in the lobby with Mr. Walcott, we chatted about my favorite German poets and my grandmother Isabel's German heritage. "You remind me of some of my family," he said. Later I was struck by the surreality of it. But while I sat there under the chandelier, the whole day efflorescing, our conversation seemed to me the most natural thing in the world.

My parents crept shyly toward us in the lobby, approaching Mr. Walcott with humble deference, bowing their heads at his chair as if they were meeting a king. He smiled as the two of them came closer, and once he glanced over their dreadlocks, he looked sideways at me and asked, "Are these your parents?"

I told him yes.

He stood up and shook their hands. Then with a glint of mischief in those eyes he said, "So which bank are we robbing?"

In the months that followed my meeting with Mr. Walcott, I never stopped clutching the unshakable hope he had given me in my writing: that I *was* a poet, and eventually something good would happen for me. Even as my college dreams still stalled, and I rode that high wave back to the shore of my disappointments, I held on to this hope. Growing up underprivileged, I had long learned that life was never a straight line. I was accustomed to its turbulent crests and falls by now, clasping, just as my parents did, to Manley's old promise that *Bettah Must Come.* About a year and a half later, in April 2006, I was a few months away from my twenty-second birthday when the email came early one morning. It was the third year of my deferral at Bennington College, and the last year I could postpone my enrollment. The Admissions Office wrote my mother to ask if I was still planning to attend the school. We wrote back to inform them that unfortunately, we didn't have the money to cover my remaining tuition. We hadn't been able to get me to Boston, either. "I'm sorry, love," Mom told me. Tears brimmed her eyes as she got up from the computer screen.

Less than an hour later we were back at the computer, blinking as we read over the reply, which seemed like a tiny sliver of promise opening.

How much can you cover? the director of Admissions asked.

My parents kneaded their heads together and came up with a nominal amount, which was just a little bit more than they would be able to afford for all four years, but which their pride bid them propose to this American school wanting to give their firstborn daughter a chance. My mother wrote back and named what they could pay.

That night I waited on tenterhooks for the college's response, and all my hope and desire and ambition thrummed through me. It was now six years since I had graduated high school, and I was still waiting for my life to begin. There had been so many maybes and could bes and what ifs, false starts and false hopes. And, even when I knew that every other young person my age was elsewhere, in school or working, I clung to the passing branches of hope. My parents, neither of whom ever held a nine-to-five job in my lifetime, never pushed me to join the traditional workforce. My father, who distrusted the world outside the gate, was resolute in preserving my purity at home and would not send me out to work in Babylon, no matter how much my family struggled financially. "Providing for the family is the man's job," he told me. I had spent all my formative years caged in, but I had spent them wildly dreaming, honing my education by my own hands, molding my own poet self from the clay, never conceding. For I was determined to write myself from out of these margins.

Now all I needed was a crack in the door. Just a crack. That's all I had been waiting for.

In the end, we didn't need to rob a bank. The email came back that morning from Bennington with three golden words.

Let's do it.

My mother and I flew out of our seats and hollered until our throats were hoarse. Those three words were more than a sliver. They held everything within them. All possible worlds, all possible selves. Each time my mother and I settled down, we would be overcome again, flying up to jump and squeal once more. After nearly six years of struggle and a river of tears wept, after cowed disappointments and all the miles of burning coals I had endured to get here, I screamed until I was hoarse, for her. The young girl who had stepped onto that rusty nail, the one who charmed a room of white men to get a scholarship to go to private school, the girl who read the dictionary and encyclopedia night after night. The girl who walked away from that glass shard to conjure her silver poem, the one who birthed herself from the veiled world into possibility. The first girl in a line of girls who looked into the frayed face of her bleak future and said no. I rejoiced now for her and for her and for her. I ran through the yard, my hair free at my shoulders, weightless with what life was in front of me suddenly, trying to imagine all the mythic details of my leaving. After all this time, I would study. I would write and dream and kiss and learn the strange and secret languages of this world.

26

The Red Door

Tʜᴇ ᴅᴀʏ Sʜᴀʀɪ ʟᴀɴᴅᴇᴅ ɪɴ Bᴀʟᴛɪᴍᴏʀᴇ to visit us, she was adamant about the first thing she wanted to do. "I just want it gone," she told us of her dreadlocks, erasing the pretense that she might have chosen any other future for herself. It was 2010, four years after I had left for Bennington College. I was now twenty-five and on the brink of graduation, Ife was twenty-one, and Shari was now sixteen. Ife and I huddled on a bunk bed in her small studio apartment, our backs bent over Shari's head, our one mind fixed on a singular goal. Unraveling. Shari wanted her locks gone but she didn't want us to cut them off, leaving her hair short. So, we spent our first real hours together in two years painstakingly trying to re-deem the hair that was matted within each dreadlock. We three pressed in close together, our legs crossed lotus on the bottom bunk, knee to warm knee, talking as we worked. Three birds appeared above us, weaving in and out, making a nest. This was sisters' work.

Ife and I no longer relaxed our hair, so we were used to pushing our hands into thickets of curls as a weekly ritual. We heard none of Ife's Johns Hopkins classmates' frolicking in the hallway, nor their meandering laughter outside in the streets. In this modest studio, we three had nothing but ourselves. Shari sat tranquil as a cat with her head bowed while we made swift work of unfastening what kept her fastened to home, bound to the one whose name we tried not to speak. Even as he weighed heavy on our minds, our hands were pulling her away from him. Sweat beaded on our noses as we untangled each nettled year from her hair. As the morning slumped into the afternoon, my fingertips reddened and stung. Sometimes the dreadlock made a sharp ripping sound as we pulled it apart and Shari's head bobbed with the force of our pulling. But she didn't flinch. This hair had been dead to her for a long time before.

This was her first time in the States. Though Shari was the youngest of the four of us, sometimes I sensed in her a belief that she might as well have been born an only child. Not long after I left, my mother—who now had not one but two daughters studying in the United States—was granted the ten-year visa she had always craved and was determined to make good use of it. She left the country often and for long periods of time, frequently visiting her siblings who had emigrated to Foreign, some of whom she hadn't seen since they were teens at White House, and who often helped her send money back to Shari in Jamaica every week. Like Ife and I had done before her, Shari spent many of these formative years locked up alone, moving houses with my father every other year, forbidden from leaving them. They had moved three times in the four years I had left for Bennington College, and were now up to the ninth rented house since the night we rolled away from White House twenty years before. Each holiday trip home, I dropped my bags in a new rented house, and tried my best to bridge the gone years with Shari, but when I bent over her unraveling head in Ife's studio apartment that day, I felt only irreparable loss. She was no longer the sweet twelve-year-old who clung to me as I had clung to her in those two years we were home alone, our two heads grown into one, watching classic movies and Miyazaki anime, listening to her favorite K-pop. In the four years I had been gone for college, my sister had grown unsentimental, her tongue acidic, speaking older and wiser than her sixteen years, and she seemed tired, so tired of it all.

We gently prodded about home, but Shari wouldn't say much about the years spent alone with our father, though they had clearly hardened her. She wanted her first experience of Foreign to be foreign and nothing at all of home. Perhaps she thought it wasn't even worth the telling—she had grown up watching the same sad play on a loop, his wildfire burning through daughter after daughter. It was nothing Ife and I hadn't already lived. He hounded Shari about not becoming a pregnant teenager the way our grandmother had. He berated her for not pressing and cooking and cleaning for him when our mother was away. He drove crazy on the road and threatened to swerve into the gully most mornings when he took her to school. But unlike Ife and me, Shari wouldn't waste her tears on him. She rolled her eyes and kissed her teeth and called him "a diva." Not only was he angry, she said, he had now become miserly, withholding the money Mom had sent for her and almost refused to pay for her crucial final CXC exams because she stopped saying "Good morning" to him. Now here she was in America for the first time, hungry for the unraveling to be complete.

While I was away at college, I used to imagine a red door by the sea that tethered me to home. I followed my homesick longing through its sunlit frame often, finding myself beached in the past, yearning for a home and a self I was still perfecting. My longing was fed by news that came to me in snatches; seeds of family gossip, triumphs and dramas, the news inevitably turning to what was lost. All of it came by my mother through the telephone; she delayed any news of loss by days or even weeks, chewing each morsel into manageable bites before she fed them to me. I accepted her as the gatekeeper of all things that pained me in this world. So that late autumn morning when the phone rang in my dorm room, I somehow knew what she was going to say before she said it.

"Do you know who died?" she asked me. Her voice was gentle as a hymn. I closed my eyes as soon as she said it.

The air had already turned crisp and I hated the cold. I pressed my fingers against my eyelids, pressing the blackness behind my eyes into red.

"Was it cancer?" I asked.

"Yes," she said, though I already knew. I never kept my promise to read poems out loud to him in the hospital. There had been no real reconciliation between me and the Old Poet, only pinches of news that came to me via Ann-Margaret when he asked her for updates about what I was doing.

I always thought if you came through you'd come through in spades. I read over his last email to me, which came three years after I last saw him and which had gone unanswered among the selfish shotgun days of my new American college life.

And now he was gone so there was no answer left to give. There was no tearing my throat or weeping, no fingerbone pointed in accusation. All I had were the many poems I wrote about him in those desolate years and all that had happened, still coiling, unresolved in my gut. And now there would be nothing more. At last, I felt nothing. He was a jawbone somewhere in the Kingston mud. He had always told me death was only a problem for the living, but how wrong he had been, even then.

A misty-eyed silence fell over our unraveling as all the bottled ache of the past years unstopped itself and flowed over. I thought of all that was happening at home without me, all I must have been losing even now, while not even knowing. I let my brooding get away from me, and I confessed to my sisters the awful thing that had consumed me the last few days.

The email, titled "Long ago and Far Away!!!" had come from a woman named Leah Sinclair, a person I did not know. I opened it with mild interest only to find that I did know her, as she was quick to remind me. She was a woman we had met at Bogue as children, and who told us to call her "Mama Lee." Running in a thunderstorm, popcorn kernels in a pan, a rainy afternoon appeared fuzzy in my mind. I was too young then to question any of it, and she was just another foreign woman visiting us with toys. But now here was an email not from "Mama Lee" at all, but from a woman who now had my own last name. My head had reeled as I read on.

> Dearest Safiya,
>
> I have tears in my eyes as I write this. Can you believe it? Hello from Mama Lee!!!
>
> Don't remember me? We spent many days running through the fields at Bogue where you, Lij, and Ife sang songs about the river. Listen to the water! Still don't remember? Leah Sinclair married Howard Garfield O'Brien Sinclair 2/9/87!
>
> I've kept up with all your successes online—big congratulations to you! Heard you were just in NYC. My son, Mosiah, and his son, DJANI, both live in NYC.
>
> I'd really love to reconnect with your mom, and hear her magnificent laugh again. Oh, what adventures we had

on my visits to Jamaica! Please, please, please send me her
email address?

And if you're up for it, we can also trade "missives."

I'll wait to hear back from you with bated breath.

Peace, love, and light,

Leah NEFERTITI Sinclair

A familiar lava coursed up my throat as I pieced this all together. I
kept reading over two details in her email as spots flashed in and out of
my eyes: That she had married my father three years after I was born, and
that she had a son who named his own son Djani. My father, who had
never married my mother because "Rasta don't believe in marriage," had
not only married this woman, but he had led her to believe she could
carry my name and my mother's name in her mouth. I brooded black
over the disrespect. That he had given her my email address, that she
thought we would ever exchange "missives," and that she really believed I
would pass on my mother's contact information to her.

I took my hand away from Shari's head now and pressed my knuckles
into my eyes. Auntie Audrey once told me she could never forgive my
father for hugging and kissing some foreign woman in the back seat of
a taxi while my mother rode with them stone-faced in the front seat like
a stooge. That he had been with that foreign woman even as my brother
was born, Lij wailing out all night in the hospital as my mother also cried.
Now here was that same woman, her cuckoo's egg landed in my morning
nest. I told my sisters about the email and passed the foul thing around
for them to see. Our repulsed silence grew into repulsed sighs. It was hard
to be surprised by what our father did anymore.

"I can't believe she had the *nerve* to email you," Ife fumed, snatching
at Shari's hair. The unraveling was now almost complete.

"I can't believe he gave her my email," I said. "I'm so upset."

"Really, Saf?" Shari said, turning her neck to look at me. "What do
you really expect from him at this point?"

She was right. I was foolish, more foolish than any of them. And even
worse, I was weak. Marred by my double axe—both sentimental and a
hopeless masochist, I kept expecting something different from my father

every time. Having loved him first, I somehow believed he could become something worthy of loving again. I believed it still, even then. I believe it still, even now.

"Please don't tell Mom about this." Ife spoke low now, her lip quivering. She made a rake of her hands to sweep up strings of fallen hair from the bottom bunk.

"I won't," I promised.

But in truth I had already told Mom. She was the first one I wrote to, seething after I got the email, and she was more than hurt to hear it. Soon her hurt turned to an anger as potent as the day she walked out the gate. It was not the marriage. She already knew about that, she told me. My father had married Leah in hopes of attaining a green card, so my mother had already moved on from the indignity of their relationship and the details of the arrangement that eventually went sour. It was the gall of this woman that stuck in her craw. The gall, to write to her daughter as if she were after something. "If someone owes her something, it's not you," my mother told me. Even then, I could hear the hurt hardening in her voice, which only hardened me too.

My sisters and I slipped back into a humming silence again, shuttering our blinds on the email, never speaking of it again. We crammed that woman's son and grandson into a box in the corner with all our dead hair and left it there.

"Finally," Shari said when we were done. Our hands swollen, her dreadlocks gone. She got up and stretched, brushed her clothes free of the stringy excess that had fallen from her untangled locks. "Now can we change the subject?"

Like everything else in her life, my mother did it herself. A week later, while in the United States for my graduation and alone in Ife's Baltimore apartment, feeling some urgency overtake her, she took a pair of scissors to her dreadlocks and cut. Those dreadlocks had been growing on my mother's head since she was nineteen years old and living in a Rasta commune deep in the hills. They had grown past the birth of four children, two miscarriages; countless unnamed students laying their sticky palms upon her head; through my father's so-called friends Mama Lee

and Reina and Primrose. They had outgrown decades of changing pres-
idents and prime ministers, had mourned the death of Bob Marley and
Peter Tosh and Dennis Brown, and had kept on growing through plane
crashes, economic crashes, and multiple space shuttle crashes. They had
seen the coral reefs by her seaside village vanish, and had weathered the
death of her own father. Those locks had held and comforted and aided
the mass mutiny of her daughters, but it was the cutting of her own
womb that made her finally do it.

Some years before, my mother had been diagnosed with fibroids and
had to undergo a hysterectomy. For her, the surgery and its recovery were
a throbbing revelation. Whomever she thought she was in the world,
and whatever that woman's purpose, was suddenly gone. She laughed like
a songbird when she called me to tell me she had cut her dreadlocks.
"Something just switched off," she told me. She returned home without
her womb, then realized that my father no longer had any hold over her.
There would be no more children by him or any man. There was nothing
else to bind her to him. Now that she was in America and finally free
from my father's gaze, she wanted to revel in that freedom. Freedom to
eat meat and drink alcohol and learn to be herself, away from him. So
she did. Here, in America, where she felt free, my mother let go of that
scared nineteen-year-old searching for purpose and found the woman she
had been waiting a whole lifetime to be. After nearly five decades spent
in constant service to the wants of others, this was the first thing she had
done just for herself, choosing the shape of her own life for the first time;
conjured, at last, by her own persistent hands.

I took long glances at my mother as I waited under the tented heat with
the other Bennington graduates. It was hard to look away from her—this
astonishing new and beautiful creature with newly shorn hair, looking
fabulous in her heels, her light frost of pink lipstick. My graduation dress
was made from traditional African fabric with a Swahili message printed
around the hem that meant *You are the light of my life.* I wore it in dedica-
tion to my mother, which made her eyes spill over with joy. She jumped
in the front row with Ife and my grandma Sweet P, who had flown over,

all of them screaming for me when they called my name. As I walked across the stage, I thought of the women who had come before me, my riverine clan of women known and unknown, whose many futures and possibilities and bodily autonomy had been taken, and I wept as I became the first girl in my family to graduate from college. Whatever came next, I promised myself, I would do for them. In my hands, their names and lives would never be forgotten. My mother clutched my diploma to her chest the entire weekend and couldn't stop laughing. Laughing at nothing at all. Seeing me come through after all this time, after six years of limbo and four years of study, had her cup brimming over. And nothing was going to overshadow that. "Mi glad bag buss!" she kept telling me. "Oh, Saf. Mi glad bag buss!"

Before I left my college behind, my mother, grandmother, and sister helped me pack and clean out my dorm room. Our hands quick as one again. I had never decorated my walls, but I had accumulated towers of books. My grandmother filled a suitcase heavy with all my books to take back to Jamaica for me. My looming countdown to return home weighed heavy as we packed. I had three months to find a job in America in my field of study or I would have to join my suitcase of books right back in my father's house.

"Did you tell him you did it?" I asked my mother now, glancing over her hair. I just assumed she had told my father about cutting her locks, but I never asked.

"No," my mother said, raising her brow and tilting her head at me. Her voice sharp as a honed blade. "Tell him for what?"

When my mother walked through the arrivals gate in the Montego Bay airport, my father saw what else my hands had unraveled. Her dreadlocks shorn and gone. "Oh Jah," I imagine him muttering to himself. Earrings in her ears. A mid-calf skirt hugging her figure. The look on her face defiant. My father's face pulled inward, downcast with hurt as he considered my mother's new appearance. His eyes grew red and wet as my parents drove back to the house. She said nothing and he said nothing back. When they crossed the threshold into the house, he brought in her luggage in that silence, one by one. My mother, however, waltzed through the house in a breeze. Everything my father once had a claim upon had been cut. There was nothing more for her to give. Nothing left except whatever she would make of Esther.

When there was nothing more in the trunk for my father to busy his hands with, he finally approached my mother in the kitchen. My father's voice was hoarse from singing the night before, and broke as he spoke.

"Makini," he said, calling her by her African name they had chosen from the naming book all those decades ago. "You used to love me once."

"Once," my mother said, and clutched her belly.

Then she laughed. The laugh of a witch in full moon, feeling the earth's voice as one with herself. All of that love had gone. That night, my mother took a set of sheets and a pillow and slept in a separate bed for the first time in her life. All she had needed was a catalyst, and Leah Sinclair's email had pushed her to the blade's edge. Inside the bedroom that once belonged to her daughters, she pushed all the furniture in the room—a bed and a dresser—to block the door. When my father came looking for her and tried to push the door, my mother thought again of that woman's email and held it closed with her back pushing against the furniture, barring my father's entry to the room. Even as he knocked and shouted for her she did not answer, for that voice no longer moved her to crumble.

The next morning my father walked through the hibiscus garden with his black machete. All night he had heard laughter echoing, not from my mother, but from its original source. His mind darkened over the root of his curse, his rotten seed and her iniquity, swatting at the pestilence that had been plaguing him for twenty-six years. As he walked, he swung the blade and spat, wondering to Jah how he had fathered his own ruin. He sought out the voice he heard cackling at him now from Foreign. The cause of his Rasta family's undoing. The one whose face snaked, scaled and hissing from the bushes—his firstborn, first in all things profane—as he readied his cutlass to chop me down.

27

Iphigenia

H E REACHED FOR THE PILLOW FIRST, and the machete second. As the earth spun away from me in darkness, all I could see was blue.

Before the lumbering crush of my father's hands at my skull, the day had begun in shining beauty. And so much blue. The morning sky was cloudless and lapis blue, so blue I had had to look away to the hills. My father woke with a nimble song in his throat, cooing for the two little birds back in his hand, the two daughters that he held and held, squeezing a song to drown out all their squirming. I dressed for work as Shari braced herself for another blank day at home, finding herself right where I had been years ago—out of high school at sixteen and waiting on a chance to go to college. My mother had flown back to Foreign with the singular aim of getting her washbelly—her lastborn—enrolled in college, come hell or high water. I had landed back in Montego Bay three months after graduating in June 2010, having failed to find a job in the United States related to my English degree. As soon as I'd landed back home, three warnings struck like a gong and I set my eye on leaving again, for good.

The first warning that calamity was on the horizon came during my first week at work, where I had begun my new job teaching English at St. James College. The moment my father had turned up the marl-dusted driveway and I returned to the same converted great house that was the site of my old haunting, I knew I could no longer have a future in Jamaica. My four years away had sailed swift and boomeranged me right back to where I had always been, except now I was teaching Mobay's rich and overprivileged instead of studying with them. There was no triumph to be found in my return. I wandered the same stuffy bedroom-turned-classrooms, noticing the old scratches on the windows, old names carved into desks. Some days it seemed that besides cutting my dreadlocks, not even I had changed. I was still stuck in amber. After dropping me off on my first day, my father had lingered in the driveway, which sent the students flocking to the windows to stare at the Rastaman in the old champagne Toyota Corolla, wondering how he was connected to their English teacher, who bore no resemblance to him. "He's my father," I told them, and ended the mystery, lest their minds run away from them.

Not more than five hours after I told them who my father was, the first warning sign arrived folded in a scrap of glossy paper, turned face-down on my desk. Some student, sweaty with mischief, had sought to disrupt. I unfolded the scrap and found myself face-to-face with my desecrated self, flung back to Mrs. Newnham's office. Before me was my eighth-grade picture, torn out of one of the old yearbooks that were kept in the school library, my smile a wound and so unsure of itself, hiding my broken tooth. There, my old uncombed hair lay black and thick atop my head, with my dreadlocks in a ponytail falling behind my back. Around my picture were the same pen scratches of cruel words, doodle of disfigured teeth, and the bubble above my head that said I HAVE NO BOOBS. I looked around the empty teachers' room. The desk I had been assigned was the same one Mrs. Pinnock used all those years ago. Her sour glare now raking at me from the ether. Every morning I sat in the same spot she had tried to rub the henna from my hands. Where she scoured her fingers until my skin turned red. Just then, something moved in the corner of my eye. I looked around to the large window behind me. Outside, an eleventh-grade boy ducked out of the frame from where he had been watching me inspect my picture. His face warped by the old glass. I could hear him sniggering now, his footfall pattering as he ran away.

Soon Shari and I had fallen into our old, conjoined rhythm. We were once again the only ones left. We clung to each other, slept together in the same room, ate together, and skirted my father as much as we could, especially when he was in a mood. We kept Lij's room empty in case he decided to come home. Much to my parents' dismay, my brother had quit law school after being told he had to cut his dreadlocks to practice law. He was now teaching English at his old high school across town, where he lived with his new girlfriend. More and more my brother seemed resolute to plant his own unruly garden without us.

Shari and I made our own language and our own sense of being. We were furthest apart in age than all our siblings; I was twenty-six and she was seventeen, but we grew closer than anyone else, bonded by our linked catastrophes, which we referred to as "the plight of SS." We discovered new, sisterish ways to be happy, while I schemed with Mom to get Shari away to college, and to get myself away for good. Before I left Bennington, an American publisher had solicited a hybrid chapbook of poems and essays from me, which I spent the summer after graduation writing, and which had now been published. With my chapbook and some money for application fees, I began applying for MFAs abroad. On the backs of my poems, I had decided, I would cross this ocean again.

By the time the second warning came, it was disguised unexpectedly in a wave of good news. My first MFA acceptance arrived on my lunch break at St. James College where I hunched over my old desk. I yelped as I read the email. Then another email acceptance came. I felt a roiling sense of right, tectonic plates shifting beneath my feet. When my father pulled into the school that afternoon to pick me up, I swept into the passenger seat of his parked car, smiling with news.

I could barely sit still in my seat. "I just got into college for my master's degree!" I told him.

Instead of praises, my father's face fell. He went quiet and stared out over his steering wheel for a long time. I glanced out to see what he was looking at. There was nothing there.

"So the I just goin go weh and leave I and I here alone?" he asked me.

He was more vulnerable than I'd ever seen him.

"What you mean, Daddy?"

"Everybody just up and gone a Foreign so. Lij tek up with woman. All of the I them just lef I man here by miself."

How silly I was. I'd expected him to be happy for me, my new possibilities. As he spoke, I should have heard the clear siren of warning of what was to come. That he thought only of himself in this moment and not my happiness, and certainly not my future. For, if he didn't want any of us to leave him, what did he really want?

"Well, what did you think was going to happen, Dad?" I asked.

He fidgeted in his seat now and looked away from my face. "Well . . . I man don't know . . . I man just thought we coulda buy a house and all ah we jus' live there . . ."

"You mean forever?" I asked him.

"Well, yeah . . ." He looked almost bashful now, having spoken this thing out loud at last.

Almost. The silent acolyte woman whose throat I cut all those years ago tried to whisper herself back into existence as my father spoke. But then I remembered my acceptances. My poems. Remembered everything that made me want to leave.

"Dad," I said, turning my body in my seat to face him now. Orange poinciana petals blew down onto the windshield of our parked car. "Someday we will have our own families that we will live with, in our own houses. We were always going to leave and make our own way. That's how it's supposed to work."

"Well, what about this family?" he asked, running his hands over the motionless steering wheel. "What about staying together? Why can't we have a place just for ourselves?" His face was almost pleading as he spoke.

"I thought you would be happy for me," I said. I turned away to watch the orange flowers falling.

The mood in the car fell silent as I looked out ahead of me, to the far glances of sea shimmering across the street.

My father turned on the ignition and started slowly rolling down the driveway, while I ignored the flock of johncrows circling their dark message overhead.

The last warning bell was the landlady's phone ringing. Three weeks after the second warning, she'd flown down on vacation from Canada as she did once a year, except this time she notified my father of her plans to move back to Coral Gardens for good. All week her high-pitched old Nokia ringtone had been piercing the air in a ceaseless cacophony from inside her quarters at the house in Coral Gardens, putting all of us on edge. We were given one month to vacate the house where my father and sister had lived for the last two years. We spent two weeks driving all over Montego Bay, searching for a place to live. When I was done teaching, my father drove my sister and me to look at new rental houses he'd found in the Classifieds, and I liked none of them. Too small. Too yellow. Too many people in the yard. Each day we returned in the evening, the landlady's cell phone would ring out incessantly, followed by her high-clucking voice rattling on all night. Her old Nokia plagued our waking hours in those sweltering weeks, insistent as an alarm, an unheeded warning.

We finally found a new house, far into the whispering hills and away from the sea again. My father desperately wanted my approval, unnerved by some dread that I wouldn't like it. I told him I liked it well enough. "But this is just temporary for me," I reminded him. His face slumped, lonely and crestfallen. Maybe that was the thing that did it. Or perhaps it was my mother's absence. She had been gone five months now, but it already felt twice as long. My father had never moved without my mother, carrying the weight of all of us in her hands. He'd never done any of the packing for our many moves and the undertaking seemed to be breaking him. I was the only one of the three of us who had to work all day, so I told my father that they'd have to do the bulk of packing themselves, and I would help as best I could when I got home. That put him in a foul mood immediately. That night, while I pored over my lesson plans, I could hear him cursing halfway across the house, which I ignored, until I heard him say my name.

The day that had begun in its beauty now fell like a dead bird at my feet, squeezed soundless in my father's hands. I snapped my books shut and walked down the hall. I stayed out of sight for a moment and listened.

"She not helping with nothing—" he was saying to Shari, who was mostly ignoring him, fixing her curls in his bathroom mirror, absentmindedly saying "Yeah," every other minute as my father kissed his teeth.

"She is damn lazy—" he hissed. As he spoke, I stepped visible into the threshold of his bedroom and stood akimbo in the doorframe. I was as tall as him and held myself straight as a lightning rod.

"I don't really know why you're talking about me," I said. "Stop treading on my name."

There was a crackle in the air. Next to me I could see Shari standing alert in the doorway of the bathroom, glancing sideways at me. My father stepped away from his dresser, where the framed picture of Haile Selassie faced me. The emperor's scorpion eyes, no longer a site of any fear.

"Girl, you better watch how you talk to I and I," my father said. The furniture bounced as he stomped toward me. "Get away from here." He made a swatting motion with his hands, as if I were a fly.

I crossed my arms and dug in, planting myself firmly in the doorway. "I'm not moving nowhere," I said.

"Move from here," my father said again, pulling the words through his teeth. His scar was shining under the bedroom light.

I laughed. "Or what?"

He kissed his teeth and stomped back to his bed, grabbing a pillow.

"You can't talk about me like this." I shook my head at him as I spoke. "I'm a grown woman. I'm not some likkle pickney you can insult anymore."

My father smiled that red smile, still trying to squeeze me to nothing. "You're nothing but a little girl," he sneered. "Get away from my door, girl. Good for nothing."

Shari was pinned to her feet now with her back to the mirror behind her, unmoving and watching us wide-eyed, fearful.

"You can't move me," I said.

"I'm so tired of you," my father growled, squashing the pillow in his hands. "Ever since you been born you been plaguing me—I'm tired of you!"

"And I'm tired of *you*," I told him, running my palm over my hair. "I cannot wait until I'm gone from here for good. Everybody is tired of you. No one can stand you. Not even our mother—"

"Stop talking, girl—" he warned, coming closer with the pillow in his hand. But I wouldn't be stopped. The threshold between us could no longer hold.

"That's why Mom left you," I said. A dark adrenaline rushed through me, my heart pounding hard and dauntless. "She's done with you. She doesn't want you anymore. Don't you know? She is already moving on," I said.

Then, just as my mother had done when she last stood in this kitchen, I laughed.

My father flew toward me in the doorframe. His hands sprung at my head, his aim resolute. He rammed the pillow into my face and swung a punch at it, connecting with staggering force. Before I knew it, I was flung down, the earth coming toward me, the walls whirling away. Shari let out an ear-splitting wail and bolted back into the bathroom, where she started calling someone on her cell phone. Blackness swam across my eyes, and the world flashed in and out of light. I was on the ground in the hallway, and my father was scowling over me. His face was entirely emptied of himself. I blinked and when I looked again he was gone. Where his fist had connected with my face through the pillow, my teeth had burst into the skin of my lip and blood flooded out. A numb shock overtook me, then rage rose in my throat. As I got up from the floor, I had one thought in my mind. I slumped back to the kitchen and eyed the largest knife I could find. I could hear Shari on the phone in the chaos, her voice panicked and high-pitched. There was only one set of keys for the house and they were in my father's room. There was no way to get out without them.

Then the landlady's cell phone suddenly rang out. A howling wind tore through the roof of me, scattering all the day's blue in a hurricane. Blood rushed in my ear at a deafening pitch. When I had left for college, I promised myself that no man would ever put his hands on me again. Now my father's blow had reopened that lifetime of wounds, all of it finally boiling over into blackness. I no longer recognized myself. I picked up the knife from the dish rack and held it tight in my hands, blade forward, determined to plunge. My heart was pounding as I walked back to my room clutching the knife in my fist and grabbed my phone to dial my mother in America. My cut lip was swelling now and stung with every word. Mom's voice was already breaking when she picked up. Someone had already called her.

"Mom, he hit me over," I cried out, my lip bleeding as I spoke. "He punched me over—"

"Saf, are you okay?" she asked. Her voice breaking.

"My lip is cut," I said. My head was dizzy. All the while I could hear my father's voice booming and raging, shouting from his room, but I could not make out what he was saying.

"I'm going to kill this man, Mom," I said, gripping the handle of the ratchet knife. "I swear to you, I'm going to kill this man. For everything he's done to you, for everything he's done to me—" I caught my breath. I had snapped. Even as I swore it, I didn't believe it. I dropped my hands to my sides and screamed with every muscle in my body. A full-throated, primal scream that drenched me in sweat.

"Oh god. Oh god! Please god." My mother was crying on the phone, trying desperately to calm me down.

I stalked back to the kitchen and slowly approached the bedroom. On the line I could hear my mother saying, "No no no no, please, Saf, no." I kept her on the line so she could hear, but I stopped talking to her. I texted Lij and told him Dad punched me down and he needed to come up here right now.

The landlady's cell phone pierced out again, cutting through the ceiling, fissuring the night air. That is when I heard my father reach for his machete. The one he kept sharpened under his bed to fight off any unexpected intruders. Through the open doorway, across the house I heard the blade scrape long and metallic against the ceramic tile floor as he pulled it out. Shari screamed a blood-curdling cry and banged with all her might against the bathroom door.

My sister's squeals stopped me cold.

I realized then that my father had locked Shari inside the bathroom in his room. I could hear him now, banging the black machete against the burglar bars of his window, his large, deep voice blasting badwords and dark threats, pulling the whole house down into a screeching clamor.

"Run, Saf!" Shari shrieked, kicking hard against the locked door. "Run! Please run!"

My father snarled ugly out of my sight. "—talk bout Makini left I man! I going kill this bloodclaat—"

As the machete clanged against the reverberating bars, Shari's voice cried, "Daddy, let me out! Please let me out!"

My stomach dropped, hearing my sister kicking at the door and begging for him to let her out.

"Shari!" I screamed from the kitchen, and edged closer to the room. "Are you okay?"

Just then her voice unleashed an unearthly wail.

"Saf, don't come here! Don't come here. Please!" She was sobbing. "He said he's going to kill you! Run! Please run!"

Mom was now crying inconsolably on the line, so I hung up. Whatever came next I would spare her from hearing.

"He's going to kill you!" Shari's voice erupted into the night and filled my ears to bleeding. In his room, my father was detailing what hurt he was going to do to me for only my baby sister's ears to hear. "Please, Saf. Please, get out!" she said, her voice tearing at itself to reach its highest animal pitch and get through to me.

I came back to myself at my sister's last warning. The terror in her voice told me she thought my father was actually going to do it. That he had locked her up so she would not see. And I was not going to make it out of this house alive. I dropped the knife, clattering on the floor. My heart thumped as I skittered away from the kitchen, away from his bedroom, and desperately tried to find a way to get out of the house. For the first time in my life I picked up the phone and dialed the police. My voice shook as I heard myself telling the police officer that my father had attacked me and was now threatening to kill me. I said the words but they did not seem real. I ran out to the veranda and hammered on the landlady's door. By the time she opened it, I was hysterical.

"What is all that racket eh—" she was saying as she opened the door, but whatever look I wore on my face stopped her voice like a stone.

"Please. I need to get out," I said. My hands shook as I spoke. "I don't feel safe and I don't have a key to get out. I have to get out now." My lips quivered. "Can you please let me out?"

"What you saying?" she asked me, her head cocked in confusion. She was in her pink floral housecoat and still held her cell phone to her ear in mid-conversation.

"My father is trying to kill me!" I screamed. "I need you to open this veranda gate and let me out!" I pointed to the white iron bars that were like a cage around the veranda.

"Oh Jesus," the landlady said, and went back inside for her keys.

Finally, she rattled open the burglar bars of the veranda gate and let me out into the front yard.

"Thank you," I whimpered, as I walked out into the chill of the night. I was wearing only a thin T-shirt and blue house shorts. The shrill of the crickets broke against my swimming ears. Sloping down toward the front gate, I kept turning back to look at the light in my father's bedroom, at his dark figure pacing back and forth across the window, the machete still pointed in his hand as he ranted. I could still hear my sister sobbing as the police car pulled up to the gate.

I heard my father curse as the police car parked at our gate, red and blue lights flashing. I knew then that the shame of the landlady seeing this would concern him more than what he had done to me and Shari. The policeman got out of the car and approached me.

"Hello, ma'am," the policeman said, coming closer. "I'm here for a domestic disturbance call. Can you step outside the gate?"

"No," I said. "It's locked and I don't have the key." The gate and the wall were both too high for me to climb.

I saw the policeman look behind me and I turned to follow his gaze. My father, who no longer had his machete, was now talking calmly with the landlady, who I'm sure had some questions for him. From his body language I knew the monster had already shifted back into the wily public man.

The police officer asked me to recount what happened. I told him that my father had punched me in the face, and then took out his machete and said he was going to kill me. That he had locked my sister in the bathroom as he was coming to do it. As the policeman listened, he nodded, holding on to his belt, heavy with a handgun and a baton.

"Is that your father?" He pointed behind me, where my father was making his way down the driveway.

I nodded.

"Good evening, Officer," my father said now with a voice of honey. "How can I help you, sir?" I crossed my arms about my chest for warmth and stepped away from him.

"Your daughter says you assaulted her earlier this evening," he said.

My father feigned surprise and shook his head. "No, Officer, she is lying. I did no such thing." He smiled as he talked, and held his hands clasped behind his back. I looked over at him as he spoke to take in what a true coward looked like.

I pressed my face at the iron bars of the gate and pulled up my cut and swollen lip, still bloody, and showed it to the policeman.

"Here is the proof. My lip is still bleeding," I said.

"Sir, how do you explain her injury?" the officer asked my father.

My father sighed and rolled his eyes. "That's nothing at all, Officer. I just swatted her away with my pillow. Just a little swat. But there was no punch, sir. She is lying."

"He said he was going to kill me," I told the policeman now, my voice pleading with him to hear me. "He locked my sister in the bathroom and she was telling me to run for my life."

"Is this true, Mr. Sinclair?" the policeman asked him. "Those are serious allegations."

My father smiled and shook his head. "This girl is a liar, Officer," he said. Every time he called me "girl" it was a calculated chisel strike, purposefully chipping me away. There in his performance I saw it plainly before me, finally. He knew what it meant to cut me down, was doing it even now as we stood before Babylon. As long as I lived under his roof, he would never respect me. He would never see me as a person with value, my gender forever robbing me of his esteem.

"I'm not a girl." My voice rang clear against the crickets. "And I'm telling the truth."

"This *little* girl is a liar, Officer," my father said. He pulled on his beard and smiled with those razor-straight teeth. "I am a musician. A Rastaman. I would never do these things."

The officer now looked at me with curious eyes, with something like pity, which quickly shifted to a half smile against the light of his face. He had decided, it seemed, which one of us he thought was lying. Just then, another car pulled up behind him. My brother climbed out of the taxi and walked toward the gate.

The policeman wrote something on a piece of paper and handed it to me. "If you want to press charges against your father, here is the date, and here is the place you need to go to bring this to court. Have a good night," he said. Then he climbed back into his car, turned down the hill, and drove away.

My father didn't wipe the lurid smile from his face until the police car had disappeared from our sight completely.

"Hail, Fire," my father seethed to Lij. He'd shaken himself back into a quiet rage, brows knitted as he talked to my brother. Eyes dark and voided, the monster had broken out of the man again, just like that.

I kept my eyes on my brother's face and he kept his eyes on mine. He wore a calm expression that I knew meant calamity. "Open the gate," Lij said to our father.

My father threw the keys to the ground and turned to walk back to the house. The keys rattled in my hands as I opened the gate. Behind me I could hear Shari running down, and when she reached us she leapt onto me in a flood of tears. I grasped her back. "Are you okay?" I asked her. She nodded, weeping.

My father was only halfway back up to the veranda when Lij got through the gate. He stomped past me and up the driveway.

"Don't believe nuttin she—" My brother shoved the words from my father's mouth. Lij loomed tall as he dashed at my father in the driveway, and for the first time, I saw fear in my father's eyes.

"Why you have fight for them, but you don't have fight for me?" Lij asked, his voice deep. He shoved my father backward, again.

"Fire, listen—" my father said. But Lij was past hearing now.

Lij shoved my father's chest again. "Eh? Why you have fight for them, but you don't have fight for me?" He pushed my father hard in his chest once more. My father tripped backward as he looked up at Lij, his eyes wide as my brother charged again. Both of their dreadlocks had swung undone from their ponytails now, falling wild about their shoulders like perilous vines.

Behind them the silhouette of the landlady peered out from behind her living room curtain, her cell phone still at her ear as the night grew damp and shrouded.

"What kind ah man go after woman, eh?" Lij asked. "Your own daughter them? Mi whole life yuh have fight fi them and you nuh have no fight fi me!" He shoved my father one last time.

My father tripped backward again on his feet, trying to cross his arms across his chest to shield himself from Lij's barrage. Looking down at me and Shari still huddling together at the front gate, he scowled. "All ah the

I them wicked!" he shouted at us, walking slowly away from Lij now. "All ah yuh deserve one another." With that, he clopped and hoofed back into the house.

Lij left him to lick his wounds and came back down to the gate where Shari and I were still clasping each other like plucked birds. My brother put his arms around us and asked us if we were okay. He was warm as a furnace when his skin touched mine, and I finally exhaled a breath I had not realized I was holding.

I showed him my cut lip. He kissed his teeth and shook his head, looking back toward the house. "Pack your bags," he told me and Shari. "Come and stay with me at Cornwall."

My sister and I clasped each other's hands tight as we slipped back into our bedroom and filled a bag. We threw everything in and rushed out of the house in less than ten minutes. Then Shari, her nerves frayed to nothing, had to slip back in to use the bathroom.

My brother lit a spliff and put his arm around me, blowing plumes of smoke into the night. We sat in silence on the ground as the stars wheeled overhead. I pulled at the grass that grew up between the driveway's concrete.

"I'm going to press charges," I said.

My brother shook his head and sighed. "You can't do that, Saf."

I looked into his narrowing eyes, iron-black and searching mine for something. I looked away.

"You shoulda never call Babylon," Lij said, making sharp pulls on his spliff. "This is family business."

"I was scared."

"Well, I'm here now. I handled it." He blew the smoke over my head. "No need to involve more Babylon." He squeezed my palm in his hands as if to say that was the last word on the matter.

Shari, who had been on her cell phone reassuring Mom and Ife that we were fine, ran her soft footsteps down the driveway just as the taxi crunched the gravel at the gate.

"He needs to face the consequences for once," I told Lij, remembering my baby sister's screams from behind the locked door. I knew this night would change her, but I didn't know then how ruthlessly. In the years to come, the baby sister I'd known best in this world would become emotionally unreachable. After she left for college, she would never set foot in Jamaica again, never speak another word to or acknowledge my father again. Though each of us would deal with our trauma in different ways, my dear Shari would soon grow detached and impenetrable; never expressing her love for any of us again.

I looked at my brother now, his dreadlocks a black waterfall running down his back, pooling behind him in the driveway where we still sat. "We can't just let him get away with this," I protested to Lij. "We can't just keep forgiving him."

My brother sighed again and gusted a last cloud of smoke before snuffing out his spliff. He peeled his woolly head away from mine and rose from me. He was twenty-four, and his eyes had now grown as fierce and fire-struck as my father's, blazing intensely when his own temper flared. As he spoke he stroked his chin, now cropped with the straggly hairs of a sparse precept.

"I hope you find someone who understands you," he said, eyes burning pitch-black as he turned and marched away through the gate to the parked taxi. He reached into the back seat to comfort Shari, who was already sitting with her bag clutched to her chest, then turned to lean on the car door leaden-faced, waiting for me.

I sat alone for a moment with the red sting of my brother's words, on the cold stone of the driveway. I lifted my face to the night air and exhaled. There was nothing left for me here. Just home, and its omen. I rose to my feet in the driveway and turned to see my father still pacing in the window of his bedroom in anger. He looked so small as he raged on, small as a boy, and not at all as I remembered him from only a half hour before. Up in that house alone, he never looked back at me, not once. If he had, he would have seen it. The moment when my body shook under the night breeze, my arms tufted wide, talons outstretched, featherweight and freed, as I turned in the driveway and flew from him.

28

Jumbie Bird

Eᴀᴄʜ ɴɪɢʜᴛ ʜᴇ ᴍᴜʀᴅᴇʀꜱ ᴍᴇ, ᴏʀ tries to. His hands tight at my throat, dreadlocks cording a black noose around my neck. I startle awake in my Charlottesville apartment, forgetting where I am. It is late August 2012. Almost five months have passed since I left home for good, and my father, except for his hands, has been a ghost of my memory since I walked out the gate at Coral Gardens. Each night he murders me, or tries to, as he lops my head clean off with his black machete. I sputter awake, weep my floodwaters open. Drown. At dawn I slip through that red door again and follow the sunlight, try to hold on to something beautiful: my toes digging into warm sand at White House, the soft velvet of a pink hibiscus against my nose, my ocean glimmering its sapphire light. But nothing takes. The pale owl of my past still chases me down. At night I wander that old veranda in Bickersteth, where the ghost of the Rastawoman is a cold breath at my back, plaguing me with the red thread I have spent a lifetime pulling. Each night she crawls back from the dark of my memory, anchoring me to a place I have stopped trying to escape. I sputter awake and decide to face her—to reclaim my story, our family history, one sister, one daughter at a time. I am trying to write it all down, the story of our lives, trying to change the fate of the next Sinclair girl in the retelling. With each word, I will recourse the river of my making. With each word, I will change that Rastawoman's fate.

For months the lonesome cold seeps in. A snowstorm blows through and takes the city's power, and takes with it my heat. I wander the cold streets of an alien country pulling at the vein of this familial ache, my inherited trauma and its lingering thread, asking the fixed question of myself: Where did it begin? Back, before Bogue and before White House. I pull that red thread past the young girl walking into the sea, past my mother dancing across Bottom Road with the positive pregnancy test, past my gone grandmother Isabel dying with the sea's crash in her ear. I ride the train with Haile Selassie, watch him step again onto the mud and clatter of the Kingston tarmac. I sputter awake, blotting the microfiche of my mind, trying to understand. Where, where. Where. Did all this trouble begin with me?

My cell phone rings. A flash of blue neon across the screen: DAD. I press decline and turn it facedown.

It is the fall of 2012 and I am learning how to be a Black woman in America. Eight months have now passed since I left home for good, and my sisters and my mother are scattered seeds on the wind. Mom and Ife are grafting whole new selves here in Foreign, and Shari is now at university in Grenada studying marine biology and wildlife conservation. I check in with them often from my carpeted dark. In my MFA program, I am one of only two who look like me. Here in America, I am a caged curio, a beast shaking the bars of her otherness. While every white writer stumbles sightless, their words directionless, their chatter thick with whiskey and Klonopin. Under their cold gaze, I have never felt more foreign. At parties they ask me if I have the ability to tan, why I don't have a Bob Marley accent, and do I like to smoke weed? All day I am prodded, all night I am probed. My skirt is lifted, my flower dissected. My silver ransacked without permission. Each day I am learning to live in a town built on the bones of the enslaved. I gasp awake in a country birthed from one terrible wound and then another, and I am unable to ignore America's own red lineage. Here, no tree is ever just a tree. Here, every rolling field has been nursed on stolen sweat, every green acre sprung from blood. For months, I pull at the terrible thread of America's past, put my ear up to the gutted voices of Charlottesville's history, trying to hear lost families in the scattering shrill of cicadas.

In Vinegar Hill, Charlottesville, the air smells parched. I walk through parking lots and sidewalks where the Black neighborhood was torched to the ground for white "redevelopment" nearly five decades before. Now nothing seems to stand except a single indie movie theater, where I sit in the dark and watch *Beasts of the Southern Wild* with the MFA program's enthralled white fictioneers. Later they will hang on my every thought about the film. Here, I find that every day is a renegotiation of my body. I am reminded of my Blackness in all spaces I enter. At the end of my street, a white neighbor marches dogged to hoist a yellow flag embroidered with a rattlesnake, coiling. Hissing *Don't tread on me*. As I pass by I wave hello, but he looks right through me and turns away. Alone in the court square I walk over a bronze plaque that says SLAVE AUCTION BLOCK. "On this site slaves were bought and sold." Here in Charlottesville, I am finally learning how to say bloodsucker. How to say baldhead. How to say heathen. Here, every street, every house, gapes another maw of trauma. Wound after wound, I cannot escape. I walk the university campus built brick by brick by the hands of the enslaved and hear students worshiping an enslaver they've pet-named "TJ" without irony. Up on the hill looms his house of hallowed violence, the domed room, the fine columns, the centuries-old facade. Every brick laid with blood. I follow the thread of this ghoulish history to the park downtown, where the statue of Robert E. Lee looms so large, citizens could spread picnic blankets in his shadow. Every place here is a place of violence, and I am heavy with poems.

My cell phone rings. DAD. I press decline and slip back into the black water engulfing my bed.

We each spend Christmas alone. My siblings, my mother, and I. There is not enough money for us to see each other this year. That December I stay shut in by choice, wandering my lonely rooms and reciting poetry out loud. All winter I let the wave carry me back to the river, remembering the folk songs of my kin. At night I follow the trail of women who came before me, slip into a tangled past where their hum seals my ears. I wander through their underworld and eat of its bounty. Soon poem after poem fills my mouth with pomegranate seeds. At night I burn a fever, unspooling red from my throat, determined to make sense of my doomed matriarchy. My inheritance. My mother lore. Bending over the page in my basement apartment, I try to write the ache into something tangible.

"*I am going to think that this kind of experience is part of the fierce initiation by which someone confirms her vocation as poet*," my professor Gregory Orr writes to me in an email.

Each morning I wake and can't let go of all that red. Instead of turning in a final paper for his poetry class, I write him a letter describing in vivid detail my father's hands at my throat, being throttled breathless in the night, the black machete. I drift until I startle awake in my bed, gasping.

My cell phone rings. DAD. I press decline and lick my blood from a shard of shattered glass.

February 2013 brings me blank pages of snow. I open my chapbook and return to that dark veranda in the thick countryside, which I first poured into an essay called "Bickersteth," and which a decade later would become the first words of this memoir. I wander around in the memory of the Rasta family in the country, how close they came to losing themselves in the fire there. I encounter myself again, a young woman in crisis, her head still bent under the terrible blade. Still trying to sever that ghost in her white georgette. Still drowned under fever, her long black reeds of hair. For days I sit with her in the cold silence of Foreign, and each night she reminds me that *only I can right this*. Under a foreign sky blustering and gray, I decide to rewrite that young woman's future. To make every word the flame, the struck match.

Bringing myself to a boil by the portable heater, I begin to work, trying in vain to weave the mother lore. I try to write down my memories but still, he kills me in the night. All winter I contemplate the bottle of sleeping pills my white poet friend gave me. All night my larynx is crushed, collapsing into silence. Sometimes Emily Dickinson comes to me in dreams. I rattle the pill bottle. I tell her I am trying to fill the gap. That like her, I long to solder the abyss. All winter I try to write them down—my family. My old life. But there are no good words, no words, only my hair coming loose in handfuls on the carpet, black snatches furring the shower drain. I wake to the dull cold of another blizzard and a concerned email from my advisor, Gregory Orr:

I have been thinking about your memoir project and I realize that I think it might be more than a little hazardous
for you to attempt it now. I think back to myself at your
age and realize I could never have handled the narrative
accounting of my life or the revisiting of scenes from it.
Not then. Remember how I twist Wordsworth's "emotion
recollected in tranquility" into a more modern statement:
"trauma remembered and revisited from a place of safety"?
That place of safety—you may not yet have that.

I tell myself he has lived through worse and would know better. I
abandon the book, abandon my memories. Turn away from myself. I
long for tranquility. Long for that place of safety. Instead, I gasp awake in
the night, my father's hands still gripping my throat.

My cell phone rings. DAD. I let it buzz until the insect sound dissolves
in my ear.

Spring blows in like a blousy bitch. Outside the grass grows long and
needful in my yard in Charlottesville, clutching my clothes when I pass
hungry through the untended gate. I sleep on my stomach and gasp
awake in the night, my larynx bones cracking under my father's hands. I
ride around town with a white writer from a Bay Area suburb who voted
for Obama, but who sings the n-word out loud to his favorite rap songs.
White America, a violence. I wrench out of his car and clamber home-
ward alone in the night. Shamble past the end of my street, where my
white neighbor, ruddy-faced, has mounted a Confederate flag above his
yellow rattlesnake. Two flags flap angrily in the wind. When a seething
hurricane blows through this side of Virginia, I pray it takes me with it.

The summer humidity holds me to choking while I pull poems out of
my ear like weeds. Almost a year and a half has passed since I left home for
good. The US government reminds me that I am a "non-resident alien." I
need their permission to work, permission to move, permission to leave.
I catch my neighbor's white wife stop short to watch me from their manicured driveway, and out of animal habit, I wave. With an icy glare, she
turns back on her heels and disappears into the house. Weeks later, the
town wakes to graffiti on the Beta Bridge: NIGGER scrawled in red next

to enlarged male genitalia. I pull that thread, following its vein down to pulping ventricle, and start to believe my father at last was right—red with baldheads, red with bloodsuckers, red about all of it. I hear his voice in my head, scorching with thunder and brimstone, reminding me that he had spent a lifetime teaching me how to say it—

This place is Babylon.

At last, I understand. There is no American dream without American massacre. Black towns burned, native families displaced, graveyards desecrated, lands stolen, lands ruined: Here is the invention of whiteness, a violence. Here is the original wound. Here I am, homesick in Babylon, and I am angry, so angry at all of it. Because, for the first time since I left home, I understand how frightened my father must have been for me, a Black daughter walking through the inferno, and now I am all alone.

By the time I sit across from Rita Dove and hang my wilted head at her desk, I am heavy with tropical rain, and all that has been brimming dark and unseemly inside me. All this fury. By the time she extends her warm hands into mine, her nails bright as papayas, eyes warm as maple and says, "Tell me what you mean when you say you are in exile," I am a river of despair, flooding the room.

That night my phone rings again. DAD. I decline. I leave it unplugged until it dies. Fall asleep unraveling myself from all this red.

That winter, from the dusk of my basement apartment, I lay unmoving as I listen to my mother's voice, softened and joyous on the vine: My brother and his wife were having a baby. A daughter. I hadn't seen or spoken to Lij since I had left Jamaica. In the bitter months after he had saved me from the machete, my brother had grown angry, believing that I should forgive my father, and that my refusal to speak to him had fractured our family. Now that I was in America, our distance only worsened, that mute ocean growing wider and deeper between us.

The news of his daughter shakes me out of my wintry stupor. While lying in bed, I try to imagine her, and something else clutches the air. Just out of the corner of my eye I see it. The flash of a white wing, making a nest of red thread around my neck. All night I can't escape it, this creature growing uncontained in the dark. A thought, beaking its way into me.

What kind of world would I be giving to my niece now? What kind of family? I try to trace the pattern of our bruised history, pulling strand after endless strand of red. Did it begin with him? My father, whose violence first bred this unfilial hurt? Had he been thrashed and then in turn had done the thrashing? How far did these wings ripple, beyond me and beyond him, beyond my grandmother, beyond and beyond? I pull and pull this thread of violence back through the generations of my family, through my marked bloodline, and beyond them, back to Jamaica's first colonial whip, back to the last Taíno dying of Columbus' smallpox, back to the first colonizer who put a shackle on a Black woman's neck, back to the first woman who said "No."

A person was either a lionheart or a weakheart in this world, my father always said, and a weakheart is ripe for the worms of Babylon. Was I a weakheart if I tried to forgive him? Or should I stand firm and keep saying no? I turned away from the calls on the blue neon screen for the same reason I struck that ghost woman down at Bickersteth; I wanted more, so much more than this fixed inheritance. I wanted to hold the world in all its mouthwatering beauty, to forge some version of myself I could believe in. I was determined to write myself back into the frame, to grab hold of the bull and stamp my name on his tongue. To never cower to my father, or any man, again. Now my niece was coming, and the way forward was clear. This book I was envisioning, I would write for her. I would write for every Sinclair girl who was still to come. For them, I would try to point the compass forward: to change the shape of our lineage, the weight of her legacy. So she who comes next would never have to know the fire. So she who comes next would always know herself.

Later that week, my phone rang again. DAD flashed neon across the screen. I moved my finger to press decline.

But when I thought of my niece, I picked up instead.

"Hello?"

"Oh, Princess," he said, his voice breaking.

I listened first and said nothing.

"It is so irie to hear you," he said. His voice was so familiar, the one I had known as a girl climbing into his guitar case. His tone so changed from the last time I heard him, was now kind and molasses-sweet.

"I've been thinking of you so much, Princess——"

In the corner of my eye, the flash of a ghostly wing. I pushed my toes into the bedroom carpet and listened, but found I could not speak.

"You there?" he asked. "How are you? How's——"

"Dad, what do you want?"

"I just want to hear your voice . . ." He was almost singing.

"Look." I closed my eyes as I spoke so I could find the lamplight of the words I needed to see my way through. "We're not going to have a conversation until you admit what you did. Until you own up to it and apologize."

My heart started thumping as soon as I said it. Beads of sweat gathered at the edges of my temples.

My father drew a sharp breath. "You're right, Princess," he said, softly. "I'm so sorry. Please forgive me."

I let the line go quiet and waited for him to say more.

"So, how are you? How are your studies?" he asked.

"Every night I have a nightmare that you are killing me. Every single night, you have your hands around my throat, or your machete at my neck."

"Oh Jah. Oh, Budgie," my father gasped. "I man so sorry for that. I could never hurt you, baby. I would never hurt you."

"But you did, Dad. You did." My throat was burning its familiar kettle now, quivering with tears. I held them in, let them evaporate with anger instead.

"I wasn't myself," my father said, a note of unfamiliar anguish in his voice. "You have to believe me. The landlady obeahed me. It was that wicked woman."

"No. No, Dad. *You* did those things. And then you told everyone I was lying. I'm not going to just pretend none of it happened. You have to own up to the truth."

"You are so right, Princess. You are so right. I already told your mother. I told her and now——" He couldn't finish. Now she was gone for good. She would never forgive him. He had put his hands on her firstborn daughter after she had put a stop to the red belt over a decade ago. My father's voice croaked hoarse on the line.

"You have to tell everyone the truth," I said. "What you did is unforgivable. What you did—" I had not realized I was grabbing at my hair until my scalp pained me.

He was quiet now.

It had been nearly two years since he had picked up the machete. "You really hurt me. And you think it's okay to hurt me. You think I will just forgive you."

"Oh, Budgie. I'm so sorry. Please forgive me. Budgie, please—" and that's when it appeared from just out of sight, not a budgerigar but a jumbie bird, a white owl stretching its large wings overhead. Buried underneath its ruffled face, a red glare. All that red string I had been pulling, a ruby glisten in its black beak. This bird, as I'd been taught as a child, was a death omen.

My spine bent under its stare.

"I man just want the I to know you always have a home to come back to," my father told me.

The bird's weight pressed in on my neck.

"The I them is all I have. All I have in this world—"

It sounded like a sudden crash of rain outside the window, my father's voice breaking into sobs.

"You and you brother and you sister them are all I have," he cried. "Please. You are all I man have in this world. Please come home, Budgie. You have to come back home."

The jumbie bird hooked its beak into my spine and would not let go.

When I rounded the familiar blue of the Caribbean Sea above the airport tarmac that Christmas of 2013, I almost touched the window, picking out my tiny birth spot of White House from the air. The white people clapped as we landed and I didn't even mind that. It was not my father but my newborn niece who convinced me to go home: Cataleya. My brother's firstborn, named for a genus of orchid. Cataleya. I spoke her name and it felt like an incantation. When I got the news of her arrival I decided right then. I would end this cycle. She would need a better nest, a better seam to follow. What kind of future was I giving her if I didn't come home to meet her now? If I didn't try? I could keep pulling the thread, spend years unraveling all that unraveled me, or I could pull it all through the needle's eye, and stitch.

As soon as I walked off the plane, the familiar heat greeted me with a humid kiss. In the airport, even the ordinary seemed beautiful then: the stacked shelves of Appleton rum and bright commercials for Digicel next to tourist posters full of dolphins and women with flowers in their hair. I rolled my bags past the customs desk and walked out into the vigorous chatter of home.

Outside, the sun pressed me into a long-lost embrace. While I waited for the taximan my father had sent to pick me up, I turned down offers for rides, drivers asking, "Ma'am, where can I take you?" with a surplus of twang. I had to reply with enough patois to assure them I was born right yah ah yard. When he arrived, the taxi driver filled me in on the details of a minor accident my father had had. "Nuttin to worry bout man," he said, and told me my father just needed to take the car into the shop to get checked, and would pick me up from my brother's that night. As we drove up Top Road to my brother's place at Cornwall, all the color my eyes had been craving flashed kaleidoscopic. Magenta pocketfuls of bou-gainvillea, those hills and hills of green stretching flush and unruly ahead of me. And to my right, the racing blue gallop of the sea.

When we pulled up to my brother's apartment, he had already jogged down the three flights of stairs to greet me. I flung myself out of the car and we crumpled into each other in the rocky driveway. "Been too long, Saf," he said. I had called him the night I heard my niece was coming, and all that had gone unsaid between us had vanished into joy then. Now the heat passed one thought between us like the dog-eared days of our gone ramping, when we could still read each other's minds. He took my luggage upstairs and I finally met her, my Cataleya, a tiny little wide-eyed thing, grabbing on to her crib. I did not expect it. Like a vase suddenly poured full with water, there was love. My bloodline stretched ahead of me, tangible and woven to hers, and everything seemed so possible. She cooed and smiled at me gummy and drooling, and I was grateful then that I had picked up the phone.

"Can I hold her?" I asked Lij. He had married the same girlfriend I had last seen him with before I left for Virginia. They had a very small wedding, when she was already pregnant, a ceremony he only told me about after it had happened. My brother said he didn't want to bother my studies to have me come down, since he knew I might not be able to afford it. Of course, there was the other unsaid thing between us. Of how we had last left things, my father waving the machete, our distance and our months-long feast of silence. But none of that troubled me now as my niece grabbed and gurgled between us. With the standing fan in my brother's modest bedroom turned on me, I handed him the gifts I brought from Foreign, a stuffed lamb for Cataleya, and a book for him: *Strong Fathers, Strong Daughters: 10 Secrets Every Father Should Know.* As he read over the cover he shook his teary head and thanked me, and his dreadlocks, which were now past his buttocks, shook too.

I asked him gently if she would grow up under the strictures of Rastafari. My brother smiled and told me, "That will be for Cat alone to choose." She would eat what she liked, wear what she liked, she would fix her hair however she wanted. "I've seen what all my sisters had to live through," Lij said. His daughter would be free to make her own way through the world.

I smiled back at him and nodded, misty with gratitude as he placed Cataleya, warm as my own warmth, in my arms. I kissed her, I cradled her and she did not cry. She only looked up into my face and grabbed for my hair. As I held her, I thought of all the pain my siblings and I had endured together, the lifetime of wreckage that had almost pulled us under. "It was worth it," I whispered in her ear. "Just to meet you."

That night, when my father and I approached his new house in the country, I was not surprised to see the jumbie bird perched pale atop the streetlight in front of the yard. Even so, I turned wide-eyed to look at my father in the driver's seat, wanting to make sense of the white bird and its meaning, but he kept driving and said nothing, as if he had not seen it. This rented house was a far climb into the verdant hills from town and swathed by thick hillside for as far as I could see. This new yard was hidden on all sides by the murmuring trees. A tall battalion of sugarcane and a bright bearing ackee tree made an unofficial fence in the backyard, and in the front was a toothsome garden of sunflowers Ife had planted in the short few months she had spent there in between visas.

The next morning my father woke early and disappeared into the small crop of cane to smoke marijuana. Something he had taken up each morning in his solitude, although I had not once seen him smoke while we were growing up. He was thinner than I remembered, and shorter. When he returned from the rambling fog, he came with Jah's bounty. He had cut stalks of cane and carried a stretched shirtful of oranges and green gage mangoes, which he peeled for me and watched me savor over breakfast. He spent most of the days I was there peaceful like this, strumming his guitar, smiling and tiptoeing around me if he thought I was writing. Some afternoons he drove me to buy my favorite beef patties and curry chicken, and even sat at the same table and talked with me as I ate the dead flesh across from him.

Meanwhile I nursed a prodigal quiet, watching the days unfeather between us. I left my bags packed, each day keeping my eye fixed on the gate, where the jumbie bird was still perched. Six nights it clasped unmoving, while I waited for my father to mention it to me. I kept expecting him to panic, to shoo it, to do anything at all with this white bird carved like a totem watching us from the road. But under owl-glare, he said nothing of the owl.

When I walked through my father's new house I felt alien, missing the home my mother had made for us. The floor was poorly swept and overrun with ants or curls of my father's hair, the kitchen cupboard and refrigerator bare. In his bedroom, my father's dresser was filled to tipping with our gold. Hillocked with past glories, he had framed our school pictures and gathered every single trophy, certificate, medal, and plaque my siblings and I were awarded over the years, our accomplishments now resting side by side with his picture of Haile Selassie. My mother's absence from home was only magnified as I admired all the awards on my father's dresser. Her hands had made every single one of them. And all of us.

In a photobook my father kept beside these medals was the beloved newspaper clipping, now pressed under the laminate, proof of my first award. Next year I would begin my doctorate program in Los Angeles, with my first full collection of poems soon on the way—poems that would win me some prestigious foreign awards, with prize amounts that would be printed in newspapers both in Jamaica and the United States.

But this clipping on my father's dresser had been my first. I shook the little memory pleasantly in my head. Not only was it an award in Maths, but when the reporter leaned into my eight-year-old face and asked me if I had a message for the young people of Jamaica, I had smiled beyond my dreadlocked shyness and said yes, I did. Then I squeaked into her recorder the message I wanted all the other children to know: "You just can't give up!" That smiling Rasta girl and her message made it to the front page of the *Jamaica Gleaner*, and now she was beaming back at me. How young she was then, how unaware of what tempest had been brewing out there on her horizon.

While drinking sorrel in his living room that evening, my father and I laughed about that day I got my Maths award. I reminded him of the poem I had recited at the awards ceremony for the politicians, how nervous I was. "The I just make me so irie," he said while pulling on his precept, not wanting the moment to pass without naming it.

Ignoring the omen outside the door, I slipped between the warped space of my memories and slept girlishly again. All while the bird's white wing flapped outside the yard, signaling what had long been oncoming. In my father's house, I would always slip back into that girl again. She was everywhere in here, and out there, in the cane. The smiling Rasta girl who had no idea what doom was coming, even though she reminded me what to do in the face of it. Guiding me to persevere, no matter the weather, to harden around my own dreams like a pearl. My father couldn't set that Rasta girl free in his mind. He clasped onto that daughter like driftwood, keeping him afloat in Babylon's torment, saving him from drowning in his life's crashing disappointment. He would never see me as I was. He would never hear me. Wherever I walked, she was there. Whenever I looked back, my father was a rootless tree, reaching for the hope he once held under the wide sky at Bogue: that Rasta family living in *umoja* who still believed in him.

The night before I returned to the States my father took me to one of his reggae shows at a hotel in Negril. I watched entranced as he jumped and flashed his dreadlocks and sang like a man overtaken by wildfire. When the band started playing the songs from his album *Rocking You*, the one he had recorded twenty years before in Japan, I squealed and rose from my seat to dance and belt out the songs of my youth. The same songs

I had carried in my head to primary school every morning. I still knew every word. My father pointed at me and smiled as I sang each song along with him. Bellowing out the righteous words of my father's music with him then, I briefly wondered if I could have ever been a true daughter of Rastafari—was there any version of that woman in white that I would have chosen to preserve? Was there any of her now, that still lived on in me? Perhaps if I had felt embraced as a woman by Rastafari, I, too, would have embraced it. But I was never allowed to sit with a circle of Rasta bredren or join in on a reasoning. They never passed my history directly into my hands. So I stayed away from it, until years later when I pulled at the first thread of this beginning. My father's eyes glistened now as he watched me singing, so I sang louder. I didn't know when I would come home again, or what future would ever be possible for us. But trilling under the crackle of the resort's night air, I wanted him to know I had been listening all this time. I might have left Rastafari behind, but I always carried with me the indelible fire of its rebellion. And when I returned to America, I would walk taller. Babylon would never frighten a daughter like me.

29

I Woman

All water has a perfect memory and is
forever trying to get back to where it was.
—Toni Morrison

There was nothing broken the sea couldn't fix, my mother always said. In 2018, six years after the night I flew through the gate and away from my father's machete in Coral Gardens, five years after I returned home to meet my niece, and sang my father's songs out loud with him, I finally feel ready to write our story. I am now in my Jesus year, and twelve years older than my mother when she received the news of her miracle pregnancy and decided to follow the path of Rastafari. Not a day laps by when I don't think of all the women in my family who bear the blood-wound fixed deep by tragedy. Whose life and deeds washed away, unsung, unknown in the tide of history. All that I write now is for them. "I just can't believe you took my dead-left life, all our hurt and history, and made something so beautiful out of it," my mother told me after my first poetry reading, where I looked down from the podium and saw her mouthing the words to every poem. "I just can't believe I have my own personal poet," she said.

I thought of her now while leafing through my debut poetry collection on the hotel balcony overlooking Treasure Beach. I was preparing to read from my book for the first time at home in Jamaica, on the biggest literary stage in the Caribbean, the 2018 Calabash Literary Festival. My mother was in Foreign and unable to see me read later that night, but her work loomed bright over the tide of my homecoming. It was her hands that had woven the moment of my return. My father and brother were driving three hours from Montego Bay to the other side of the island to see me read for the first time. It was June and the weather was bewitching in its beauty. The sea glimmered in the distance. The coconuts shined a deep green, full of fresh water. The festival organizers had given me a special hotel room built right over the ocean, where I could sleep and wake with the sound of the sea in my ear. When my father and brother arrived, I led them to sit out on the deck where the waves licked at the wooden balcony. They had come to my room bearing gifts, thick stacks of photo albums that they brandished like peace offerings, sun-bleached picture after picture of our family's past. I squeaked and thanked them, cradling the photographs. Five years after abandoning my memoir project in Charlottesville, I had slowly begun writing our story again, and these pictures would be anchors and buoys to my memory. We immediately started leafing through the albums in a raucous reverie, laughing and pointing.

There went the years running ahead of us, self after self: me at two years old, arm in arm with my father in our bed at White House, smiling from ear to ear. Me and Lij at eight and six years old, radiant with our budding dreadlocks, our mother's young face wide-eyed next to us, peeling an orange she'd plucked from the tree at Bogue. Me and my siblings as preteens, our locks shoulder-length, huddling together in a ragged pose, glistening and grassy from ramping. As we flipped through the years, my brother, now thirty-one, rewove the old stories with me, pointing to our young selves, reclaiming them.

Then there she was.

Pale flash of my teenage self. Her gaunt face lit up like a ghost, her eyes so large I almost fell into the pooling doubt. Just like that, the reverie seamed shut. Her glance housed a rift in time, like the day Lij and I had returned to Bogue in a fit of Sehnsucht and found that the home we remembered was never really there. To our shock, the once mighty yard was now a small stony crop of land; our heads were towering above the branches of the once giant trees, and the house was a tiny shamble, crumbling to weeds. My brother and I had sprinted away from there and vowed to forget it as soon as we left, to hold our paradise as it had lived on in our minds.

I touched my hands to the plastic sleeve, the tangible sadness of her gaze, and closed the album. I looked out at the waves, which lapped at the balcony. There were some years I thought I might never go home again.

Some years I went six months or more without talking to my father. Some days I was unsure if our relationship could ever be healed. But I always felt compelled to try. My father stroked his beard and gazed at me the way I gazed at the sea. He touched my hand gently. "Jah know, Budgie," he said, his voice quiet. "I man spent so much of the time worrying about you and you sisters them, but ah really wish I had been cooler. Wish I coulda see that I and I had nothing to worry about." I closed my eyes as he spoke, sitting for a time with the breath of it. When I gathered the words to thank him, my voice was only a whisper. My father gently handed me the stack of albums and told me he was leaving them permanently in my care. "Out of all of us, I man know the I will take the best care of them," he said, his face quiet with a dew-swept calm I had never seen before. I was the keeper of my family's stories now, which they all treated with a rare kind of reverence. My father smiled solemnly and nodded, as if he had known all this time, and known it deeply, after hearing me talk about a "memoir"—the purpose for all the mournful words I had been saving to speak since the night I flew away from him and the machete six years before. That all our dimmed and luminous hours would be etched in ink, the pale owl gathering the fluted bones of the unsaid in the dark.

The festival stage was a flood of lights so bright I looked out ahead of me and saw only black. Standing alone in the spotlight, mosquitoes made a halo around my head, while the night rang loud with its jam-band of crickets. The podium had been adorned with blooms of red ginger and bright anthuriums, conch shells, horns of driftwood, fiery heliconia and birds of paradise spilling among the greenest leaves. I was home. The ocean behind me was unlit but I could feel it, my blue floral dress waving like a semaphore in the sea breeze.

I'd spent an hour in the mirror rehearsing the sequence of my read-ing in my head, my stomach in knots as I steeled myself for what I was planning to do. Ignoring the buzz of warning in my ears, I memorized the words I intended to say to my father, speaking them out loud to myself for the first time, growing more nervous as the hour drew closer, trying to prepare myself for what was to come next.

Pouring out ahead of me now was the crowd, which I'd watched pile in before the event began. They had come in the hundreds, stretching far beyond the festival tent, ready to hear the poems of their prodigal. Beyond the blare of the stage lights, I could see the dim outlines of their faces; illumined, waiting for me to speak.

"Smile, Jamaica," I said to them, as I took my phone out and snapped a picture of the crowd, referencing the name of our popular morning television show. Everyone laughed, and my nerves calmed.

Though there was only darkness the farther out I looked, I could hear the people murmuring, a wave carrying me along. My nails, which were painted marigold yellow, shined as I clutched the pages of my poetry collection, published almost two years before. My face felt hot, incandescent against the stage lights, and the night air blew cool against my arms. As I looked out into the crowd I thought of her. The young girl who had written a poem to nurse her wounds, then felt herself at home for the first time, there on the page. "This is an incredible moment for me," I told the audience.

"I remember coming to Calabash for the first time when I was a young poet. At seventeen or eighteen," I said, "And I remember looking at the readers on the stage that night and being inspired to keep going. I thought, *If I keep going, one day I'll be up there.* And now, I'm here." I smiled. Like a blessing of rain breaking, the crowd applauded.

My father and brother were in the second row, closer and clearer in my sight line. They both made the Sign of the Power of the Trinity with their hands, and when my eyes caught theirs, my heart skipped. They nodded at me in reassurance. "My father and my brother are here," I quavered, "listening to my poetry for the first time, so if I get a little emotional, that's why."

And so I began. With a poem called "Home." Though I couldn't see them, I could hear the audience coming alive as I read the poems I'd written from that cold basement apartment in Charlottesville, while starved with homesickness. Every word, every line, I had made for them. Poems nested in bougainvillea, filled with hummingbirds and sugarcane, flush with shame-a-ladies and one long orange peel. I sang poems for the wild goats and the runaways, for our blue fern gully, for our shantytowns. I read a poem for White House and Bogue-mud, a poem for my grandfather and the fishermen, poem for my gone grandmother Isabel. A poem for my sisters, poem for my brother, poem for my mother and her hands.

I read poems for the sea, poems for my family, page after page. When I read a poem about sex, I instructed my father to plug his ears on my cue, which he did, playing along effortlessly, while the audience cheered.

I glanced out into the lights and readied myself for my last poem. The poem for my father. I couldn't look at him, but I imagined a blaring starshine around his face. "I grew up in a pretty strict Rastafari household," I said. "You might not know from looking at me, but I still have some Rasta in my heart."

I could feel my father watching me as I spoke, though I couldn't yet face him. I waded out into the dark, trying to find the right words.

"A lot of us in the Caribbean have deeply complex relationships with our fathers, and so do I. This poem is for my father," I said, voice quiet. I looked out into the second row and found my father ghostly lit, barely visible.

"This is the first time I'm reading this poem with my father in the audience," I said. Though I couldn't see his expression, my heart thumped as I said the words. I held my palms open and upward like a prayer.

"And so, Father, I say to you—I hope you hear me." I looked down into my father's face and began.

> Father unbending, father unbroken.
> Father I was forged in the fire of your self.
> Father your first daughter now severed at the ankles,
> Father your black machete.
> Father a flag I am waving/father a flag I am burning.
> Fathering my exorcism. Father the harsh brine of my sea.
> Making sounds only the heart can feel.
> Father a burrowing insect, his small incision.
> Daughter entering this world a host.
> Father the soft drum in my ear.
> Father
> Let me in.

I read for an audience of one. As I read, I was a lionheart, braving the fire. With each word I spoke, feathers fell from me like canefield ash. The ghost owl and its weight lifted, no longer resting heavy on my chest. Like

a mist on the wind, the pale silhouette of the woman in white blew away
with a sigh. Feeling weightless now, the heat of the gone talons burned
my shoulders as I read, and I knew. There was no more red thread. No
more red. I had pulled it loose and given it my best words. Here on the
page, blank as a beach, my mind's waves rippling. Home was poetry and
what it had forged of me.

When I was done, the wind swept me from my trance, as the audience cheered and wept. I don't remember leaving the stage or walking
toward my family in the audience.

My father found me first, and pulled me into a deep embrace, an embrace that could nudge a seed skyward from the dirt, the kind of embrace we
had not shared for more than a decade. He squeezed my arm, and we both
breathed deep. Already I could feel it rising, the warm quiver in my throat.
He held my shoulders and looked at me, for perhaps the first time in our
lives, his eyes dampening. Then he held me close and whispered in my ear.

"I'm listening," he said. "And I hear you."

I could barely answer him then, when I heard those words. The tears
stung my eyes as I took it all in, nodding against my father wordlessly and
crying. The words hung their gentle atmosphere above us. I held him in
gratitude, saying nothing. It was enough, then, just to hear it. I looked into
his eyes, wide and pleading, and I knew he meant it then, as much as he
could mean anything. I wanted to believe it, desperately needed to believe
it, even if I didn't know how long his words would hold, or what might
come next. I am still learning that one doesn't always have to be a lionheart. I am slowly trying to forgive, trying hard to revise the man he once
was in my mind. So I hold close to those words and would stay a century
in this moment if I could, my father's breath my breath, his light all mine.

My feet did not touch the grass all night. My heart swam full as the
moon above me. Its glow touched my father's face, and he looked as
unburdened and young as the nectarine days we both thought we had
lost. As he and I moved arm in arm through the crowd, a Rasta bredren
touched his shoulder and asked him, "This your daughter, Rasta?" And
my father looked back at him, still clutching my hands, flashed his radiant smile and said, "Yes, Fire, this is my daughter."

There was nothing broken the sea couldn't fix, my mother liked to say. And now, in these pages, she can see it—there, in our sea village of the lonely and unclaimed, a young girl had been gathering a life, glittering trail of sea-glass, conch and ancient driftwood, all what good may come of us, page after page. Back home in Montego Bay, I woke at dawn thinking about that young girl again. What the night at Calabash would have meant to her. What it meant to her now. Walking down to the beach, I watched the sea shimmer against the horizon. I waded out into our sea, the water warm as a womb as it rose up to me. I pushed out and kicked my legs against the blue to swim. Out and farther out I struck, heading for the distance. Halfway toward the buoy, I heard a faint cry of my name. I turned back toward the shore and saw what had been waiting three decades to be found.

Behind me, walking into the sea was my smallest self, a baby girl throwing herself into the waves. Behind her I saw my mother, flying in footsteps to pluck me from the water. My mother's cut foot trailed a red spool of blood in the sand, weaving to the small figure of my mother as a girl, crouched and digging for food, waiting for the sea to offer her something to believe in. Wandering behind my mother I saw her gone mother, watching the sea in a wind-worn dress. Out in the distance was another young woman, and another, each walking beside their own mothers and sisters now, tall women, stern women, a woman whose name I did not know, her upturned face a copper sun, marking me. I bobbed transfixed, neck-deep in waves, watching the women weave and stretch for miles and decades beyond me, beyond and beyond, marking a line that trailed out from our little strip of beach and into the sweltering city, up into the hills and the green backbone of our country. Walking behind her and behind her, I saw them—all the women who had put one foot in front of the other and pushed their hands into the dirt. Women who had survived. The women who made me.

I threw my throat to the sky and accepted at last what I had been gifted. There was no one and nothing ahead of me now but the unending waves, the sky outpouring its wide expanse of horizon, and all this beckoning blue, all of tomorrow's sun, all mine.

Acknowledgments

When I first began thinking about telling this story, back in 2013, my agent Janet Silver was the first person who not only believed in its vision but, more importantly, believed in me at a time when I felt the most alone in the world. She never rushed me, never worried after the pages. Even when I doubted that I would find the emotional fortitude to wade out into this telling. Janet, thank you for your patience and unwavering belief, which helped give me the confidence I needed to write this book in my own time. None of this would be possible without you. Thank you for not only being my fiercest advocate, one of my closest confidants, but for also becoming a second mother to me. I am forever lucky, forever grateful that our paths crossed in this life.

To my brilliant and insightful editors, Dawn Davis and Kish Widya-ratna, thank you for helping to sharpen my poet's mind on the page, for your grace and patience when I disappeared for long and silent months at a time to work on this book. Thank you for your guidance and for helping to push me to be my absolute best, word by rigorous word. Your wisdom and encouragement these last three years have been an indispensable gift.

My greatest thanks to Jon Karp for his enthusiasm and support of this book. Thank you to the lovely Anne Tate Pearce, Stephen Bedford, and Chonise Bass for all their tireless effort and support. Thank you to Jackie Seow and Rex Bonomelli for the book's incredible cover and wonderful design. Thank you to Maria Mendez, Yvette Grant, LaSharah Bunting, Stacey Sakal, Jaime Wolf, the wonderful and enthusiastic marketing and sales team, and the entire Simon & Schuster team that have rallied around this book with such care and helped to bring it into existence. Thanks to my Fourth Estate team in the UK, to my foreign rights agents Erin Files, Chelsey Heller, and Caspian Dennis for advocating for this book worldwide.

My deep and unwavering gratitude to my mentor Rita Dove, whose late April phone call to a young Jamaican girl on the knife-edge of her existence offered me both hope and certainty in where I was meant to go next, and changed the trajectory of my life. Thank you for always reminding me how to move with grace, to always change the spaces that I move through for the better.

Thank you to my professor and advisor Gregory Orr, who was the first person to encourage me to write this memoir from a place of safety. I'm indebted to you for that sage advice. Thank you for always reminding me that the hard and luminous hours are as vital in making a poet as tranquility.

To my most unwavering literary advocate and mentor, David St. John, thank you for helping to make space for me and my work in so many crucial ways over the years; thank you for being my wisest and most steadfast supporter in all my endeavors. To Kwame Dawes and Shara McCallum, thank you for paving the way for me and other Jamaican poets, and for always offering me your help, advice, and encouragement no matter the hour. My deepest thanks to Mrs. Newnham, Mrs. Charleston, and all my English teachers throughout the decades who encouraged me to put pen to paper, to trust in my voice, and to keep writing.

A very special thank-you to Justine Henzell for her infectious passion and tireless support of the arts in Jamaica, and a big thanks for inviting me to the Calabash Literary Festival in 2018. Justine and Kwame, thank you for calling me back home when I needed it the most.

I am indebted to the MacDowell residency, who offered me much-needed time, and a beautiful light-filled space to finish the final edits on this book. I am also grateful to the Elizabeth George Foundation and the Jeannette Haien Ballard Prize for their financial support of this book. Thank you to Natalie Diaz, Jeffrey Cohen, and the folks at ASU for their wonderful support of my work. I'm immensely grateful to E.C. Belli and Liz Clark Wessel at Argos Books for giving the first seedling of this book a home.

My deepest thanks to Courtney Hodell for being such a wise and generous advisor, and to the Whiting Foundation and their team for the years of support. Thanks also to Jonathan Walsh and Danny Stein for their sage financial advice these last few years. I'm immensely grateful to my publicists Whitney Peeling and Michael Taeckens, who have been hearing me talk about this book for more than six years and never stopped believing in its possibility.

Thanks to my dearest poet-sister Ann-Margaret, who was such a lighthouse to me in those grey days past, when I most needed to find my way back. Thank you to the auntie-poets, Gwyneth Barber Wood, Delores Gauntlett, and Verna George, for giving such kindness and encouragement to a young poet who was still new to the literary world. Thank you to Derek Walcott, for offering me a lamplight of hope when I needed it most, and for confirming to a young Jamaican dreamer that she *was* a poet.

My immense gratitude to all my literary sisters, my coven: Mary-Alice Daniel, Jean Ho, Wayétu Moore, Nicole Sealey, Rachel Eliza Griffiths, and Julia Adolphe (my sister in song). Thank you all for giving me safe haven, for the laughter, the advice, the listening ear, the shoulder to cry on, and the dazzling inspiration of your genius minds. I have found a literary family in each of you. Your sisterhood has made my world.

My dear Amanda Sullivan, soon our friendship will be older than the sun, and I am so grateful to live in a world that has your light in it. You have always shown me how to be my best self, and I am forever blessed to call you my sister.

Grandma Sweet P, I'm eternally indebted to you for showing me how kindness kindles light in this world. Thank for all the laughter-filled evenings of our dog-eared summers. Thank you for filling my childhood with sun. To my dear Auntie Audrey, where would I be without you? Thank you for shaping my world so acutely and showing me what a strong and independent woman could look like. To all my aunties, especially Auntie Jackie, Auntie Pansy, and Auntie Sandra, thank you for ushering me into this world with warmth and kindness.

My deepest thanks to Ika and Isha Tafara, and to all the bredren and sistren of Rastafari who showed me my roots and my history, who helped me to understand all the power I possess. Who showed me how to walk taller in Babylon.

Dad, thank you for instilling this steadfast rebel in me (even when you didn't like her very much). Her fire is your enduring gift to me.

Thank you for the wildfire of your song. The way has been rocky, but I hope we keep working on it.

I'm grateful beyond words to Mitchell S. Jackson, my first reader for every chapter of this book. Thank you for tirelessly and patiently reading countless drafts of these passages, talking me through every subtle and neurotic poet's change. Thank you for always encouraging me, for giving me the best literary pep talks, and for your unfailing belief in my voice.

My siblings, my heart-root. Mi love unnu bad. This book would not exist without you. I would not exist without you. Thank you for bearing with my constant trawling of your memories as I wrote this book, and for graciously and judiciously answering all my questions about details and minutiae we left buried in that old garden so long ago. To Lij, my first ragamuffin partner in this life. You've always pushed me to be my best (by besting you) and I wouldn't be the same without your tenacious brilliance. You made me a big sister and I am eternally blessed for it. Still can't beat me in Scrabble though. My dearest Ife, thank you for always showing me the countless ways I can be good and kind and patient in this world. Thank you for the gift of your humor, your wit, your unmatched intelligence. When you sing, the world stops to listen. So never stop singing. Shari, my youngest sis, my twinnie, you are a rock star and firebrand in my eyes. I wish I had a tenth of your tenacity. Thank you for always showing me how to be strong. My dearest siblings, my blood, my kindred. I am indebted to you three for putting up with your big sis who keeps digging up the roots of that old garden, hoping to make something bloom. All that I write and make and dream is for you.

Grandma Isabel, from you came the poems and the conch shell dialect and the ocean of our future. I wish you could have been here to see it.

Mom, there is not enough space in these pages to thank you. You, who dreamed me into existence, who fed me from your mouth like a baby bird. You, who gave me the sea and all its sapphire history, who first taught me to read the green language of blooms, who taught me the name of every fruit and flower, who reminded me to marvel at every living and natural thing. You, who nurtured my love of words, who handed me my first book of poems, and who taught me to read the sea like a poem. This book is for you. You made me the poet and writer and daughter that I am. Thank you for all you have gifted me. This—all this dazzling and wondrous beauty, word after word—is what your hands have made.

My dearest niece Cataleya, one day you will be old enough to read this, and I want to thank you for changing the shape of our family's life for the better. Our world is more radiant with you in it. I hope when you look into these pages, you will better understand your history and see something of yourself in these words, and all the women who came before you. But, Cat, I also hope you see nothing ahead of you but startling blue, a world that is only yours for the shaping.

To Jamaica, my first and truest love. This book is my song to you, and to all the beautiful, hardworking, brilliant, unknown, and unsung Jamaican women who first pushed their hands into the clay and made me.

Note on Rastafari History

While writing this book, I supplemented my own firsthand knowledge of Rastafari with research and oral histories collected mainly from my father and brother on Rastafari livity and tradition, and on Rastafari vernacular, which I am calling "Rasta Poetics." I give thanks to them for the time and knowledge they shared with me. In addition to the insight they provided, the following archival resources were helpful in supplying further historical details and background information for Haile Selassie's visit to Jamaica in Chapter 1, "The Man Who Would Be God":

Ben Cosgrove. "Haile Selassie in Jamaica: Color Photos from a Rastafari Milestone," *Life* Magazine, 1966. Photos by Lynn Pelham.

"Emperor Haile Selassie's Visit to Jamaica—April 1966," Jamaica Information Service archival video.

"Wild Welcome for Negus," the *Daily Gleaner* Archives, April 22, 1966.

In addition to the oral histories I collected and the firsthand knowledge gleaned from my lessons growing up, supplemental information on the Coral Gardens Massacre, Bad Friday, and the history of the persecution of Rastafari in Chapters 1, 3, and 8 was aided by these articles and texts:

Horace G. Campbell. "Notes and Comments: Coral Gardens 1963: The Rastafari and Jamaican Independence, a Personal Recollection," *Social and Economic Studies* 63, no. 1 (2014): 197–214.

Carolyn Cooper. "Bring in all Rastas, dead or alive!" the *Gleaner* Online, April 7, 2013.

"Rastas beaten, forcibly trimmed of their locks after Coral Gardens," the *Jamaica Observer*, December 16, 2015.

Jenny Jemmott, *The Parish History of St. James*, the Jamaica National Group, in collaboration with the Department of History and Archaeology at the University of the West Indies.

About the Author

SAFIYA SINCLAIR was born and raised in Montego Bay, Jamaica. She is the author of the memoir *How to Say Babylon*, winner of the National Book Critics Circle Award and a finalist for the Women's Prize for Non-Fiction, the OCM Bocas Prize for Caribbean Literature, and the Kirkus Prize. *How to Say Babylon* was one of the *New York Times* 100 Notable Books of the Year, a *Washington Post* Top 10 Book of 2023, a *TIME* magazine Top 10 Nonfiction Book of 2023, one of the *Atlantic's* 10 Best Books of 2023, a Read with Jenna *TODAY* Show Book Club pick, and one of President Barack Obama's Favorite Books of 2023. *How to Say Babylon* was also named a Best Book of the Year by the *New Yorker*, NPR, the *Guardian*, the *Los Angeles Times*, *Vulture*, *Harper's Bazaar*, and Barnes & Noble, among others, and was an ALA Notable Book of the Year. The audiobook of *How to Say Babylon* was named a Best Audiobook of the Year by Audible and *AudioFile* magazine.

She is also the author of the poetry collection *Cannibal*, winner of a Whiting Award, the American Academy of Arts and Letters Metcalf Award, the OCM Bocas Prize for Caribbean Poetry, the Phillis Wheatley Book Award, and the Prairie Schooner Book Prize in Poetry.

Sinclair's other honors include a Guggenheim fellowship and fellowships from the Poetry Foundation, Civitella Ranieri Foundation, the Elizabeth George Foundation, MacDowell, Yaddo, the Bread Loaf Writers' Conference, and the Fine Arts Work Center in Provincetown. She is currently an associate professor of creative writing at Arizona State University.

Silver

Silver flows through my veins

Into my hands when I caress the strings of
                of my guitar
Silver is the moon I swallowed
on a dry dreary night when I willed it so
silver is the rain in May
wholesome and lithe, and falling into me

Our springtime sarabande kisses me sodden

up then I'm happy
down then I'm sad
Silver   I cry   Silver

Silver encases my heart
like a drunk jeweller quenching a cigarette
silver is my lips against the ice
my tongue upon the frost
my sweet staccato
my praline dress
my stuck umbrella on a sunshiny day

Silver is the witty wind
coaxing my eyes to sleep
upon the blurred pastel pages
of a slipshod butterfly
Silver is a legerdemain
Legs like a leprechaun that feeds on leer
                     and lemons
a quire of my deepest thoughts
the inkling of my most secret soul

It is the palsied web
of the crestfallen spider
the ugly dewdrop ring
that scars my finger like acid
dusk that brings the sidereal night
resting its echo upon the wing
of a firefly that drinks the silver from my eyes

Silver is my billowing meerschaum
is the flicking goldfish fin in the silent sun
silver are the wispy strands in my hair
lined silver spiralling through the universe
Silver chose me
like starlight to the naked eye

the words I bleed are silver
the time that dances minuets
upon my broken sylvan skin,
is silver in a lancer's armor

when my stomach bursts
and I disgorge eternity
silver stands beside me
fondling the viol

The weight, the wind, are uxorious
for they are solely silver
ever heading my way

My ears are filled with a pixie's dreams
like honey   only Silver
when the days of maiden's trouble subside
silver peels away

My belly swells
and it'll be a while
but I know more silver
is welling
inside.